TWAYNE'S WORLD LEADERS SERIES

EDITOR OF THIS VOLUME

Samuel Smith, Ph.D.

American Writers on Education before 1865

American Writers on Education before 1865

ABRAHAM BLINDERMAN

State University of New York at Farmingdale

TWAYNE PUBLISHERS

A DIVISION OF G. K. HALL & CO., BOSTON

Library of Congress Cataloging in Publication Data

Blinderman, Abraham, 1916-
    American writers on education before 1865.

    (Twayne's world leaders series)
    Bibliography: p. 221-28.
    Includes index.
    1. Educational literature — United States — History.
    2. Educators — United States — History.   I. Title.
    LA205.B65   370'.973   74-22037
    ISBN 0-8057-3503-8

For Rita,

whose mandolin airs, songs, and art
have sweetened our lives

Contents

About the Author

A "G.I." student at Brooklyn College and New York University, Abraham Blinderman earned his B.A. in English in 1948 and his M.A. in 1950. From 1950 to 1963 he worked as a high school teacher and studied intermittently for his doctorate at New York University. Finally, in 1963, he was awarded the Ph.D. degree at New York University.

In his quarter of a century of teaching, Dr. Blinderman has taught in junior high schools, vocational, technical, and academic high schools, two- and four-year colleges, evening departments of high schools and colleges.

Since 1966, when the *University Review* of the State University of New York carried his first article, Dr. Blinderman has written about fifty articles for academic and general publications, including *College Composition and Communication, U.S. Camera, The Christian Century, The Teachers College Record, The Water Skier, The History of Education Quarterly, The National Jewish Monthly, The New York State Journal of Medicine, Newsday,* and *The American Journal of Psychoanalysis*. In addition, he has published teaching manuals for Prentice-Hall and Glencoe, a chapter "Shamans, Witchdoctors, Medicine Men, and Poetry," for *Poetry the Healer,* edited by Jack Leedy, M.D. The University of Miami Press will publish his forthcoming edited work on criticism of Upton Sinclair.

Since 1970, Dr. Blinderman has won these academic honors: a Research Fellowship granted by the Research Foundation of The University of the State of New York; a National Endowment for the Humanities Fellowship for a year's study; and the Chancellor's Award for Excellence in Teaching. In 1974 he was nominated by the college as its candidate for one of the eight Distinguished Teaching Professorships named by the State University of New York.

Preface

My interest whetted in educational history by Adolphe E. Meyer's distinguished teaching at New York University, I accepted Dr. Sylvia Bowman's invitation to outline a book on the educational thoughts of American writers. That was about five years ago, and what was then a seemingly unrealizable inspiration has almost imperceptibly evolved into being as *American Writers on Education before 1865*. The manuscript of my second volume, *American Writers on Education after 1865*, which has been edited, will also be in print soon.

Dr. Bowman and I thought that this book was needed, since we knew of no historical studies of American authors on education that span two centuries of writing. Hundreds of admirable works on the history and philosophy of education are available and many more are steadily forthcoming, but we believed that the book we had in mind would be unique and would fill a gap in educational scholarship. We hope that this book will be helpful to faculty and students in the educational and liberal arts disciplines, and, because education is everybody's concern, that it may have popular appeal as well.

To avoid bulging the book to encyclopedic expanse, I was compelled to exclude many of the authors included in exhaustive bibliographies, such as Spiller's *Literary History of the United States*. Starting with John Trumbull's still readable "The Progress of Dulness" (1770), I scrutinized the writers of the Revolutionary, post-Revolutionary, Jeffersonian, Jacksonian, and pre-Civil War periods for references to education. As seems customary in the literature of any age, the writers disparage the schools, students, teachers, administrators, trustees, and public attitudes toward education. Many of the caustic criticisms of the schools that are aired today are found in the pages of such early writers as Philip Freneau, Hugh Henry

Brackenridge, Washington Irving, Ralph Waldo Emerson, Henry Thoreau, Orestes Brownson, and Walt Whitman. Their consensus is that schools are parsimoniously funded, teachers are poorly prepared intellectually and morally to guide youth, curriculums are often worthless, and the public is apathetic educationally. Disenchanted with their teaching experiences, Freneau, Longfellow, Amos Bronson Alcott, Melville, Emerson, Thoreau, Walt Whitman, Louisa May Alcott, and Margaret Fuller gave up teaching for writing.

The Founding Fathers were more positive in their educational views than the novelists, poets, and essayists who wrote dispraisingly of schooling, although Louisa May Alcott had unstinted praise for her father's maligned progressive ideals in *Little Men*, a novel that celebrates Bronson's educational utopianism. Franklin, Washington, John Adams, Samuel Adams, Jefferson, Benjamin Rush, and Madison believed that a republic could not flourish without an enlightened electorate. Among them, Jefferson stands out as a superb master of prose of whom Henry Adams wrote: "His writings often betrayed subtle feeling for artistic form, — a sure mark of intellectual sensuousness." Collectively, this group of earnest statesmen asked for a national university, free public education, vocational and technical education, scholarships for deserving students, education for girls, and liberalization of the traditional classical curriculum.

Important as state papers and letters are in the propagation of educational doctrine, the fictional writer reaches a much wider audience than the statesman for advancing his philosophical and political beliefs. Louisa Alcott, in illustration, has reached millions of young readers — and undoubtedly, millions of adults, too — with *Little Men*. Unwittingly, millions of Americans have applauded Amos Bronson Alcott's progressivism in his daughter's romanticism. But Louisa's saccharine portrayal of the altruistic Bhaer in *Little Men* is offset by Washington Irving's incomparable pedagogical rogue, the scheming but cowardly Ichabod Crane. Millions of Americans have read "The Legend of Sleepy Hollow," Irving's hyperbolization of the impecunious rural schoolmaster, a characterization that must have embarrassed many early-nineteenth-century teachers.

In the preparation of this book I have had invaluable encouragement and assistance from my mentor and friend Dr. Adolphe Meyer, with whom I have corresponded since 1963; from Dean Hyman Lichtenstein of Hofstra University, an administrator who loves

Preface

teaching, and Professor Louise M. Rosenblatt of New York University, both of whom joined with Dr. Meyer to sponsor my candidacy for fellowship grants; from Mrs. Gertrude Langsam of Adelphi University in Garden City, New York, contributor of many helpful communications on writers relevant to my work; from Professor Raynor Wallace of my college, who has generously shared his thoughts on education and literature with me for many pleasant years; from Parker Van Hoogenstyn, reference librarian at Farmingdale, who has diligently supplied me with leads to writers I had bypassed; from Prescott Harmon, reference librarian at the Levittown Public Library, Levittown, New York, a gracious guide to the perplexed scholar; and from my son, Mark, a part-time instructor at Farmingdale, who has assisted me in searching for facts and in classifying them. I am indebted also to Dr. Samuel Smith, whose calm optimism and gracious speech succeeded in seeing me through this book; and to Robert Reimann, who read my manuscript so painstakingly and effectively, I am deeply appreciative, his ubiquitous red pencil notwithstanding.

Had I not received a research fellowship from the Research Foundation of the State University of New York in 1971, and a year-long fellowship from the National Foundation for the Humanities in 1972, I doubt that I would have completed the manuscripts for both volumes at this writing. I am grateful to both research foundations for the material support they gave to my project.

Finally, I should like to thank those members of the Sabbatical Committee at Farmingdale who voted to grant me a year's leave of absence even though they themselves had applied for similar leaves. I hope that I vindicate their unselfishness in this book.

ABRAHAM BLINDERMAN

Levittown, New York

Chronology

Date of
Birth

1706	Benjamin Franklin	1794	William Cullen Bryant
1722	Samuel Adams	1795	James G. Carter
	George Washington		Samuel R. Hall
1735	John Adams	1796	Horace Mann
1737	Thomas Paine	1797	Mary Lyon
1743	Thomas Jefferson	1799	Amos Bronson Alcott
1745	Benjamin Rush	1800	George Bancroft
	John Jay	1803	Orestes Augustus Brownson
1750	John Trumbull		
1751	James Madison		Ralph Waldo Emerson
1752	Timothy Dwight	1804	Nathaniel Hawthorne
	Philip Morin Freneau	1807	Henry Wadsworth Longfellow
1753	Alexander Hamilton		
1754	Joel Barlow		John Greenleaf Whittier
1757	Royall Tyler	1809	Elizabeth Palmer Peabody
1758	Noah Webster		
1762	Susanna H. Rowson		Edgar Allen Poe
1769	De Witt Clinton		Oliver Wendell Holmes
	Samuel Miller	1810	Margaret Fuller
1771	Charles Brockden Brown	1811	Wendell Phillips
1775	Lyman Beecher		Henry Barnard
1783	Washington Irving		Henry David Thoreau
1787	Richard Henry Dana		Frederick Douglass
	Emma Hart Willard		Horace Greeley
1789	James Fenimore Cooper	1819	James Russell Lowell
1790	Fitz-Greene Halleck		Herman Melville
1791	George Ticknor		Walt Whitman
1793	Samuel Griswold Goodrich	1822	Donald Grant Mitchell
		1823	Edward A. Sheldon
	James Hall	1827	Lew Wallace

1830 Emily Dickinson
1832 Louisa May Alcott
1834 Charles William Eliot
1835 Mark Twain
      William T. Harris
      John Muir
1836 Bret Harte

1837 William Dean Howells
      Edward Eggleston
      Francis W. Parker
1838 Henry Brooks Adams
1842 Sidney Lanier
      William James
1843 Henry James
1856 William J. Grayson

CHAPTER 1

Educational Beginnings from George III to Andrew Jackson

B UOYED by their faith in a God who had blessed their perilous passage to the new Jerusalem, Englishmen of all Christian denominations in the colonies did not forget their Benefactor after they had rooted themselves in the strange but promising land peopled by heathens whom they would either bring to Christ or destroy. To perpetuate the faiths that had inspired them, colonial theologians and statesmen uncompromisingly decreed that their schools be religiously oriented, and to support this educational parochialism the clergy sought political and financial assistance from affluent merchants and planters.

Religion and Education in Colonial America

Nominally, the Protestant sects believed in the Reformation doctrine of freedom of conscience, although in practice they punished one another for supposedly advocating heresies. The Puritans baited Quakers and Catholics who desired to settle among them and sometimes they lashed out in violence against peaceful non-Puritans. Intellectually, the Puritan never solved his dilemma of conscience. How could he justify his right to freedom of conscience and yet deny the same right to those who saw God's ways differently?

Piety and prosperity were the hallmarks of the successful Puritan. Jonathan Edwards preached that in addition to teaching young Puritans the common branches of learning, the masters were obligated to promote the religious thinking of their charges and to steer them to conversion should they stray from salvation's path.[1] In 1723, Harvard's library reflected the dominant intellectual tone of Massachusetts Bay Colony since 60 percent of the books on its shelves were theological. Other colonies also experienced political and religious interference in educational administration.[2] In Pennsylvania, for example, the Episcopalians, although small in numbers, were a powerful educational and political force. Dr. Smith, president of the College of Philadelphia and a member of the Church of England, irritated the Presbyterians, who complained that he and his faculty were converting young collegians to Episcopalianism, a religion which supposedly gave them a taste for high life and a passport to perdition. But the dissenters at Harvard, Yale, and Princeton troubled the affluent Episcopalians; Yale especially grieved them because of its alleged aversion to bishops, kings, and religion, and its preference for republican principles of government.[3]

Colonial Views on Education

Colonial society in 1750 comprised four major social classes: slaves, indentured servants, small farmers and urban laborers, and wealthy merchants and large planters. Aided by their intellectual and organizational acolytes, the prosperous merchants and planters controlled the legislatures, courts, law-enforcement agencies, and churches. Nevertheless, there were many educational prophets in the mid-eighteenth century who championed the school as the best agency for instituting social change. William Smith argued that education has more than a vocational aim in his "A General Idea of the College of Mirania" (1753). His theory of the function of knowledge is reminiscent of Milton's humanistic educational philosophy: "The Knowledge of what tends to neither directly nor indirectly to make better men and better citizens, is, but a Knowledge of Trifles; it is not learning but a Specious and ingenious sort of Idleness."[4] Smith avoided the dilemma of later republicans who believed in the paradoxical political credo of Reverend Jeremy Belknap, a leading Unitarian minister of the Revolutionary period. "Let it stand as a principle that government originates from the people," proclaimed Belknap, "but let the people be taught . . . that they are not able to govern themselves."[5] Belknap had eminent supporters for his aristocratic political bias. Edmund Randolph, Elbridge Gerry, Robert Sherman, William Livingston, Alexander Hamilton, and George Washington expressed doubts about the ability of the people to govern themselves and young Gouverneur Morris epitomized their fears of democracy in his reaction to mass unrest: "The mob begin to think and reason. Poor reptiles! . . . They bask in the sun, and ere noon they will bite, depend upon it. The gentry begin to fear this."[6]

In his definitive study of colonial education, Lawrence A. Cremin praises eighteenth-century American educational institutions for attempting to solve their major problem of "how and how much to make life as it was and would be, rather than life as it had been, the central fact of the curriculum."[7] Franklin advocated middle-class ideals, which represented change and progress in a society that still cherished aristocratic and feudal values. Progressive English liberals of the seventeenth and eighteenth centuries were widely read in the colonies, seeding the minds of the intellectually curious with notions of natural rights, political equality, and educational liberalization. The growth in population and wealth encouraged Americans to found nondenominational dissenting academies based on England's excellent schools, but these academies were generally located in large, commercial cities.

In 1755, Archibald Kennedy of New York wrote movingly in defense of freedom of opportunity in education: "In countries where Liberty prevails the Road is left open for the Son of the weariest Plebian to arrive at the highest Pitch of Honors and Preferment, there will never be wanting the great Emulations, and of course, great men."[8] Similarly, James Otis, a brilliant New England lawyer, renowned as an orator, classical scholar, and pamphleteer, argued for a wider diffusion of learning since "the ideas of earthly superiority, pre-eminence, and grandeur are educational; at least acquired, not innate."[9] Otis's comments conflicted with the views of those colonists who favored a state ruled by aristocrats. If traits of leadership were acquired through education and not heredity, then restricting education to the sons of the wealthy made no sense. It took some time before the ideas of Kennedy and Otis were generally approved.

Weaknesses of Colonial Education

The elders in the Massachusetts Bay Colony pioneered in elementary education. Their main purpose was to arm the innocents with enough of the Gospel to delude omnipresent Satan. Historians are not generally impressed with the quality of colonial education. There were few opportunities for the education of the young in the generations preceding the Revolution, and the costly duplication of schools occasioned by the demand of each denomination for its own school retarded education.[10] Generally, colonial teachers were neither learned nor inspiring, but in Boston at least schoolteachers were well paid and seem to have been a higher type of man than some who disgraced their profession in other parts of the colonies.[11] Primary schoolmasters in New England were unhappy men, held in low esteem by their employers. Adolphe E. Meyer sums up their lot succinctly: "Usually his appointment ran for six months or so, whereupon he put away his books and birches to devote his surcease from intellectual cares to earning his keep in some less exigent calling, say, as a cow tender or plowman, or even a keg washer."[12]

In 1755, John Adams, not yet twenty, became the master of a grammar school in Worcester. A century later, Charles Francis Adams described his grandfather's experiences: "His condition, as the teacher of a school, was not and could not be a permanent establishment. Its emoluments gave but a bare and scanty subsistence. The engagement was but for a year. . . . It was an expedient adopted merely to furnish a temporary supply to the most urgent wants of nature, to be purchased by the devotion of time, which would have otherwise been occupied in becoming qualified for the exercise of an active profession. To his active, vigorous, and inquisitive mind this situation was extremely irksome."[13]

But New England's culture was never so ignominiously lampooned as poor New Amsterdam's was in Washington Irving's scathing hyperbole: "Happily for New Amsterdam . . . the very words of learning, education, taste, and talent were unheard of; a bright genius was an animal unknown." Thomas J. Wertenbaker supports Irving's low regard for colonial Dutch culture: the Dutch had few libraries, either public or circulating, they were not habitual readers, and they supported neither Dutch newspapers nor magazines. According to Van Wyck Brooks, New Amsterdam boasted of but two poets, one of whom left the Muse for commerce. Competent teachers refused to migrate to a raw province whose educational directors exacted hard physical and mental labor from their poorly paid masters. After the Dutch yielded to their British conquerors, their children depended on charity schools or apprenticeships for their education. Secondary schools came late in New York, and King's College did not emerge until 1754 — more than a century after Harvard had opened its doors to its first class of Puritan matriculants.[14]

In the Southern colonies elementary education was poor in quality and inadequate. Incompetent instructors in field schools and charity schools were paid with victuals or tobacco. Reverend clerks taught in their homes, but these makeshift parson's schools were of little value to their apathetic students. The Yankee scholar, prized as a tutor by the plantation owner, was accorded many social advantages by his employer. He dined with the family, assisted at family councils, and if he was more adept than hapless Ichabod Crane in courtship, he might even win not only the hand of the planter's daughter but also a handsome dowry that went with the bride.[15]

As the colonies prospered in the third quarter of the eighteenth century, education made noteworthy advances. For example, Benjamin Franklin helped elevate Philadelphia to the most civilized place in colonial America. (His role in establishing an academy, a college, and a library in Philadelphia will be discussed in Chapter Three.) Education in New York City was praised in 1759 by Andrew Burnaby, an English traveler. He admired the colony's enthusiasm for learning, epitomized in the opening of King's College, which on an austerity budget managed to accommodate twenty-five students, seven of whom had taken degrees. Crèvecoeur added his accolades for the college in 1770, warmly approving its library, architecture, and scientific apparatus, but John Adams withheld his approval of the school in 1774, finding fault with its one building and dearth of students.[16] Generally, as the nation approached revolution, colonial writers and statesmen took pride in its educational achievements compared to the state of education abroad. John Trumbull (whose lampoon of colonial college education is discussed in Chapter Four) nevertheless boasted that "perhaps there is no nation in which a larger portion of learning is diffused through all ranks of people."[17] Even those who did not go to college were eager readers, and for one lad who sought his degree scores pursued self-education.

Education and the Revolution

Colonial education was disrupted by the American Revolution. Eighty thousand loyalists went into exile during the war. Since many of them were well educated it is reasonable to conjecture that their flight from the colonies appreciably retarded educational development in America. The young republic rejoiced in the departure of England's proud civil, military, political, and ecclesiastical hierarchies from its shores, but it would sorely miss — when it most needed them — the thousands of talented royalists who in conscience could not join the revolutionists.[18]

The pro-Revolutionary forces were an odd coalition of poorer classes, wealthy Southern planters, and Northern politicians lacking wealth and status.[19] But the military successes achieved with major

French assistance were not converted equally into political victories for the social classes who had fought for independence. The delegates who assembled in Philadelphia in 1787 to compose a national constitution were an elite group representing the monied classes. Almost 50 percent of the delegates were college graduates, ten bearing Princeton's imprint. Sixty percent were lawyers, most of them British born, who in addition to their British tradition were heirs also of Continental culture — the Greek and Italian Renaissances, the Reformation, and the *philosophes*.[20]

At the Constitutional Convention, the delegates painstakingly debated various plans of government submitted. The final draft of the Constitution borrowed freely from the principles of Hobbes, Locke, and Montesquieu. Authored chiefly by propertied men, the document neatly limited the powers of a potential revolutionary majority and protected funded, landed, slave, and business property. To the Founding Fathers liberty was associated with property, not with democracy. Men lacking property, they thought, cannot be reliable citizens.

Richard Hofstadter has described the convention as "a fraternity of types of absentee ownership," an assemblage of aristocrats who were products of private education and hostile to public schools and charity schools. They had major political problems to solve, and education, not an immediate concern, could wait for future disposition.[21] The sections on property rights in the Constitution were soon to be made Gospel by Justice Marshall's conservative decisions on property rights. Although his decision in the famed Dartmouth College case (1819) was a victory for the conservative philosophy of government, his defense of Dartmouth's royal charter as an inviolable contract not subject to New Hampshire's desired modification ensured a bright future for American private colleges.[22]

American Statesmen on Education

Philosophically, American statesmen were advocates of public education for the masses. Convinced that only an enlightened citizenry might transform the colonies into independent states, John Adams wrote George Wythe in 1776: "Laws for the liberal education of youth, especially of the lower classes of people, are so extremely wise and useful, that, to a humane and generous mind, no expense for this purpose would be thought extravagant."[23] John Madison envisioned our political institutions as models for newly emerging states in the western hemisphere and appealed to his countrymen "to prove by their establishments for the advancement and diffusion of knowledge, that their political institutions, which are attracting attention from every quarter, and are respected as models by the new-born States in our own Hemisphere, are as favorable to the intellectual and moral improvement of man as they are conformable to his individual and social rights."[24] Madison's words were echoed by De Witt Clinton, governor of New York and a strong supporter of public education. Dismayed by the low esteem for schoolteachers in his state, Clinton in 1822 expressed a view that could be used today by collective bargaining representatives of teachers' unions: "To elevate the standard of education in the common schools, it is indispensable that the qualifications of teachers should be improved. The inhabitants of the school districts ought to be impressed with the great importance of affording such compensation, as will imbue men with great talents to fit themselves for the situations of teachers, as a profession for life."[25]

Clinton applauded "those solid and enduring honours which arise from the cultivation of science and the acquaintance and diffusion of knowledge," for they will "outlive the renown of statesmen and the glory of the warrior."[26] Agreeing with his contemporaries on the need for education of the "mass of the people," Chief Justice Marshall warned in 1827 that pauperism and famine will follow when the supply of labor exceeds the demand. Happily, it would take many decades before the population grew out of hand; in that interval mass education would serve well, but the future fretted him: " . . . as our country fills up how shall we escape the evils which have followed a dense population?"[27] This Malthusian dilemma still haunts our politicians, scholars, and scientists, and especially the victims of technological unemployment. Justice Marshall anticipated our own disturbed age. Mass education, massive population, and the cybernetic revolution have vindicated the implications of his prophetic query.

Education in the Post-Revolutionary Period

"The whole problem of education is one of its cost in money," wrote Henry Adams after reviewing his effectiveness as a professor of history at Harvard in 1871, a sweeping generalization that is shared by philosophers and school boards alike.[28] And there was very little money in the colonies after the Revolution. In 1783 land and property lay waste, trade was almost nil, the national debt was a foreboding $75,000,000, and the central government was in an anarchic condition. Education suffered woefully during and immediately after the war. First, charity schools ceased operation; then private schools closed their doors. Education came almost to a standstill. Only a privileged handful of students were able to seek out tutors or schoolmasters.[29]

The states carried on petty commercial wars with one another, contested territorial boundaries bitterly, and refused to contribute to the payment of the national war debt. The decline of business, the refusal of people to accept paper currency at par with gold, and the enmity between farmer and businessman created economic paralysis.

The burdens of the new nation were awesome and its founders were not inclined to initiate educational programs while the nation's fate was still in doubt. "All in all," concludes historian Adolphe E. Meyer, "the young republic's notable deeds were political and economic rather than educational. This was almost inescapable. To get the nation solidly on its feet, to forge its wrangling factions into the union of a single people, to give it strength and substance — such was the main and overwhelming task. All else was secondary."[30]

It would seem so. True, Franklin and Jefferson, as presidents of the American Philosophical Society, offered prizes for the best essays on national systems of education, although it is worth noting that nothing developed out of the winning essays submitted by Samuel Knox and Samuel H. Smith.[31] In *Liberalism and American Education*, Professor Hansen lauds the philosophical contributions of Thomas Paine, "the master teacher of the American nation in the principles of democracy."[32] But save for Jefferson, the patriarchs of the Revolution were not overly stimulated socially or politically by the gadfly of the Enlightenment. Jefferson enshrined many of the Enlightenment's precepts in the Declaration of Independence and fought diligently to have them legalized in the Bill of Rights. Yet, he advocated gradualism in granting democracy to the people, since, like Franklin, he believed that masses must be educated before they could participate effectively in governing the nation. Washington and John Jay entertained similar reservations regarding the wisdom of granting the people immediate political power.[33] The aristocratic colonial inheritance of the Revolutionary patriots, humanitarians, and educational reformers inhibited them from liberalizing the schools and endowing them with new social and cultural functions.

Opposing educational innovations in the newly founded nation were men like Fisher Ames, a congressman from Massachusetts who saw democracy as a damnable institution inimical to liberty. Ames deplored the leveling process; only a nation ruled by a wealthy class that patronized an elite and subservient intellectual minority might produce geniuses.[34] Interestingly, some educational historians discount the professions of the Founding Fathers for mass education, characterizing them as conservatives who cared very little for the intellectual elevation of the people. Professor Cubberley noted that only once during the Constitutional debate was education brought up.[35] Perhaps, had Benjamin Rush (whose educational views are discussed in Chapter Three) attended the Constitutional Convention, he might have convinced the delegates to support public education as a bulwark against the excesses of popular liberty.[36]

Public apathy was responsible for much of the national neglect of education. Contributing to this attitude, according to Professor Cubberley, were the simple rural life of the people, their homogeneity, the isolation of their villages, the lack of universal manhood suffrage, and the public acceptance of illiteracy.[37] But John Adams's and John Trumbull's praise of colonial literacy as well as Wertenbaker's detailed account of colonial culture seem to contradict Cubberley's statement on colonial illiteracy. Charles and Mary Beard praise the colonial booksellers and libraries that were frequented by numerous men seeking self-education. Franklin boasted that "the libraries have improved the general conversation of the Americans, made the common tradesmen and farmers as intelligent as most gentlemen from other countries." Unfortunately, no records of the extent of colonial literacy exist, but the fact that one hundred thousand copies of Thomas Paine's first call for independence were immediately sold is collateral evidence of Franklin's optimism on colonial literacy.[38] The combination of school tutor, library, bookseller, and parental teaching in the educational process undoubtedly reduced illiteracy in the colonies significantly. Excerpts from the diaries of Revolutionary soldiers reveal quaint grammatical usages and variant spellings, but even today poor writers may be excellent readers. Elijah Fisher, after being released from a New Jersey prison ship, recorded this amusing intelligence in his diary for April 10, 1783:

I leaves Mr. Frances and so goes about the City to se it and went into Nombres of these shopes and would say your servant gentlefolks, I wish you much Joy with the nuse of peace. I hope it will be a long and lasting one, some of them would be very well pleased with it and would wish me the same (and others would on the other hand) and said that their surcomstances poor at preasant but now hoped they would be better. I said what then do you think of us, poor prisoners that they have neither Money nor frinds and have been long absent from our homes, then some of them would pity us and give is something some half a dollar, some a quarter, some less, some nothing but frowns.[39]

Elijah was a private. Andrew Jackson was a general. A comparison of Private Elijah Fisher's composition with a letter written by General Jackson suggests that neither would earn a passing grade in a contemporary composition course. In 1819, Jackson wrote the following to Andrew Donelson:

There is nothing so beatifull in writing as a plain easy stile. Mr. Madison excelled in this, and altho Mr. Jeffersons writing has met with the approbation they meritted — I have always thought that the chasteness of Mr. Madison excelled any American author I ever read.[40]

Two voices spoke up for educational innovation in this transitional period — one from the South and one from England. Thomas Cooper proposed a "full, complete, really free system of education at every grade at the public expense, open to every citizen, without exception, without money, and without price."[41] Here indeed was a prophet! Who would be excluded from an educational utopia modeled after his? But perhaps the sagest advice to American educators came from an Englishman, Richard Price. Dr. Price's succinct statement on university aims is especially valuable: "The end of education is to direct the powers of the mind in unfolding themselves; and to assist in gaining their just bent and force. And, in order to do this, its business should be to teach how to think, rather than what to think; or to lead into the best way of searching for the truth, rather than to instruct in the truth itself."[42] Price's philosophy of education was enlightened and consonant with the rationalistic spirit of the times. To the Puritan whose theocratic dogma precluded him from treading beyond the bourn of his stern Calvinistic field, Price's scientific concern for the truth was an incomprehensible and heretical flirtation with Satan. Price wrote his dictum on education in 1785. But the new nation was neither physically nor intellectually ready for the adoption and advancement of educational ideals that, alas, are still not respected in some educational systems and institutions.

At the beginning of the nineteenth century, only New York and

New England were strongly committed to public education. Before 1800, New Hampshire, New Jersey, Delaware, Maryland, Virginia, South Carolina, Kentucky, and Tennessee did not provide for education in their state constitutions. A handful of liberals fought vainly for tax-supported schools, "but the ruling classes stood against them to a man."[43] As late as 1819 Congress objected to a proposal to grant public lands for the endowment of state universities. Congressman Poindexter of the Committee on Public Lands opposed the proposed cession by the federal government of 100,000 acres of land to each state for the establishment and support of universities because:

1. No states had submitted bills of necessity for such grants.
2. The grant of 2,300,000 acres of land to the states would hinder further settlement of the states by withholding land from a free market.
3. Such grants of land are not in accord with republican principles — they are monopolistic, depriving small farmers of the right to buy small acreage.
4. Educational grants should be in money, not land.[44]

The Status of the Teacher

How did the teacher fare in a war-ravaged land? Traditionally a humble recipient of society's miserly stipends, he might, if he possessed the altruistic selflessness of Chaucer's poor clerk of Oxford, sublimate his material and egoistical deprivation into priceless acts of elevating love for his pupils. But teachers then as now were concerned with salaries, conditions of labor, and hopes for advancement. Few cared to resign themselves to pedagogical martyrdom. And why should they live in penury, despised and humiliated by their employers?

Schoolmasters were depicted by fictional and scholarly writers as sadistic disciplinarians, subservient to the dignitaries who hired them. For example, in *The Adventures of Robin Day*, Robert Montgomery Bird fictionalizes a student riot at New Castle Academy allegedly motivated by the boys' displeasure with their tyrannical master.[45] The Reverend Samuel Miller portrayed Southern schoolmasters as "ignorant and vicious adventurers, administering a profession shunned by dignified men."[46] Many of the Southern schoolmasters were unloved Yankees whom Fitz-Greene Halleck typed in his poem "Connecticut":

> Wandering through the southern countries, teaching
> The ABC from Webster's spelling book;

> Gallant and godly, making love and preaching,
>   And gaining by what they call "hook and crook."
> And what the moralists call over-reaching
> A decent living. The Virginians look
> Upon them with as favorable eyes
>   As Gabriel on the devil in paradise.[47]

Schoolteachers were aware of the low regard the public had for their profession. Alexander Wilson, an 1814 immigrant, earned his bread in the new land as a weaver, a peddler, a schoolteacher, and a naturalist. Occasionally, he dabbled in doggerel, a verse of which he dedicated to the unjustly maligned schoolmasters of his time:

> Of all the professions this world has known,
> For clowns and cobblers upward to the throne;
> From the grave architect of Greece and Rome,
> Down to the framer of a farthing broom;
> The worst for care and undeserved abuse,
> The first in real dignity and use,
> (If skilled to teach and diligent to rule)
> Is the learned master of a school.[48]

"If skilled to teach and diligent to rule!" How many prominent Americans looked back to their early schooling with loathing for their masters! Lyman Beecher bitterly recalled his barnyard school. His first teacher, Mr. Bishop, was "a poor creature who didn't know what else to do, so he kept school."[49] Samuel Goodrich of "Peter Parley" fame hated his school and his teacher at Ridgefield, Connecticut. In 1799, he was taught by Delight Benedict, a sallow, sullen spinster. In Goodrich's tenth year the undelectable drills in reading, writing, and arithmetic were given by Master Stebbins. Goodrich appraised his early eighteenth-century schooling as follows: "The art of teaching as now understood . . . was neither known nor deemed necessary in our country schools in their day of small things. Repetition, drilling, line upon line, and precept upon precept, with here and there a little of the birch — constituted the whole system."[50]

Foreign Travelers on Early American Education

Foreign visitors to post-Revolutionary America were not impressed with what they saw of the lower schools. Moreau de St. Méry, a Frenchman who traveled in America from 1793 to 1798, witnessed little of educational value for the twenty-one boarders and forty-five day scholars attending the Academy of New Utrecht. All of these scholars were served by one Negro, one Negress, her two children, and a young white domestic. The master of the school would not or could not discipline the children, who learned only what they wished to. The parents of the anarchical scholars were interested solely in the cost of tuition and in having relief from the capers of their unruly children. When home for vacation, the cunning lads asked to be returned to school if they found life at home too Spartan.[51]

Another English traveler, Henry Wansey, visited the Academy of Flat Bush in 1794, and deplored its utilitarian goals. His criticism of the school, namely, that it aimed to develop practical men who shunned the broader avenues of speculative and abstract learning, is still a popular foreign attitude toward American schooling.[52] But a notice of a school opening in Jamaica, New York, on May 1, 1792, stresses the classics, as the tuition rates imply:

Attendance will be given at Union Hall, on Monday morning, the 21st of May, by Mr. M. Gilston, a gentleman of approved character and abilities. The prices for which tuition may be had are: for the Latin and Greek languages, mathematics, etc., six pounds per annum; reading, writing, and arithmetic, 3.4 pounds; reading and writing, 2.8 pounds; reading only, 2 pounds. The matriculants were advised to deport themselves well and to especially obey these rules:
1. Every scholar when the tutor, or any other gentleman, comes in or goes out, shall rise with a respectful bow.
2. Every scholar shall be particularly careful to treat all men, and especially known superiors, with the greatest modesty and respect.[53]

But foreign observers of American education were too narrow in their appraisal of American schools. Since most of them were cultured aristocrats who compared American academies with long-established schools in Europe, their criticisms tended to overlook the peculiar responsibilities of American schools to help the struggling young republic to overcome its technical, agricultural, and commercial problems. Although Latin and Greek retained their traditional role in the secondary schools, English grammar, oratory, elocution, mathematics, astronomy, surveying, and natural philosophy increasingly challenged the classics for curricular supremacy. Girls were admitted to more progressive academies, but public opposition to sexually integrated schools led to the founding of female academies. In these institutions girls might dabble in needlecraft, embroidery, oil painting, sculpturing, and musical studies. Later, they might even study pedagogy to prepare themselves for teaching.

The Classics Attacked

The hold of the classics in the American schools was strong, but Franklin and others attacked the undue stress given to the classics by American schoolmasters. Thomas Paine had disparaged classical studies for schoolboys in *The Age of Reason*. In that pamphlet he contended that learning is a knowledge of things, not a knowledge of language. Why destroy a student's joy of learning by burdening him with onerous Greek and Latin studies? Let him study the natural sciences and the living languages; it is natural for a child to have curiosity which, if properly channeled, will open delightful and meaningful scientific worlds to him. Unfortunately, Paine continued, the church stands as a barrier to these brave new worlds of learning. Fearing that a truly liberal and scientific education would encourage students to question its theological premises, the church has always restricted formal learning to the study of dead languages.[54] In 1816, Edward Tyrell Channing of Harvard, a teacher who inspired many of his students to write professionally, scored the schools' excessive indulgence in the classics. He argued that the untrained schoolboy, "fed on the best of classicism, develops distaste for his native tongue."[55]

Undoubtedly, many enlightened Americans agreed with Benjamin Rush that the emphasis upon the classics in the schools had created an aversion in the public mind for institutions of learning. The new land could not afford to indulge its youth in ornamental learning; there were resources to discover, industries to build, and lines of communication to develop. Even the colleges were wasting their energies in teaching dead languages, lamented the Reverend Samuel Miller. At a time when science was flourishing and intercourse between nations was mounting, would it not be wiser to minimize the classics in deference to the vigorous interest of the nation in natural science and modern tongues?

In 1780, William and Mary appointed a professor of modern languages, and not much later, Harvard permitted its students to substitute French for Hebrew. Successively, Columbia, Rhode Island College, the University of North Carolina, and Williams College included French and other modern languages in their curriculums. Concurrently, interest in Anglo-Saxon and English linguistics was spurred by Jefferson, who prepared a simplified Anglo-Saxon grammar, and by Noah Webster, who attempted to simplify English phonetics in his *Compendious Dictionary of the English Language*. Naturally, as the schools attended increasingly to scientific, modern language, and English literature studies, the classics slowly lost ground in the curriculums. But the champions of the classics did not submit to the innovaters meekly, for decades were to pass before the classics were almost universally repudiated as requisites for matriculation in the nation's colleges.

Some Accolades for Post-Yorktown Education

The post-Revolutionary period was not without its advances in education. Lawrence Cremin praises the role of education in the new republic, noting that European nations in 1783 began to reappraise American institutions inspired by American education. Perhaps the innovative Americans might teach them something of value.[56] Jared Ingersoll, writing in 1823, approved of the education he observed, but, unlike Cremin, he attributed the advance of American education to the stability of its political system. Ingersoll praised also the unique American system of funding education, dating back to Plymouth Colony, which set precedents for inclusion in the constitutions of newly admitted states of provisions for founding schools, academies, colleges, and universities.[57]

New England and the Middle Atlantic states had devoted educational defenders. In his epitomization of post-Yorktown culture, "A Brief Retrospect of the Eighteenth Century," Samuel Miller singled out Massachusetts and Connecticut for their support of common schools that reflected "the general spirit of activity and enterprise which is inherent in the national character of New England." The Middle and the Southern states excelled in chemistry, natural history, and medicine, whereas Massachusetts and Pennsylvania emphasized mathematics and natural philosophy.[58]

Modern educational budgeteers have reason to envy the financial acumen of Philadelphians who in 1823 taught five thousand children the three Rs at the almost painless cost of three dollars a year per student.[59] A contemporary critic of Southern literature, Jay B. Hubbell, defends the better academies of the South, especially the school run by the Reverend Moses Waddell that nurtured John C. Calhoun, Hugh S. Legaré, George McDuffie, Augustus B. Longstreet, and William H. Crawford.[60] A British traveler lauded the vitality of American education, comparing it favorably with Old World learning that is essentially a process of "unlearning superstition infused from cradle to adolescence." American education on the other hand is fresh and vital and the American "in his infancy, manhood, or age, never feels the hand of oppression. Violence is positively forbidden in the schools, in the prisons, on shipboard, in the army. . . . "[61]

Postwar Decline of Higher Learning

The most important pre-Revolutionary attack upon college education was authored by John Trumbull, a New England satirist whose poetic diatribe "The Progress of Dulness" epitomized the colonial criticism of higher learning. (His still readable doggerel, which castigates collegiate education as fraudulent, stupid, and incongruous, is discussed in detail in Chapter Four.) Franklin, who scorned much of the pedantry of classical scholars, denigrated Harvard as an intellectual cesspool where rich students paid the poor "grind" to do their studies.[62] But Paul Goodman credits Harvard with becoming a democratic and dissenting community after Increase Mather ceased to dominate its affairs.[63] Also one must cite William and Mary for the remarkable achievements of many of its alumni. These include, in addition to Thomas Jefferson, six of the eleven members of the Committee of Safety, eleven of the thirty-two drafters of the Declaration of Rights, and four of the seven Virginians who signed the Declaration of Independence.

The success of the Revolution, however, did not encourage an educational rebirth in the nation's colleges. As the glow of the Revolution paled so did the ardors of some of its inspirers. Noah Webster, an agnostic revolutionary, abandoned his iconoclastic stance for orthodox Calvinism and conservative Federalism. Washington and Jefferson opposed shipping off supposedly impressionable youths to foreign universities where they might become contaminated with alien principles. Benjamin Rush (a physician-statesman whose views are discussed in Chapter Three) urged in 1788 that thirty years after the establishment of a national university all officeholders must have academic degrees. This proposition certainly was in conflict with the democratic ideal of rugged individualism. The conservatism of college administrators, especially in New England, had little to do with the popular slogans of the Revolution. The Hartford Wits, mainly Yale men, adhered to their rigid Federalism, and attacked liberal leaders vehemently. Even

Ethan Allen, a popular war hero, was denounced by Timothy Dwight of Yale and by Sparks of Harvard as a vulgarian and an atheist.[64] Daniel Webster pontificated that the nation's peace and security depend more upon religion and government than upon reason, a strange admission that reason and government might not be compatible.[65] As an example of the collegiate conservatism of that time, in 1786 college boys formed a cavalry regiment to help suppress Shay's Rebellion, an uprising of irate farmers that for a short time threatened to become another revolution.[66] William Lane Allen, in his novel *The Choir Invisible,* depicts undergraduates whose chief interest is the merry pastimes of tavern life, where they intermittently drank, wenched, and read Tom Paine's *Age of Reason.*

Early nineteenth-century authors censured the colleges mercilessly for a variety of reasons. In his Phi Beta Kappa address at Cambridge in 1816, Frances Calley Gray criticized American colleges, comparing them unfavorably with European universities that had superior curriculums taught by eminent men.[67] Three years later Richard Henry Dana, Sr., disparaged university scholars as traditionalists who hated innovation.[68] George Tucker attributed the large number of mediocre men in the colleges to the flight of superior dons to greener intellectual pastures.[69] Embittered by the public's lack of interest in higher learning, William Ellery Channing attacked the materialism of his fellow citizens: "We want universities worthy of the name where a man of genius and literary zeal may strengthen himself by intercourse with kindred minds. We know it will be said we cannot afford these. But it is not so. We are rich enough for ostentation, for intemperance, for luxury. We can lavish millions on fashion, on furniture, on dress, on our palaces, on our pleasures, but we have nothing to spend for the mind."[70]

Francisco de Miranda, a South American traveler, concluded after visiting Harvard in 1786 that the college was "better calculated to form clerics than capable or educated citizens."[71]

Included among the school's many other critics were scores of its native sons. Harvard graduate George Dennie was a prominent essayist and editor. As an undergraduate he was degraded ten points in class rank for alleged disrespect to Professor Crosby. In a letter to a classmate, Dennie defended his action as a necessary criticism of the inept faculty. Although he later successfully petitioned the faculty for reinstatement, he never forgave Harvard for compelling him to perjure himself for its forgiveness. In a letter to a classmate in 1790,

Dennie wrote: "The cursed impertinence of a mock examination being over, a lying petition read, and the last acts of a pigmy despotism exorcised, I forsook Cambridge with bitter execrations, and repaired to Lexington for sweet air, to dine with Temperance, and to build anew my tottering fame." In 1800, Dennie wrote that Harvard was "a sink of vice," "a temple of dullness," and "a roost of owls."[72]

Another eminent Harvardian, Rufus King, one of the signers of the Declaration of Independence from Massachusetts, found the college lacking in competent classical scholars and misguided in its preference for science and modern poetry. Students ignorant of the elements of numbers were vainly taught higher mathematics when they should have been taught true moral and intellectual values by a classical scholar who would "create an era in our system of Education."[73] A year later, in 1821, the great orator and educator Edward Everett, impressed with his educational experiences in German universities, deplored Harvard's mediocre tone in a letter to Judge Joseph Story, a Harvard Overseer: "But I find that the whole pursuit, and the duties it brings with it, are not respectable enough on the estimation they bring with them, and lead one too much in contact with some little men and many little things."[74]

But Harvard had to contend with problems other than scholarship. The rigid discipline initiated by President Willard triggered many student disorders. Examples of these student "rebellions" were meticulously documented by Eliphat Pearson, professor of Hebrew, in his diary for the years 1788 - 1797. The professor's list includes instances of noisy chambers, hurling of snowballs at instructors, intoxicated students, cutlery thrown at tutors, blown-out lights, broken chapel windows, stone-throwing, firing of pistols, rioting in town, Bible stealing, hooting and whistling at lectures, and interruption of chapel prayers.[75] Even Josiah Quincy, later to ascend to the presidency of Harvard, participated in a riot originating in the Commons. The enraged students smashed all the crockery and most of the furniture in the dining hall. This vandalism led to the suspension of the apprehended rioters.[76]

According to Moreau de St. Méry, Princeton matched Harvard in student irresponsibility. In 1794 he wrote in his notebook:

It would be indeed pleasant to be able to speak highly of the curriculum of this college [Princeton]; but when one has not been brought up in the American way, praise is difficult. Any system that, due to the heedlessness of its masters, fails to impose any restraints on its youths, and indulges them in the customary indolence of Americans, cannot but produce vicious results. These effects are visible at Princeton College, where sport and licentious habits are said to absorb the pupils more than study.[77]

Some Accolades for Post-Yorktown Colleges

But along with all the criticism, early American colleges were praised by some writers too. Educational historians, past and present, honor William and Mary for its pioneering in elective and honor systems, departments of political economy and modern history, and a school of public affairs. In addition, William and Mary founded the Phi Beta Kappa society and wisely encouraged its students to become proficient in the social graces. In its great law professor George Wythe, teacher of Thomas Jefferson, John Marshall, Henry Clay, and James Monroe, the college boasted a legal scholar second to none.

Lyman Beecher, whose critical comments about his grammar school education were discussed earlier, had kinder words for Yale. Taught in 1793 by Roger Minot Sherman, a great teacher who had inspired him, Beecher found much to learn at Yale, even though the library housed only two to three thousand books.[78] Yale was also praised handsomely in verse by one of its sons, David Humphreys, a Hartford Wit, a colonel in the Revolutionary Army, and an ambassador to Spain:

> Say, in what state, so soon imbibed by the youth
> Th' eternal principles of right and truth?
> Where education such instruction spread?
> Where on the mind such influence morals shed?
> Where modesty with charms so fair appear'd?
> So honour'd age, and virtue so rever'd?
>
> Thou fount of learning where I drank, thou Yale!
> Fount of religion and of knowledge, hail!
> There, happy parents bid our thirsting youth
> Quaff copious immortality and truth;
> While Dwight with soaring soul, directs their way,
> To the full well of life, in climes of endless day.[79]

Princeton was regarded favorably by John Melish, an English traveler who noted its reputation "as one of the best seminaries in the United States."[80] Francisco de Miranda appraised it as "a well regulated college for the education of youth, the advantages of which are known in all this America."[81] To the west, Timothy Flint, author and educator, ranked Indiana College, founded at Bloomington in 1829, with the best colleges anywhere offering classical curriculums.[82]

Education of Blacks

Meanwhile, the black man, slave and free, was practically ignored educationally by his white masters. The index of Cubberley's *Public Education in the United States* (1919) carries but one reference to the education of America's large black population. But, appearing in the same year as Cubberley's textbook, C. G. Woodson's detailed *Education of the Negro Race* gave notice to white historians that they had omitted a chapter in their books — black educational history — which all historians would eventually have to consider. Cubberley's own words on race and nationality seem to ignore the existence of blacks in America:

Assimilation is a blending of civilizations and customs to create that homogeneity necessary for citizenship and national feeling and may be promoted by education and social institutions and wise legislation; amalgamation is a blending of races and blood, and is a process of centuries. Through assimilation of all our diverse elements we are preparing the way for that future amalgamation of racial elements which will in time produce the American race.[83]

But Cubberley limits his "melting pot" components to Saxon, Celt, Teuton and Slav, Latin and Hun. No Indians, no blacks, no Semites, no Puerto Ricans are included in his brief for the evolutionary creation of an American race.

"A little learning is a dangerous thing" seems to have been the educational thinking of Southern whites toward blacks in the colonies. Since they never intended to offer the blacks equal educational opportunities, they denied black children even a little learning in security's name. Learning would incite the slaves to rebellion and make them unfit for servitude.[84] Ironically, in 1770, the same year that Georgia reenacted the law of 1740 "which forbade under penalty anyone to teach slaves or employ them in a writing capacity,"[85] Phillis Wheatley, a former slave and a leading colonial poet at seventeen, addressed the youth of the University of Cambridge in New England poetically:

> Students, to you 'tis given to scan the heights
> Above, to traverse the ethereal space,
> And mark the systems of revolving worlds.[86]

In 1800 the Charleston City Council gave authority to the police to "break down gates, or windows, in dispersing any gatherings for the mental instruction of the blacks."[87] In 1826, the council resolved that "to be able to read and write is certainly not necessary to the performance of those duties which are required of our slaves, and on the contrary is incompatible with the public safety."[88] In 1832 Alabama forbade any person to teach any free person of color or slaves; to enforce this ordinance slaves were forbidden to congregate, an act designed to prevent black schooling. New England, too, hindered blacks from founding their own schools; the citizens of Hartford, Connecticut, vehemently rejected the plans of the city's blacks to form a school for their children in 1830.[89]

Generally, whatever education was permitted for the blacks was of inferior quality. In rare cases a "house slave" was carefully educated by a master who encouraged him to develop his innate talents; but for every Phillis Wheatley who was loved, instructed, and guided by her owners, there were scores of self-educated blacks whose lives were constantly burdened with the anxieties peculiar to unloved aliens. Where rudimentary formal schooling was available for blacks, as in Maryland, most of the teachers were indentured servants.

In the North some attempts were made to educate blacks. Elias Neau, a Frenchman residing in New York City, opened a school for blacks as early as 1704. In Philadelphia, Anthony Benezet, a Quaker sympathizer, founded a similar school and left monies in his will for further aid to black education.[90] The Polish patriot and Revolutionary hero Thaddeus Kosciusko had great compassion for black people. He gave liberally of his time and money to educate blacks and provided funds in his will for the purchase, liberation, and education of blacks. Unfortunately, his heirs interfered with the original intent of his will, leaving much of his projected philanthropy undone.[91]

A formal campaign to win support for the education of blacks in New York City commenced in 1785 with the work of the New York Manumission Society. The goal was "mitigating the evils of slavery, to defend the rights of the blacks, and especially to give them the elements of an education."[92] Alexander Hamilton and John Jay supported the society's educational aims and, two years later, free public schools for blacks were opened. In 1834 these schools merged with the Public School Society of New York.

The Quakers in Philadelphia were the first whites to offer blacks the same educational privileges that they themselves enjoyed; in 1784 they employed Sarah Dwight to teach sewing to black girls.[93] The civic-minded Dr. Benjamin Rush deplored the reluctance of masters to educate their black servants. But in 1798, Moreau de St. Méry reported wonderingly that in Philadelphia "there are schools called African assigned for the education of colored children."[94]

Sunday schools in the large urban areas of the North gave blacks an opportunity to learn to read and write without duress, for how could good citizens object to religious instruction that would teach blacks humility?[95] Slave owners tacitly admitted that some slaves were literate; notices on fugitive slaves bore these pathetic legends: "Can read writing"; "can read and write a little"; "can write a pretty hand."

Ironically, the chief source of financial support for pauper schools in Washington City until 1844 was lotteries and a tax on slaves and dogs.[96] The sons of poor free men were taught by the profits exacted from the black man's toil. The Enlightenment had brought reason to men, but it had not kindled compassionate fires in their hearts. The heroes in the struggle to humanize mankind were few. Not many college presidents were as principled as Edward Everett, who resigned in protest against the Harvard Corporation's refusal to admit a qualified black applicant.[97] Morris Birbeck took a more expedient course in his appraisal of a small college in Washington, D.C., in 1817: "From the dirty condition of the schools, and the appearance of loitering habits among the young men, I should suspect it to be a coarsely conducted institution. . . . There are also a considerable concourse of free negroes, a class of inhabitants peculiarly ill-suited to a seat of education."[98]

Early Education of Women

Although the white American male showed intellectual contempt for females by disenfranchising them until the twentieth century, he was slightly more magnanimous in granting them educational privileges. Jehovah and Jesus were males and, save for infrequent outbursts of Mariolatry among its adherents, the Christian Church has always been male oriented in principle, organization, and practice. How many writers of the Testaments were women? How many in the upper hierarchies were women? How many theological chairs have they occupied in the universities?

The pioneering American woman knew her place. She cooked, raised children, prayed, and sometimes fought beside her husband when the Indians atttacked. A bit of quaint verse on a colonial sampler illustrates the "male chauvinism" of the period:

> One did commend me a wife both fair and young
> That had French, Spanish, and Italian tongue.
> I thanked him kindly and told him that I loved
> none such,
> For I thought one tongue for a wife too much.
> What! Love ye not the learned?
> Yes, as my life,
> A learned scholar, but not a learned wife.[99]

The young women born at Plymouth Colony were generally illiterate; it was a rare Priscilla who could sign her name.[100]

In the later colonial period private schools for girls offered the traditional academic subjects, but they added courses in dancing, needlecraft, painting, millinery, and hairdressing to ensure that American females would be charming helpmeets to their prospective husbands.[101] Abigail Adams saw merit in music, dancing, and painting courses for girls; however, she urged that these liberal offerings be balanced with religious studies to guarantee that young ladies have proper respect for God and the Sabbath.[102]

Plymouth opened its first female school in 1789. But it was not until 1828 that the public schools in Massachusetts admitted girls on an equal footing with boys.[103] After Yorktown the Moravians established a boarding school for girls in Bethlehem, Pennsylvania, and in 1821 Emma Hart Willard founded the Troy Female Academy, a unique school for its day that encouraged girls to study science, mathematics, metaphysics, and scientific housewifery, the forerunner of modern home economics. Mrs. Willard stressed charm and "femininity" in her school, but not in the fatuous tradition of the finishing school. She intended to develop personable young ladies, conversant in many disciplines and equal to men in culture and accomplishment.[104] The better female academy served as an adequate substitute for the college to the daughters of the prosperous. Colleges were not for women; to a man, biased college presidents responded negatively to qualfed girls who sought admission to their schools. One such episode occurred at Harvard in 1849 during the tenure of President Jared Sparks. For the first time a young lady dared apply for admission to Harvard. An excerpt from Sparks's letter, April 25, 1849, reveals his graceful administrative obdurateness:

As the institution was founded . . . for the education of young men; all its departments arranged for that purpose only, and its rules, regulations, internal organization, discipline, and system of teaching designed for that end, I should doubt whether a solitary female, mingling as she must do promiscuously with so large a number of the other sex, would find her situation either agreeable or advantageous. Indeed, I shoud be unwilling to advise anyone to make such an experiment, and upon reflection I believe you will be convinced of its inexpediency.

It may be a misfortune that an enlightened public opinion has not led to the establishment of Colleges of the higher order for the education of females, and the time may come when their claims will be more justly valued, and when a wider intelligence and a more liberal spirit will provide for this deficiency.[105]

The nation would not attain "a wider intelligence and a more liberal spirit" toward the higher education of women for almost a half century. In 1820, the American male's attitude toward female education in general was in accord with the thinking of Frances Wright, an Englishwoman who had traveled widely in the new nation. Pleased with the wide education given to "Eastern ladies," she recommended that it be shorn of some of its ornament — French, Latin, dancing, and drawing — to have it equal the education of males.[106] Anticipating, perhaps, the enormous westward trek of Americans that would exact inordinate physical and mental discipline of the wives and daughters of the land questers, Mrs. Wright commented: "Now, though it is by no means requisite that American women should emulate the men in pursuit of the whale, the felling of the forest, or the shooting of wild turkeys, they might, with advantage, be taught in early youth to excel in the race, to swim, and in short to use every exercise which would impart vigor to their frames and independence to their minds."[107]

Conclusions

An editorial in the *Boston Recorder,* January 15, 1829, informed the American people that all was well with the state of the nation. Proudly optimistic, this journalistic tribute to the country's peace and prosperity might have been the editor's admonition to President Jackson to curb his radical penchants. Why institute change at a time of national felicity?

The chief glory of the end of the year 1829, is the situation of the Union. We refer to the unequalled prosperity and security of the American people; their advancement in numbers and wealth; the increase of their reputation and influence abroad; the new and extensive conquests which they have made over the wilderness; the diffusion of knowledge and the means of education; the constant enlargement of a horizon embracing the best prospects of national weal and glittering with the lights of cultivated reason.[108]

"The diffusion of knowledge and the means of education"! This shibboleth of the Founding Fathers was not forgotten by their descendants, but defining the "best means of education" was as difficult then as it is now. Should schools be privately or publicly funded? Should they be parochial or secular? Should they innovate or conserve traditional values? Should girls be educated beyond the secondary level? And to what extent should blacks, both slave and free, be advanced from illiteracy?

Religiously oriented at first, colonial schools and colleges tended to drift away from parochialism as public school societies gradually gained public approval in many states. But the vexing problem of taxation for education persisted; farmers especially were hostile to compulsory education, for of what value was book learning to their sons when harvests had to be reaped and fields needed plowing? Conservatives generally regarded learning for the masses with dismay, for surely the education of the poorer classes might lead them to adopt dangerous democratic notions.

Secular thinkers like Franklin and Paine opposed the classical curriculum of the academies, but traditionalists fought tenaciously to retain their beloved ancients in the schools. (Franklin held that Latin and Greek should be studied only as useful tools for the professions of theology, law, and medicine.) Gradually, vocationalism crept into the academy, but the academic bias for classical studies remained in the schools until the late nineteenth century. Girls attended local primary schools where they learned the three Rs, but few attended secondary schools until the 1820's. Before 1800 not even one girl was admitted to a college, but excellent female academies provided middle-class girls with a wide variety of meaningful courses. Blacks, slave and free, were neglected educationally. In the South there were practically no educational facilities for blacks. In the North, religious sects, notably the Quakers, undertook to teach blacks rudimentary subjects and trades. A kind master sometimes taught a pet slave, but in most cases educated blacks were self-taught.

In his "Brief Retrospect of the Eighteenth Century," Samuel Miller praised the cultural and educational accomplishment of the young republic in view of the turmoil and destruction that the nation had recently experienced. Throughout the land, colleges, academies, and lower schools strove to enlighten the young. Printing presses, book stores, libraries, and newspapers supplied the public with an abundance of literary fare; scientific, medical, historical, and agricultural societies promoted both practical and speculative projects in their respective specialties; and twenty-five colleges, including medical schools, were graduating four hundred professionals annually.[109]

But for all its educational advances the nation would not enjoy mass public education and reasonably cheap college education until its citizens were fully enfranchised. By 1828 only thirteen of the nation's thirty-three states had granted full manhood suffrage; slaves and women were excluded, of course, from the ballot. The election of Andrew Jackson in 1828, the first President not bound to the aristocracy, reflected the people's distrust of the propertied and educated classes. The extension of the suffrage to all white males gave the people an opportunity to vote for public education financed by the state. The propertied, enfranchised voters were able to pay for their children's education; the disenfranchised laborer and agricultural worker could not. Early substitutes for public education had failed: in turn, chartered school societies, subsidized religious and benevolent schools, schools supported by lotteries or land grants, subsidized pauper schools, and tax-exempt schools were not sufficiently endowed to provide education for the children of the poor. With increasing male enfranchisement, the struggle for free, tax-supported, nonsectarian, and publicly directed schools was begun.[110] Unfortunately, American writers did not regard the opening skirmishes by the common man and his articulate leaders as significant enough to celebrate in literature.

CHAPTER 2

A New Country's Literature

U NTIL Washington Irving, James Fenimore Cooper, Nathaniel Hawthorne, Ralph Waldo Emerson, Henry Thoreau, Herman Melville, and Edgar Allan Poe had won European acclaim for their writing, American authors were neglected by native critics. Representative criticisms of American literature attributed the mediocrity of post-Revolutionary writers to their obvious imitation of their British peers; to a lack of a leisure class in America to subsidize genius and talent; to the inadequacy of American collegiate training in classical learning; to the importation of inexpensive English books and journals; and to the limited number of free libraries and book shops in most parts of the country.

As late as 1854, a critical history of English and American literature numbering 489 pages included a monograph of only fifty-nine pages on American literature.[1] Johann Schoepf, a foreign observer of American life in 1788, predicted that America could not hope for a brilliant surge in learning and the birth of a meaningful native literature for many decades. Some eminent Americans agreed: Walter Channing lamented the nation's lack of a national character and its delight in acquiring foreign books; Edward Tyrell Channing belittled our borrowed "gaudy patchwork" literature; and Charles Brockden Brown despaired that our bonds with England discouraged American genius.[2]

Can a new nation afford to luxuriate in aesthetic and cultural pastimes before it has attained a comfortable surplus of life's necessities? Not so, thought Benjamin Franklin in 1749 when he proposed the founding of an academy in Philadelphia. (The school will be discussed in Chapter Three.) After the Revolution, Francis Calley Gray, a wealthy Boston lawyer who devoted much of his time to civic and literary pursuits, concurred with Franklin's views. He saw that wars and economic want were deterrents to the advancement of letters.[3] This theory was stated more picturesquely by Moses Tyler: "No man is likely to be in the mood for aesthetics who has an assassin's bullet at his head."[4]

The nation would have to wait for its cultural maturation until the leisure and encouragement accorded to men of genius in many European states would be enjoyed also by American writers and artists. Meanwhile, there was an exodus of scholars, artists, and scientists to Europe for the fame and fortune denied to them in America.

The Colleges Do Not Promote Culture

American writers found the universities wanting. Charles Henry Dana, Sr., scored the colleges for their vocational bias; George Tucker berated them for having inferior libraries, incompetent professors, and insufficient numbers of students; Samuel Miller deplored the incompetent college teaching, shortsighted trustees, and prejudiced populace that withheld financial support from the colleges.[5] Charles Brockden Brown, one of the better novelists of the period, specifically attributed the extravagant rhetoric of the nation's best-trained scholars to the poorly administered classical teaching in the colleges.[6]

The schools and culture could wait for funding. There were more immediate projects facing the colonial farmer than financing parsers in Greek and Latin and patronizing versifiers of rhymed and unrhymed iambs. The post-Revolutionary farmers and workers were pragmatic, utilitarian, and averse to purely aesthetic and intellectual dilettantism.[7] Only the clergy expressed an interest in intellectualism, but the colonies produced no important speculative thinkers and no great artists.[8] Even after the Revolution the commercial tone of the nation persisted; wealth was the goal of most people and only through enterprise could one attain affluence. Learning alone would not bring wealth; America offered too many seductive commercial opportunities to those intellectually or artistically inclined, weaning them away from their impoverished and unpromising disciplines.[9]

Not only were American critics unduly hostile to native authors, but important writers were also unfriendly to their peers. Bryant dismissed most of the pre-Revolutionary poetry as valueless, but he praised Trumbull's "Progress of Dulness." Philip Frenau was no more than a "writer in verse of inferior note," and the Connecticut Wits were mere practitioners of patriotic and nationalistic rhymes.[10] Fisher Ames compared Joel Barlow and Thomas Paine unfavorably with Homer and Plato, respectively; Washington Irving searched vainly for one dramatic writer of merit; and Philip Freneau complained of the dearth of imaginative books.[11] Johann Schoepf agreed with the American critics: "America itself has contributed little to the augmentation and embellishment of what it has received."[12] Schoepf was niggardly in his listing of American greats. He conceded the genius of Franklin the philosopher, Rittenhouse the mathematician, Neal the painter, and Dickinson, Paine, and Jefferson, political writers.[13] Schoepf was undoubtedly myopic in his survey of American culture; perhaps he traveled too speedily through the states.

Cultural Taboos

A nation's cultural mores may inhibit its aesthetic maturation. John Trumbull, who criticized the college establishment in "The Progress of Dulness," wrote the following about novels:

> We grieve that reading is confin'd
> To Books that poison all the mind;
> Novels and plays (where shines display'd)
> A world that nature never made.[14]

Two years later, in 1774, the Continental Congress classed plays with the evils of gambling and horse racing, a singular pairing indeed, and this virtuous assembly of statesmen banned fiction not much later.[15] Royall Tyler, himself a novelist, cautioned fiction readers to beware of the moral turpitude of novels, especially English ones.

Book Stores and Libraries

The availability of books in the early republic seems to be debatable. There was a want of books, few public libraries, and not one good all-American library.[16] But in 1823 Jared Ingersoll noted that libraries were improving and that booksellers were announcing increasing numbers of American titles.[17] Americans were hungry for newspapers, magazines, and educational works. The schools were producing their own literature — respectable state histories, geographies, and topographical books,[18] and publishers were busily issuing theological, political, and educational works.[19] For example, 100,000 copies of Paine's *Crisis* were sold while the issue was still fresh from the press.[20]

Pioneering American publishers like Mathew Carey encouraged

unknown writers, corresponded prolifically with them, and shipped books beyond the Mississippi even as Indians and whites disputed ownership of the land.[21] One of Carey's prize salesmen, Parson Weems, wrote spiritedly to Carey (July 10, 1810) for more titles: "This is no time to be wrangling. The Country is in darkness. Men's minds are uninform'd, their hearts bitter, and their mannars savage. Humanity and Patriotism both cry aloud. Books, books, books." His order illustrates the somber reading preferences of his clients:

Buck	*Theological Deity*
Russell	*Seven Sermons*
Whitfield	*Sermons*
Bunyan	*Visions*
Webster	*Blue-Backed Speller*
Rippon	*Hymns*
Bunyan	*Pilgrim's Progress*
Webster	200 small grammars
Josephus	*History of the Jews*

No More Plays

Eleven years later Weems was still peddling books and advising Carey on which titles to publish. Pious and patriotic, Weems recommended to Carey that the lives of Washington, Franklin, and other national heroes "be made into schoolbooks," and to influence Carey to issue a series of moral guides for the young, he appealed to the publisher's moral and pecuniary sensibilities: ". . . every Parent knows that, after all his labors for his son, that son may quickly be thrown to the Dogs and the dung hill by his Drinking, Gambling, Wenching and Dueling: hence, with all considerate Parents, there is good hope that short, cheap, *ad captant* pamphlets on these most interesting subjects will ever be popular."[22]

In Praise of American Writing

In "Letter XXIII" of Cooper's *Notions of the Americans* (1828), the author defends American literature and institutions against the unceasing denigrations of domestic and foreign critics. Published in 1828, the year of Jackson's ascension to the presidency, the book was an optimistic prediction of American greatness. American literature would become independent of British influence and American authors would publish numerous original works.[23]

In his Phi Beta Kappa Address (1815), William Tudor advised

American writers to memorialize existing American themes, for in the Revolution, the Confederacy of Indian Tribes, the French Empire in America, and the nation's resources, climate, and landscapes there were endless topics for literary exploitation.[24] Longfellow thought that the native writer's love of nature would grace our literature with beauty and poetic feeling,[25] and Charles Brockden Brown, in his preface to *Edgar Huntley*, called the reader's attention, and not without just pride, to his employment of new themes in his novels:

One merit the writer may at least claim; that of calling forth the passions and engaging the sympathy of the reader by means not hitherto employed by preceding authors. Puerile superstition and exploded manners, Gothic castles and chimeras, are the materials usually employed for this end. The incidents of human hostility, and the perils of the western wilderness, are far more suitable and for an American to overlook these would admit of no apology.[26]

In 1819 Richard Henry Dana, Sr., credited Washington Irving with forming our literary standard.[27] In 1829 Samuel Knapp published the first attempt at a literary history of America entitled *Lectures on American Literature with Remarks on Some Passages in American History.*[28] Knapp had an ample literary harvest to reap from for his book: John Trumbull, Joel Barlow, Timothy Dwight, Fitz-Greene Halleck, Philip Freneau, Ben Franklin, Royall Tyler, Hugh Brackenridge, James Fenimore Cooper, William Cullen Bryant, Charles Brockden Brown, Thomas Paine, Daniel Webster, George Bancroft, and a handful of Southern writers. And, of course, the distinguished political works of the Founding Fathers could not be excluded from literary scrutiny.

The Founding Fathers in Literary History

But are the political addresses, orations, and debates of the Revolutionary statesmen valid literary works? Darrel Abel characterizes much of America's writing from 1765 to about 1790 as expository essays concerned with transitional ideas, more properly belonging to social and political history than to literary history.[29] But Charles and Mary Beard see more than fine expository prose in the papers of the Revolutionary statesmen. James Otis, the Adamses, Hamilton, Jefferson, and John Dickinson had an admirable prototype for their persuasive writing in John Locke's prose and "they had only to use English rhetoric and precedent in forging their own greater argument; but in actual fact they went beyond the rule and thumb, giving to their noblest writings some of the gravity of Roman orators, some of the rhythm and cadence of Latin poets."[30]

Early American writers, namely, Samuel Miller, Jarod Ingersoll, George Tucker, and Washington Irving, wrote appreciatively of the literary quality of American state papers. Included in these valuable papers are thousands of letters of leading Revolutionary statesmen, perhaps the most significant contribution to American letters of the founding period, for who can read, for example, Jefferson's letters, and not be impressed with his almost Faustian grasp of his "wide, wide, world," his encyclopedic intercourse with the world's greatest minds, and his deep concern for educating almost all classes of men? Adrienne Koch praises the writings of Franklin, Jefferson, John Adams, and Hamilton as a "massive literature which is the epitomization of the American enlightenment." The papers of these statesmen numbered almost three hundred volumes in 1965 and these collections are still growing. The count compiled by Adrienne Koch in 1965 is impressive:

The papers of John Adams, John Quincy Adams, and Charles Francis Adams	100 vols.
Julian Boyd edition of Thomas Jefferson	50 vols.
Leonard Labaree edition of Benjamin Franklin	40 vols.
Hamilton papers	40 vols.
Madison papers	40 vols.

Educational Value of the Political Debate

Besides being a political war, the great colonial debate between Tory and Whig was a potent instrument for public education. Newspapers, pamphlets, almanacs, and broadsides proliferated; orators transmitted written polemics to vast audiences; and an excited public avidly read satirical essays, hortatory letters, atrocity tales, blaring headlines, and inspirational poems. For the less literate there were pointed cartoons and provocative engravings to ponder. This literature of exhortation was evident in Cooper's time as well, for he noted the American penchant for polemical, political, theological, and historical writing.[32]

The Jacksonian Watershed in American History

The Jacksonian period was a great watershed in America's development. The frontier man had triumphed over the New England aristocracy, and he would encourage major political and social reforms. The area of the nation had doubled; seven new states gave the nation new power and resources. In this era American literature had its proper beginning: Bryant, Irving, Cooper, Halleck, and Noah Webster were in their prime and soon Emerson, Hawthorne, Longfellow, Lowell, Poe, Whittier, and Bancroft would have world renown. Literary magazines flourished in all parts of the land; among the leading magazines that featured American writers were:

	Year Established
U.S. Literary Gazette	1824 - 26
U.S. Review and Literary Gazette	1826 - 27
Graham's Magazine	1826
Western Monthly Review	1827
Western Monthly Magazine	1830
Southern Review	1828

Conclusions

American writers had to struggle to divorce themselves from British themes, rhetorical style, and mannerisms. Beset by strictures against fictional and dramatic writing, handicapped by the influx of cheap books from abroad, and unprotected by copyright laws, American writers had difficulty achieving recognition.

The Revolutionary conflict encouraged political writing — pamphlets, broadsides, and newspapers were read more eagerly than books. The struggle for independence and the trials confronting the postwar republic motivated American writers to eschew fiction and poetry for the more pressing political tracts that they used persuasively. As the letters of Parson Weems reveal, theological books were in great demand, but as the Revolutionary issues gradually waned in significance, fictional writers found an eager clientele for their novels and plays. Hugh Brackenridge, Royall Tyler, Charles Brockden Brown, Washington Irving, and James Fenimore Cooper were popular authors. Poets, too, had a following.

Although public education was not discussed at the Constitutional Convention, the state papers of the important leaders of the early republic touch on educational topics frequently. From 1775 until the end of the century, the literature of politics includes more references to education than the literature of belles lettres. In the mid-1820's, as more mature American writers gained prominence, the trend reversed. The American Renaissance in literature was in fiction, poetry, drama, and the essay, and with the passing of the geniuses of the American Revolution an era in glorious political writing passed also. There hasn't been another like it since.

CHAPTER 3

The Founding Fathers
View Education

A ND say finally, whether peace is best preserved by giving energy to the government or information to the people. This last is the most certain and the most legitimate engine of the government. Educate and inform the whole mass of people. Enable them to see that it is their interest to preserve peace and order, and they will preserve them.[1] [Thomas Jefferson]

Benjamin Franklin Champions Education

In 1750, Franklin wrote to Samuel Adams of his educational dreams: "I think with you, that nothing is more important for the public weal, than to form and train up youth in wisdom and virtue. Wise and good men, are, in my opinion, the strength of the state; much more so than the riches or arms, which under the management of ignorance and wickedness, often draw on destruction, instead of providing for the safety of the public."[2] Interestingly, Franklin, Jefferson, and John Adams strongly advocated public education as a deterrent to war; unfortunately, as public education increased in Western nations, so did the number of wars.

An examination of the textbooks read in the years 1930-1938 by students participating in World War II might convince a modern historian that public education as presently constituted can be no panacea for wars and other social blights afflicting mankind. Can the nations agree to a course of education that would prevent war? Do they really care to prevent war?

Benjamin Franklin looked upon the wars of his age and preached that "there never was a good war or a bad peace." That was in 1773, but after Lexington and Concord he had to live with the realities of political action. An admirer of Lockean social psychology, Franklin rejected the prevalent belief in innate ideas for the environmentalist's argument that men were molded by their experience and surroundings. Consequently, an enlightened people would institute good political and social systems that in turn would ensure the development of good people.

John Adams was less sanguine regarding education's power to bridle the evil in man. In his *Discourses on Davila*, a work disliked by Hamilton and Jefferson, Adams viewed education's promise pessimistically:

The increase and dissemination of knowledge, instead of rendering unnecessary the checks of emulation and the balances of rivalry in the order of society and constitution of government, augment the necessity of both. It becomes the more indispensable that every man should know his place, and be made to keep it. Bad men increase in knowledge as fast as good men; and science, arts, taste, sense, and letters are employed for the purposes of injustice and tyranny as well as those of law and liberty; for corruption as well as for liberty.[3]

Perhaps education might have been discussed at the Convention had the more radical revolutionary leaders, namely, Jefferson, John Adams, Thomas Paine, John Hancock, Samuel Adams, Christopher Gadsden, Patrick Henry, and Willy Jones, been present at the proceedings,[4] but Franklin's silence on education in Philadelphia was an understandable intentional or unwitting oversight which is insignificant when compared with his exemplary participation in the educational and cultural life of the new nation. Undoubtedly, as he observed his earnest peers grinding out a unique national Constitution, he must have felt assured that they would not neglect the education of the nation's youth after their political midwifery chores were over.

As a boy of ten Franklin (who had attended the prestigious Boston Latin Grammar School for a year and had led his class in scholarship) enrolled at George Brownell's business school in Boston where, however, he failed in arithmetic! For two years thereafter Ben learned the tallow trade under his father's tutelage, but, discerning literary propensities in his son, Josiah Franklin sent him off to serve as an apprentice printer to James Franklin, his older brother, then twenty-one. Now his education began in earnest. He read avidly and experimented in prose writing.

Silence Dogood Lashes Harvard

At sixteen he was ready for authorship, but did not dare submit his "Silence Dogood" papers to his brother for possible inclusion in the *New England Courant*. Instead, he slipped his first "Silence Dogood" paper under the door of the *Courant* office, and to his delight, saw his essay in print in the April 2, 1722, issue of the newspaper. His pseudonymous essays, fourteen in all, ran in the *Courant* from April 2, 1722, to October 8, 1722. At sixteen, the unlettered lad was a widely read author.

Silence Dogood, a woman born on a ship sailing to New England, was bound to a minister who had her trained in needlework and educated in writing and arithmetic. In addition, he gave her free use of his library. This is reminiscent of the liberal education given to young Phillis Wheatley, the slave girl purchased by the Wheatleys of Boston, who later gave the poetess her freedom. Silence, admirably schooled in the liberal arts, becomes Franklin's fictional critic of mediocrity at Harvard, suppression of free speech, religious hypocrisy, and blind zeal.[5] Her fourth essay is a dream vision of Harvard College, a snobbish school for the rich that hires impoverished tutors working for pittances. At commencement time, "every Beetle-Scull seem'd well satisfy'd with his own Portion of Learning, tho' perhaps he was e'en just as ignorant as ever." Nor does Silence spare vain parents who send their incompetent sons to college instead of indenturing them to tradesmen as useful apprentices. She meditates "on the extreme Folly of those parents who, blind to their Children's Dulness, and insensible of the Solidity of their Skulls, because they think their purses can afford it . . . well needs send them to the Temple of Learning . . . from whence they return, after Abundance of Trouble and Charge, as great Blockheads as ever, only more proud and self-conceited."[6] Silence has more complaints. The scholars are idle and mercenary. Seniors write papers for lower classmen — a criticism still valid — and the Philistine graduates turn out to be merchants, travelers, and other allied nonentities.

Was Franklin bitter at sixteen because he could not be a Harvard man? Was his denigration of Harvard based on his experiences with Harvard graduates? By 1753, Franklin's war with Harvard was over. One does not quarrel with a temple of learning that awards him an honorary degree of Master of Arts.[7] In less than two decades John Trumbull was to blast the higher learning in New England in his poetic satire "The Progress of Dulness," a piece remarkably akin in theme to Franklin's "Silence Dogood Papers."

Franklin's Educational Aims

Franklin's educational aims were both practical and visionary. As a humanist he believed that wars and persecutions represented a bestial side of man that education might suppress. The old education had not weaned man away from his carnivorous antics. Therefore, why not abandon both religious education and traditional education for more enlightened philosophies? For an emerging commercial nation it might be wiser to adopt new techniques in teaching where "emulation and pleasure replace fear, and worldy prosperity and recognition replace divine sanctions."[8] To prepare the young for careers in the bustling business civilization of eighteenth-century America, Franklin proposed that they should be encouraged to form useful habits, master business skills, and follow the practical sciences. The curriculum, therefore, should stress utilitarian English, mathematics, commercial history, science, and health. To ensure that the profit-minded youths would not worship Mammon unduly, Franklin recommended a sufficient dosage of moral science for each student, a sop perhaps for those who deplored his apparent lack of educational piety.[9]

To those who opposed his plan for the mass education of the young, Franklin replied that if only a few of the many being educated were successful, the cumulative effect of the eminent upon society would be significant. Furthermore, he reasoned that it is easier to educate youth than to try to cure adults of bad habits.[10]

Franklin's Educational Proposals

Franklin had many opponents of his plans for public education, especially among the formally trained graduates of traditional schools. But firm in his belief in self-education, he championed a curriculum that would make respectable those educational values consistent with the needs of a flexible, changing society.[11] In 1749, he thought that Pennsylvania was sufficiently stable politically and economically to encourage the advancement of the finer arts and sciences;[12] accordingly, he wrote his "Proposals" anonymously, modestly "avoiding as much as I could according to my usual Rule, the presenting myself to the Publick as the Author of any scheme for their Benefit."[13]

Although Franklin unequivocally preferred a utilitarian curriculum and an easy concise writing style to pedantic, note-laden scrivening, David B. Tyack sees a possible hoax in Franklin's swamping of his own proposals with endless footnotes from the tomes of Milton, Locke, Obadiah Walker, and George Turnbull.[14] Was Franklin writing with tongue in cheek or was he — humble and unlettered — trying to impress his academic and political audience with his awesome learning? Probably the former; the advocate of concise and plain speech could hardly assume a style reprehensible to him. Most likely, Franklin is a "genuine specimen of American common sense, a common sense so large, even at times so disproportioned, as to appear almost lop-sided and 'funny'." It is in his hidden censure of pretentiousness and fraud in his candid, earthy idealism that we see the prototype of the humor employed by the great majority of his successors.[15]

Franklin's "Proposals Relating to the Education of Youth in America" was a progressive educational tract for its times, and it still offers sensible recommendations. The academy, surrounded by meadow and orchard, should have a well-stocked library, an abundance of maps and globes, and a variety of scientific instruments in modern laboratories. Headed by a learned, patient, and compassionate rector, a competent and tolerant faculty would guide the temperate student body through practical curriculums aimed to create young men sound of body and mind. Gymnastics and swimming would develop their bodies; useful and ornamental studies would attend to the maturing of their minds. To prepare them for their post-adolescent jousting with the ogres of a competitive world, the academy provided courses in composition, drawing, perspective, arithmetic, accounts, geometry, and astronomy. Mastery of grammar would give their language clarity and conciseness — it was hoped. The course in reading was not so much concerned with silent speed reading as it was with elocutionary niceties. To acquire skill in writing, students were encouraged to correspond with one another, a technique still used by contemporary teachers. Of course, then as now, the tutor was expected not only to correct compositions but also to justify his corrections.

All this teaching and learning was to be administered painlessly and joyfully received. The classics, if taught, were to be offered in translation. Geography, a compendium of ancient customs, morality, and history reflecting mankind's virtue, spirit, and fortitude, was an admirable course for the youth's formative years, but it was to be subservient to the course in modern political oratory. Religion would be taught to foster notions of civil order and proper liberty in the spirited child. Naturally, lest the questing lad be enticed by licentious reveries, he was to be prescribed potent doses of religious antidotes to moral poisons.

Franklin encouraged debate as an initiator of logical thinking in youth. In pursuit of victory and praise in debate, students would employ logic vigorously. He recommended the study of foreign languages as preparation for training in specific occupations: Latin and Greek for divinity students; Latin, Greek, and French for future physicians; Latin and French for prospective lawyers; and French, German, and Spanish for merchants. Languages were not for all students, but they were available for those who desired to master them.

Learning, then, is a useful occupation. A student should know both the history of his mother country and the history of its possessions. Because trade was expanding, a wide-awake boy would profit by reading industrial histories and biographies, by understanding the principles of horticulture and commerce, and by studying natural history, including the health sciences. In pedagogy, Franklin advised tutors to teach oral reading, vocabulary skills, and the use of the dictionary, and he stressed the importance of the teacher's models in oral reading and writing. He favored prizes and praise for deserving students to stimulate the apathetic. And to ensure excellence in teaching, he divided the faculty into departments; for example, there would be a mathematics master, an English master, and so on for each of the remaining disciplines. Proud of his proposals, Franklin believed his projected academy could prepare students for any college. In his "Paper on the Academy," Franklin proposed another function for the academy.

That a number of the poorer sort will hereby be qualified to act as Schoolmasters in the Country, to teach children Reading, Writing, Arithmetick, and the Grammar of their Mother Tongue; and being of Good Morals and known characters, may be recommended from the Academy to the Country Schools for that Purpose; The Country suffering at present very much for want of good Schoolmasters, and oblig'd frequently to employ in their Schools, vicious imported Servants, or concealed Papists who by their bad Examples and Instructions often deprave the Morals or corrupt the Principles of the Children under Their care.[16]

Franklin strongly believed that "men should be taught as if you taught them not." He advised teachers: "In fact, if you wish to instruct others, a positive and dogmatical manner may occasion opposition and prevent a candid attention. If you desire improvement from others, you should not at the same time express yourself fixed in your opinions."[17]

For those who could not attend school, he cited his own life as an example of successful self-education; in addition, he advocated adult education as a means of providing a forum for the peaceful resolution of the rivalries of liberals and conservatives. Adult education would encourage self-education, the best education of all.

The Academy of Philadelphia opened its doors on January 7, 1751. The twenty-four trustees elected Franklin to serve as president of the Academy until 1756. But the trustees did not give Franklin full reign in curriculum planning. Traditionalists, they insisted that Latin and Greek be taught, although Franklin had set forth his preference for teaching in the vernacular. Considering the classics useless vestiges of aristocratic and theological learning, he nevertheless had to offer classical studies, especially for undergraduates preparing to enter the professions.

Franklin on Education of Minority Groups

An admirer of women, Franklin believed that "if women were educated as men they would be as reasonable and sensible," but they were, unfortunately, usually uneducated and courted with flattery and nonsense.[18] Always practical, he recommended that widows should study accounting rather than music or dancing, but for his daughter Sally, he provided an education in French, bookkeeping, arithmetic, and music.[19]

To prepare emancipated blacks for civil freedom, Franklin urged in 1789 that they be given employment and their children be given an education "calculated for future situations in life."[20] Earlier, the large number of German immigrants settling in the colonies had disturbed him; but anticipating the American "melting pot" dream, he proposed that the Germans be more equally distributed among the British and that English schools be established wherever the Germans were too thickly settled.[21]

Franklin's Influence

For a time Franklin toyed with the notion of creating a new alphabet. Noah Webster, America's first great lexicographer, was not interested in Franklin's "A Scheme for a New Alphabet, 1768." After all, who was Franklin? Certainly not a man of erudition. Yet, in 1789, Webster trimmed his sails, acknowledging in his "Dissertation on the English Language" that Franklin's early ideas on the improvement of orthography had been sound.[22]

How influential was Franklin in advancing American education? Interestingly, some critics argue that countless readers of Franklin's *Autobiography* were disenchanted with plans for public education because of his strong emphasis on self-education in his convincing book. If an unlettered Franklin could rise to the heights of statesmanship and scholarship, why not others? In 1838 the anonymous author of *The Life of Benjamin Franklin* praised *Poor Richard's Almanack* as an educational boon to the poor who could not afford many books.[23]

Important as Franklin's Academy was to the progress of practical education in America, his greatest influence upon American education in his time was through the media of his newspapers, pamphlets, and almanacs. For example, the only book in thousands of colonial homesteads was *Poor Richard's Almanack*.[24]

Franklin is praised by Dr. Victor Robinson, a medical historian, for his contributions to American culture and science.[25] The founder of our first philosophical society, first circulating library, first hospital, and first medical school, Franklin was also one of our earliest printers and booksellers. Dr. Robinson praises his writings on hygiene, gout, sexology, and the common cold, but he declines to mention Franklin's scatalogical essays. In addition, the versatile Franklin invented bifocal spectacles, a flexible catheter, and the Pennsylvania fireplace.

Benjamin Rush: Physician, Statesman, Educator

Dr. Benjamin Rush, a contemporary Pennsylvanian and signer of the Declaration of Independence, was the most prominent doctor in Philadelphia. Unfortunately, "he fussed over the baby until he spoiled it,"[26] and some medical historians attribute George Washington's death to the excessive bleedings administered to the dying President by disciples of Rush who attended him in his final hours.

Rush sought to introduce schools in Pennsylvania that would be modeled after the schools of Scotland. Since 1696, church and state had cooperated effectively to provide universal elementary education in Scotland. Some of these schools offered secondary education as well and sent boys directly to the university. Because of this enlightened national attitude, the high level of education and intelligence in Scotland was not equaled in any other part of the British Empire.[27]

Writing to Representative Clymer of Pennsylvania, Rush proclaimed his faith in the effectiveness of educational innovation:

For the benefit of those persons who consider opinions as improved, like certain liquids by time; and who are opposed to innovations, only because they did not occur to their ancestors, I shall conclude my letter with an anecdote of a minister in London, who, after employing a long sermon, in controverting what he supposed to be an heretical opinion, concluded it with the following words, "I tell you, I tell you my brethren — I tell you again — that an old error is better than a new truth."[28]

In his essay "Education Agreeable to a Republican Form of Government," Rush praises education as a purger of prejudice and superstition in religion, a boon to liberty, a promoter of just laws and good government, a teacher of manners and the art of conversation, and a stimulater of agriculture and of manufactures.[29] Every citizen should be given an opportunity to acquire knowledge and to prepare himself for a meaningful place in society.[30] The school must inspire him with love for republican principles and encourage him to live temperately, enjoy manual labor, and restrain his tongue.[31]

In his general educational aims Rush evidences both Hamiltonian and Jeffersonian strains of political philosophy. If man is to have liberty to develop his mind and to shape his character "in the pursuit of that happiness which the republic had been established to protect and to sustain," he must be well educated to exercise that liberty wisely.[32] Yet Rush wrote also that the essence of republican education is "to establish a government to protect the rights of property and to establish a system of schools which should encourage the virtue of its care."[33]

Rush on Religious Education

Rush, unlike Franklin, invoked the aid of religion to bolster his educational theories. Religion to him was the moral basis for any republican scheme of education; since the Old Testament refutes the divine right of kings and the New Testament "inculcates those degrees of humility, self-denial, and brotherly kindness which are directly opposed to the pride of monarchy and the pageantry of a court," a Christian must be a republican.[34] Religion prevents crimes and civil disorders. Why not, then, at a small expense, help eliminate crime by teaching religion in school? The Bible is a compendium of teachings of equality, respect for the laws, and all those virtues which constitute the soul of republicanism.[35] The free schools, if religiously oriented, would teach the poor moral conduct and ardor for industry. As the poor prosper, taxes go down, vice declines, and crime is reduced. Both boys and girls would be taught the obligations of the Christian religion, but to ward off antisectarian activists, the children would be taught in religious groupings and the supervisors would be of their own faith.[36]

The curriculum for grades one through twelve would include

reading, writing, arithmetic, and useful foreign languages. English was to be stressed as preparation for the commercial professions; history and chronology, economics and chemistry enriched the curriculum.[37] Latin and Greek, available to fourteen-year-olds, were the last subjects to be taught. Why waste the dead languages on students who would never read or write Latin or Greek?

Rush on Schoolmasters

Rush also envisioned a new type of schoolmaster, well versed in knowledge and in the ways of mankind. The existing schools were a disgrace to human understanding and their masters were ignorant or prejudiced.[38] What virtues should the ideal master possess? He should be a prudent man, ever in control of his passions, firm in class, but amiable in his associations with students between classes. He should be a dispenser of rewards to the diligent, but to the recreants he should be a benign reformer who admonishes them privately or detains them after class with their parents' knowledge. Expulsion from school should be only a last resort.[39]

But why is it, Rush inquired, that humane scholars cannot be attracted to the teaching profession? Unfortunately, too many people associated the job with despotism and violence.[40] Furthermore, the prevalence of error among the educated classes made the task of educational reform disheartening.

If the land itself would not produce dedicated teachers, there were alternatives. Although he was wary of sending young Americans to study abroad lest they be corrupted in Europe's immoral capitals, Rush did not hesitate to invite foreign scholars to take up schoolmastering in the United States. He urged European scholars to consider teaching in the Middle and Southern states. Rush pointed out that the new country offered great advantages to teachers, "provided they be prudent in their deportment and of sufficient knowledge; for since the establishment of colleges and schools of learning in all our states, the same degree of learning will not succeed among us which succeeded fifty years ago."[41]

Rush on Discipline

Rush was against corporal punishment in the classroom. Physical abuse of students, he said, deprives young people of all incentive to learn. Their fear of future punishment makes them slavish, and permanent brain damage can be inflicted by the master who specializes in thumping heads and pulling and boxing ears. A sensible teacher can discipline a class without recourse to brutality. Indeed, corporal punishment is so contrary to the spirit of liberty that laws should be passed punishing child beaters.[42]

To cope with disciplinary problems, Rush advocated student participation in extracurricular activities. Agricultural contests, competitions in manual arts and athletic games that were rigorously supervised were among Rush's panaceas for student mischief.

Yet, what Rush prescribed for other men's sons was not good medicine for his own son. Fearful lest his son be contaminated by what he viewed as immoral campus life at Princeton, Rush wrote to his friend Walter Minto that he would send his son to the New Jersey college on condition that he study at Minto's house and enter the college only for academic reasons. Alas, neither Rush's solicitude nor Minto's supervision deterred young Rush from damning himself by playing cards on the Sabbath.[43]

Rush on Higher Education

Rush had visions of an expanding system of higher education in Pennsylvania. The university center would prepare its clients for law, medicine, theology, natural philosophy, economics, and political economy. He proposed small colleges at Philadelphia, Carlisle, and Lancaster to prepare students for the university. He feared that large universities would invite dissipation; hence his support for smaller colleges that might be supervised more closely.

The university would provide masters for the colleges, and the colleges would train teachers for the free lower schools. The cost of education would be sustained by universal taxation. Bachelors, childless people, and even orphans would be taxed, because all would inevitably benefit from an educated public.[44] Rush, like Washington, believed firmly in the establishment of a national university to prepare youths for public service.[45] To prevent quacks from entering public life, only graduates of this university would be employed in public service.[46] The proposed curriculum would include courses in government, law, foreign policy, history, agriculture, manufactures, mathematics, natural philosophy, chemistry, natural history, philology, rhetoric, literary criticism, French, and German. The students would participate in athletics and manly exercises. Also, four intelligent young men would be sent abroad to select choice extracts of European culture for diffusion among American provincials. And two more youths would be set loose to explore the virgin land for its hidden natural resources.[47]

Rush, like Franklin, saw the need for educating large numbers of German immigrants who were ignorant of the law. He appealed to the trustees of Dickinson College to appoint a German teacher and urged the college to show the German immigrants that men should live for other purposes than "simply to cultivate the earth and accumulate specie."[48] Later, Rush advocated that a German college be organized to educate the sons of German farmers who were hostile to learning. To counteract the growing fear that German youth would leave their farms, he argued that learning would increase the incomes of farmers, make their work more productive, and add to the nation's strength.[49]

Rush on the Education of Blacks and Women

Dr. Rush championed the educational rights of blacks and lashed out at their masters who refused to educate and convert them.[50] Girls should be taught the usual branches of female education and their instructors should be careful to inculcate in them the principles of liberty, democratic government, and patriotism.[51] But the nation's interests were not yet significantly concerned with the problems confronting all the blacks and half the white population — the women.

Basically, Rush and Franklin entertained similar educational philosophies. Both saw the need for universal elementary education, a less rigorous secondary education, and a functional education for those who would not seek college matriculation. Rush stressed religion in education; Franklin did not. Both tried sincerely to elevate those not so gifted as themselves.

Samuel Adams on Public Education

Samuel Adams knew the power of the word; his Committees of Correspondence had been of immeasurable value in solidifying colonial opposition to the Crown. A believer in public education, he wrote to James Warren in 1775 in praise of the common schools of New England as the foundations for the achievement of public virtue.[52] As governor of Massachusetts in 1794 he asked the state legislature to support public education because an instructed youth would have a disinterested passion for truth. If educated in the art of government and jurisprudence, the youth of the land would be armed intellectually to detect errors in the administration of government.[53]

Samuel Adams saw that the academies would eventually be monopolies for the rich. For this reason he fought vigorously for grammar schools for all.[54] In an exchange with John Adams, who feared that other nations would not pay for universal education and so undermine the basis for world enlightenment, Samuel Adams wrote:

It would not be fair to conclude that, because they have not yet been disposed to agree in it [universal education], they never will. It is allowed that the present age is more enlightened than former ones. Freedom of inquiry is certainly more encouraged; the feelings of humanity have softened the heart . . . and bigotry if not still blind, must be mortified to see that she is despised. Such an age may afford at least a flattering expectation that nations, as well as individuals, will view the utility of *universal education* in so strong a light, as to induce sufficient national patronage and support. Future ages will be more enlightened than this.[55]

There is beautiful idealism in this extract, but history has been more favorable to the second President's pessimism than it has been to the governor's optimism.

Washington and Higher Education

The Father of His Country was devoted to the advancement of education, but he was concerned more with national education than with universal education. According to Samuel Blodget in his *Economica*, Washington urged the establishment of a national university in 1775.

As President, Washington did not forget his commitment to the national university. In a speech to Congress on January 8, 1790, the President spoke of education as a national duty and recommended that Congress authorize funds for the construction of a national university.[56] Again on December 7, 1796, he proposed a national university that would be staffed with the finest professors. Here, leaders would be prepared; instructed in the science of government, the graduates would in turn educate the future guardians of American liberty.[57] The thinking of George Washington and Benjamin Rush on the national university is strikingly similar.

In his will Washington left fifty shares that he held in the Potomac Company to help establish a national university within the limits of the District of Columbia

to which the youths of fortune and talents from all parts thereof [The United States] may be sent for the completion of their education, in all the branches of polite literature, in arts and sciences, in acquiring knowledge in the principles of politics and good government, . . . and by associating with each other in forming friendships in juvenile years, be enabled to free themselves in a proper degree from those local prejudices and habitual jealousies . . . which, when carried to excess, are never-failing sources of disquietude to the public mind, and pregnant of mischievous consequences to the country.[58]

Washington also left monies to the lower schools — four thousand dollars to the Academy in Alexandria to educate the children of the poor and orphans, and one hundred shares in the James River Company to benefit Liberty Hall Academy in the County of Rockbridge, Virginia.[59]

Washington on Religious Education

Washington, like Jefferson and Madison, was firm in his stand against state aid to parochial schools. In a letter to George Mason in 1785, Washington opposed a legislative bill to support religious education:

Although no man's sentiments are more opposed to any kind of restraint upon religious principles than mine are; yet I must confess that I am not amongst the numbers of those who are so much alarmed at the thoughts of making people pay towards the support of that which they profess, if of the denomination of Christian; or declare themselves Jew, Mahomitans or otherwise, and thereby obtain relief. As the matter now stands, I wish an assessment have never been agitated. And as it has gone so far, that the Bill could die an easy death; because I think it will be productive of more quiet to the State, than by enacting it into a Law, which, in my opinion, would be impolitic, admitting there is a decided majority for it, to the disquiet of a respectable minority. In the first case the matter will soon subside; in the latter, it will rankle and convulse the State.[60]

Washington's disinterested liberalism is further evidenced in his attitude toward the enslaved blacks of America. He hoped "to see some plan adopted by which slavery may be abolished by law," but in 1785 he wrote to Lafayette that the Virginia legislature was almost deaf to petitioners for abolition of slavery.[61] In his will, however, Washington provided for the freedom of his slaves and advised masters to prepare the children of slaves for freedom by educating them academically and vocationally.[62]

John Adams Supports Public Education

Throughout his life, Washington's successor, John Adams,

appealed to Americans to support public education liberally. The young mind is malleable and can be made virtuous and meaningful by early education and discipline.[63] Since the people have been given understanding by their maker they have "an indisputable, inalienable, indefeasible, divine right to that most dreaded and envied kind of knowledge — I mean of the characters and conduct of their rulers. Rulers are no more than attorneys, agents, and trustees, for the people."[64] And the knowledge gained by the people must be tenderly cherished: "Let us dare to read, think, speak, and write," said Adams. He must have startled many of his fellow aristocrats by his contention that "the preservation of the means of knowledge among the lowest ranks is of more importance to the public than all the property of all the rich men in the country."[65] To Dr. Benjamin Waterhouse he wrote that all studious students succeed, that genius is often a product of accident, poverty, distress, envy, jealousy, or love. Rum and drugs sometimes stimulated flagging intellects; Thomas Paine, for example, needed liquors to stimulate his creativity.[66]

Meanwhile, though, the aristocracy ruled the nation because only the aristocracy was educated. The three or four thousand graduates of Harvard who for two centuries since the college's first commencement governed Massachusetts and dominated its schools and universities, churches, courts, agriculture, finance, and scientific institutions, had influenced America's historical destiny far more than the uneducated masses. Only one American in ten was well educated in sciences and letters.[67] Adams seemed content with this despite his philosophical stand on the education of the poor.

In Revolutionary times Adams was an unequivocal defender of the right of the university to challenge political authority. But in 1776 when he detected a strong note of anti-intellectualism in the nation, he did not excuse the educated classes. In a letter to J. D. Sergeant he advised the learned "to lay aside some of their airs of scorn, vanity, and pride, in which it is a certain truth that they sometimes indulge in."[68] A month later, he continued on this theme in a letter to Joseph Hawley of Philadelphia:

Knowledge is among the most essential foundations of liberty. But is there not a jealousy or an envy taking place among the multitude, of men of learning, and a wish to exclude them from the public councils and from military command? . . . How has it happened that such an illiterate group of general and field officers have been thrust into view by that commonwealth? . . . [69]

In his inaugural address, Adams still spoke enthusiastically on behalf of the expansion of the nation's educational program, but the schools now had a sacred trust to "preserve the Constitution, to shield the nation from political sophistry, party intrigue, and the pestilence of foreign influence."[70] Adams warned Jefferson against importing foreign professors who most likely would turn up as prejudiced Episcopalians or Presbyterians.[71] To justify his refusal to grant visas to visiting French scientists, Adams reasoned: "We have too many French philosophers already, and I really begin to think, or rather suspect, that learned academies . . . have disorganized the world and are incompatible with social order."[72]

John Adams on School Discipline

In the matter of school discipline, Adams felt that praise was better than punishment but that praise should not be excessive. He denounced corporal punishment.[73] The churlishness of his first Latin and Greek master encouraged him to spend his time in "shooting, skating, swimming, flying kites, and every other boyish exercise and diversion I could invent." But he was never mischievous under his kind second master. Soon, this excellent teacher influenced him to love his studies and neglect his sports.[74]

Although Adams was proud of New England's schools and colleges, he ultimately doubted the potential of education to reform society. In a letter to John Taylor, he wrote:

You may read the history of all the universities, academies, monasteries of the world, and see whether learning extinguishes human passion or corrects human vice. You will find in them as many parties and factions, as much jealousy and envy, hatred and malice, revenge and intrigue, as you will find in any legislative assembly or executive council, the most ignorant city or village. . . . Knowledge, therefore, as well as genius, strength, activity, industry, beauty, and twenty other things, will forever be a natural cause of aristocracy.[75]

Madison on Public Education

Madison believed that popular government could not exist without provisions for public education. He desired education for all and thought the wealthy should be taxed to subsidize the education of the poor.[76] But since he feared national education systems would present constitutional difficulties, Madison preferred to leave school planning to local authorities.[77] When Kentucky provided liberal appropriations for a general system of education, Madison rejoiced.

But when Jefferson's bill to establish universal elementary education in Virginia was defeated, Madison wrote to his saddened friend that the bill was too expensive.

Madison, like Washington and Rush, saw great virtue in a national university that would disseminate enlightening opinion, foster patriotism, attenuate sectional animosities, and facilitate national harmony.[78] He also wrote: "The capacity of the female mind for studies of the highest order cannot be doubted, having been sufficiently illustrated by its works of genius, of erudition, and of science." Women deserved an improved system of education, but women's liberation was not a major national concern in 1821 when Madison penned his hopes for a more liberal male attitude toward their "cabin'd and confin'd" opposites.[79]

Madison and Religious Education

Washington, Franklin, Madison, and Jefferson opposed public support of sectarian education. (Jefferson's ideas on the subject will be discussed later in this chapter.) Of the four, Madison seems to have been most aggressive in his political wars against support for church schools. As early as 1775 he wrote to Monroe opposing the Committee of the Continental Congress that wanted to sell land for support of religious education. Madison called this legislation unjust, foreign to the authority of Congress, and "smelling so strongly of an antiquated bigotry."[80] His strongest attack upon government-supported parochial education was set forth in his "Memorial and Remonstrance Against Religious Assessments" (Virginia, 1785). Basically, Madison opposed a bill that would establish a provision for teachers of the Christian religion. Because each man should worship as he sees fit, civil society cannot abridge man's religious rights, nor can legislatures make religion subservient to it, since religion is exempt from authority of society at large.[81]

Furthermore, he went on, a society which can establish Christianity to the exclusion of all other faiths can also infringe upon the rights of many of Christianity's sects. By the same token, those who believe have the responsibility to guarantee comparable freedoms to disbelievers.[82] In addition, argued Madison, religious establishments always supported tyrants and never guarded people's rights. Subversive rulers have always made profitable use of the clergy. If, in America, the church and state become one, immigrants will suffer and a new Inquisition will ensue.

Madison never retreated from this stand. Writing to Edward

Everett of Harvard in 1823, he commented on "the difficulty of reconciling the Christian mind to the absence of a religious tuition from a university established by law, and at the public expense," adding that the difficulty was probably "less with us than with you. The settled opinion here is that religion is essentially distinct from civil government, and exempt from its cognizance; the connection between them is injurious to both."[83]

In 1947, Justice Rutledge referred to Madison's firm stand on separation between church and state in his dissenting opinion on the parochial school bus case.[84] The Founding Fathers are quoted frequently by partisan factions in American cultural, political, social, and economic debates, but legions of patriotic Americans would probably be bewildered were they to read Washington, Franklin, Madison, and Jefferson on state support of religious education.

Jefferson on the Need for Public Education

Thomas Jefferson's educational views are located in fragments among his correspondence, in his *Notes on Virginia,* and in his state papers. Fortunately Jefferson's correspondence has been carefully scrutinized, annotated, and anthologized.

Distrusting the sagacity and morality of rulers, Jefferson vehemently insisted in *Notes on Virginia* that the people are the only "safe depositories of government." Naturally, to ensure that the people choose and supervise their rulers well, "their minds must be improved to a certain degree." At this point, Jefferson advocated what he had never proposed as the nation's chief executive — an amendment to the Constitution "in aid of public education."[85] Education was Jefferson's lifelong passion; in 1814, he wrote to John Adams of this unwavering obsession: "There are two subjects, indeed, which I shall claim a right to as long as I breathe, the public education and the subdivision of counties into wards. I consider the continuance of republican government as absolutely hanging on these two hooks."[86] And ten years before his death he reiterated his faith in education as the antidote of "bigotry . . . the disease of ignorance of morbid minds" and as "enthusiasm of the free and buoyant."[87] Education, then, is the inspirer of intellectual freedom, a coveted prize of reasonable men whose visions are not hallucinated by the stimuli of license.

Particularly incensed against religionists who impede innovation, Jefferson lashed out at the priestcraft-educators who "look backwards, not forwards for improvements," including in his indictment John Adams, who supposedly said that the science of our ancestors could not be advanced.[88] True education is dynamic, never static. To his famed teacher George Wythe, Jefferson wrote these oft-quoted words in 1786: "Preach, my dear Sir, a crusade against ignorance; establish and improve the law for educating the common people."[89]

Jefferson resolved the question of who was to be educated by advancing his doctrine of natural aristocracy, "the most precious gift of nature for the instruction, the trusts, and government of society."[90] On the other hand, aristocracy founded on heredity and affluence lacks the virtue of talents.[91] In a letter to his friend Mr. Correa (November 25, 1777), Jefferson wrote romantically of uplifting the talented sons of the poor to their rightful rank in society — a dream memorialized in the line: "Many a rose is born to blush unseen." Conceding that his notion of natural aristocracy "may be an utopian dream," Jefferson concluded his thoughts to Correa on natural aristocracy as a true romantic: " . . . but being innocent, I have thought I might indulge in it till I go to the land of dreams and sleep there with the dreamers of all and present time."[92]

Jefferson was very blunt in his plans of selectivity. In his educational winnowing process, the most favored lad from each proposed elementary school would be chosen to attend grammar school, and from these celebrities, the best would be called to grace the halls of higher learning. Summing up, Jefferson wrote with candor of his plan: "By this means twenty of the best geniuses will be raked from the rubbish annually, and be instructed at the public expense, so far as the grammar schools go." Finally, ten of the "best geniuses" educated in the grammar schools would be chosen to sit with the young aristocrats at William and Mary.[93]

According to Dr. James Conant, Jefferson derived his ideas on schools and universities from Scotland, perhaps from John Knox's *Book of Discipline*.[94] Jefferson's 1779 bill for education in Virginia resembled Knox's plan for education. Knox proposed that each parish should provide elementary education up to the child's eighth year, that advanced students be given a grammar-school education for three or four years, that higher grammar schools be instituted for advanced students, that the complete education of worthy students be subsidized, and that no scholar be barred because of his political convictions.[95] But Knox was much too progressive for the mid-sixteenth-century establishment of his country. The noblemen found his plan too costly, and they objected to any educational plan that would depend upon church and monastic foundations for its base.[96]

Jefferson remembered his teachers enthusiastically, especially Dr. William Small of Scotland, a professor of mathematics and philosophy at William and Mary. It was Small who kindled a lasting love for learning in Jefferson, and another eminent teacher at the same college, the aforementioned professor of law George Wythe, probably influenced Jefferson's political thinking considerably.[97] Jefferson's readings, of course, were as influential in shaping his education thinking as were his teachers. He was acquainted with all the intellectual movements of his day.

Professor Cubberley attributes many of Jefferson's educational ideas to his interest in French revolutionary conceptions, an idea that might have merit because of Jefferson's known advocacy of radical French ideas.[98] But Jefferson championed Pestalozzi as well,[99] and saw in Governor Clinton's program of public education in New York a feasible model for Virginia.[100] For a possible source of Jefferson's higher educational views, Conant cites the plan of Pierre DuPont de Nemours for a national education system in the United States that would include a national university. Jefferson proposed a similar plan in 1806, but Congress refused to further the President's project.[101]

Jefferson's Educational Projects

In 1779, at the request of the Virginia legislature, Jefferson drew up three education bills, only one of which was to be enacted. The first bill proposed to divide each county into hundreds of wards, each of which would support an elementary school guaranteeing at least three years of education for each child. The second bill aimed to reform education at William and Mary, enlarge its sphere in science, and develop it into a university; and the third bill provided for the establishment of a library.[102] To ensure that his doctrine of natural aristocracy would be applied in the public school system, Jefferson's bill added incentive awards for poor but talented students. From each school, the school Visitor would choose the best student from a poor family and send him to one of twenty proposed grammar schools. Here the scholar would compete with his more affluent peers in the mastery of Greek, Latin, geography, and the "higher branches of numerical arithmetic." Of the subsidized scholars, after a test run of one or two years, twenty of the finest would be chosen for a six-year tour of learning. And of these hardy survivors, one-half would be sent home joylessly to their provincial wards; the other half, truly an elect, would be sent on to three more years of learning at glamorous William and Mary.[103]

Bill one was voted down; and bill two was also rejected, according to Jefferson because Dissenters felt that a reform of the constitution of William and Mary under the hegemony of its Church of England partisans would give the Anglicans the upper hand in the college's control.[104] The defeat of these two bills also meant that Jefferson's plan for helping poor but worthy students was not adopted.

Jefferson and the University of Virginia

Defeated in his fundamental aim to advance elementary and secondary education, Jefferson began his long but successful battle to establish a major university in Virginia. His goals for higher education were set forth in the famous Rockfish Gap Report of 1818. It stated that a university has many functions: one, to develop statesmen, legislators, and judges on whom so much of our national prosperity and individual felicity depend; two, "to make leaders and citizens . . . on an exalted intellectual scale"; and three, to prepare men in "various specialized depths for their individual roles in a future more complex society."[105] But Jefferson warned against indiscriminate admissions to higher education; to avoid overcrowding professions with mediocre men, he favored the formation of state-sponsored vocational guidance programs, another of his farseeing educational plans that was prematurely proposed.[106]

As rector of the University of Virginia, Jefferson took a personal hand in the school's construction. He opposed a single, huge building for the university; instead, he planned an academic village arranged in an open square of grass and trees. Each professorship would have a small and separate lodge offering a dry passageway to all the schools.[107] As the building proceeded, Jefferson inspected its development daily. When illness prevented his inspections, he set up a telescope on his terrace to follow the progress of the construction.[108]

The building finished, Jefferson dedicated himself to filling the school with eminent teachers and concerned students. He aimed to make his university equal to Yale and Harvard. For a time he feared that his university project would be curtailed by the economy-minded legislature. He expressed this concern in a letter to George Ticknor in 1817; happily, these doubts were unfounded; but Jefferson's contempt for the "ordinary character of our state legislature, the members of which do not generally possess information enough to perceive the important truths, that knolege is power, that knolege is safety, and that knolege is happiness"[109] betrays his feelings for statesmen who minimize the role of education in a republic. Happily, Jefferson was able to recruit first-rate men for the faculty: George Blaetermann, professor of modern languages and Anglo-Saxon; Thomas Hewett Key, professor of mathematics; Robert Dunglison, professor of medicine and anatomy; Thomas Emmet, professor of natural history; George Tucker, professor of ethics; and John Lomax, professor of law.[110] These able teachers were lured away from their posts in England, Germany, and Scotland.

Jefferson as Student Counselor

Long before the University of Virginia opened its doors, Jefferson had lauded American college education, citings its advantages over European education to the son of a friend of his, J. Bannister, Jr. At William and Mary, for example, a student could elect classical curriculums, modern languages, mathematics, and natural philosophy, a course that included chemistry, agriculture, and natural history. True, European universities taught modern languages better, and medical students had to go abroad to study, but no other school in the world had a law professor as esteemed as George Wythe, Jefferson's own teacher at William and Mary.[111] Furthermore, he warned young Bannister of the immoral English who drank, betted, and boxed, and of other immoral Europeans who indulged in debauchery, passions for whores, and adultery — vices of a privileged aristocracy that debased the human mind.[112] Two years later, Jefferson served as a guidance counselor for T. M. Randolph, a young man who sought his advice on how to prepare for the law. His mentor recommended that he remove himself to France, live with a French family, and acquire a fluent command of the language from the women and children with whom he boarded. Three years in French universities would be sufficient preparation for him to continue his studies in Virginia with the estimable George Wythe.[113] Yet, only a month later (August, 1787), Jefferson wrote from Paris to Colonel T. M. Randolph that law study is almost entirely a study of books which can be read anywhere, that is, if the preparatory reading of the law were capped by a year's study with George Wythe.[114] Four years later Jefferson commended Edinburgh as the best school for Americans desiring to study abroad; its republican spirit would put American youth at ease. Geneva was an excellent school for the sciences, but its republicanism was marred by aristocratic tendencies.[115]

Jefferson's Ideas on Curriculum

On the basis of a letter to George Ticknor of Harvard (July, 1823), Dr. James Conant hypothesizes that Jefferson was willing to try an elective system at Virginia requiring only minimal qualifications for students to enroll in subjects of their choice.[116] Other letters — one to Francis Wayles Eppes — also reveal Jefferson's willingness to experiment with an elective system: "This will certainly be the fundamental law of our university to leave every one free to attend whatever branches of instruction he wants, and to decline what he does not want."[117] In addition, there would be no grading at the university, no attendance taken, and a minimum of faculty specialization.[118] Pomp at ceremonials would be minimized, as would the granting of honorary degrees, titles, or other honors.

Another project of Jefferson's, the district college, never took root in his own time, but the hundreds of community colleges in America today attest to his prophetic insights regarding education. The object of the district college — there would be nine for the state — was to prepare local students for the university.[119]

The Jeffersonian curriculum is a blending of the utilitarian and the philosophical. According to Jefferson, from the age of eight to fifteen the child's mind is not adapted for strenuous labors, but during that span the memory is sharp and can be readily employed in learning languages.[120] Of the modern languages, Italian is delightful but the least useful, whereas Spanish is essential because of our future commercial and political relationships with Spain.[121] French, too, is important for the educated man because of the many untranslated scientific books in French.[122] But Jefferson never downgraded the classics, which he enjoyed reading in their original Latin and Greek, because he regarded them as models of pure taste in writing.[123] Though he saw no need for the merchant, the mechanic, and the agriculturist to master the classical tongues, Jefferson wrote to John Brazer of Harvard in 1819 that " . . . it may truly be said that the classical languages are a solid basis for most, and an ornament to all the sciences."[124] For the University of Virginia, Jefferson proposed in 1819 that Anglo-Saxon be offered "to recruit and renovate the vigor of the English language, too much impaired by the neglect of its ancient constitution and dialects."[125]

Disliking oversimplified textbooks for children, Jefferson thanked America's pioneering publisher Mathew Carey for the copy of the *American Monitor* that Carey had sent him in 1801. Jefferson believed that a child's capacity to comprehend what he reads is generally underestimated by adults. Children, he advised, should be given good books to read — books that teach them to read and think.[126]

Jefferson's Quarrel with Sectarianism in Education

Jefferson never minimized the theocratic tendencies in American history. To exemplify his ideas, he used the metaphor "A wall of separation between church and state."[127] A Unitarian, he believed implicitly in freedom of thought, including "one's right to profess, to refuse to profess, and the right not to profess — on religion."[128] Robert M. Healey has charged that Jefferson's objection to ministers of the gospel serving as Visitors to the public schools and his plan for selecting the University of Virginia faculty "point to an unconscious but powerful drive to put his own religious beliefs in a position of unusual strength to receive a hearing from the students."[129] Yet in 1856 George Ticknor and Robey Dunglison had defended Jefferson. Both insisted that Jefferson had never inquired about a professor's faith and had never discussed religion with them.[130] At the University of Virginia students were permitted to attend services of any religious school within the neighborhood; furthermore, the students from the parochial schools could enroll at any school of the university and were entitled to the same rights and privileges enjoyed by all other students.[131]

Jefferson, indifferent to the hue and cry of the clergy and the legislature, appointed Dr. Thomas Cooper, the English scientist and educator, to the faculty of the Central College. Since he was a Unitarian and had become a victim of the Alien and Sedition Acts, Cooper was immediately attacked by those who feared his alleged radical views. Angered, Jefferson lashed out at the clergy, especially the Presbyterians, but he finally yielded to public pressure by agreeing to an equitable settlement of Cooper's contract. If Jefferson was indiscreet, the clergy was even more so for its crusade not only against an individual teacher but against the college as a whole.[132] The issue of radicalism was raised long after Jefferson's death by the *New York Review and Quarterly Church Journal*. In the March, 1837, issue, the editor charged that Jefferson had created a university machine to convert students to his pernicious views.[133]

In a letter to his nephew, Peter Carr, Jefferson clarified his religious beliefs, revealing his opposition to religious education. He advised the young man to avoid courses in moral philosophy; it was enough to read books without wasting time in class on abstractions. Question everything about religion, even the existence of God. Scrutinize scriptural writers carefully: for example, did the sun stand still at Joshua's bidding? Even the identity of Christ should be questioned, since there are variant views about his existence.[134]

A secularist in education, Jefferson wrote in his Act for Establishing Religious Freedom in Virginia that "to compel a man to furnish contributions of money for the propagation of opinions which he disbelieves, is sinful and tyrannical; that even the forcing of him to support this or that teacher of his own religious persuasion" is depriving him of freedom of conscience. Obviously, in his ill-fated plan for public education in Virginia Jefferson insisted upon secular control of the ward school, but it is likely that had his plan been approved, dominant sects in some wards might have insisted upon hiring teachers of their own persuasion.

Jefferson on College Discipline and Teachers

Jefferson was opposed to the office of college president, although he believed that the governing body of an educational institution had the right to demand adherence to its political and constitutional bylaws by the faculty. He feared that a college president might become despotic and warned the trustees of the University of Virginia to "avoid too much government by requiring no useless observances, none which will merely multiply occasions for dissatisfaction, disobedience, and revolt."[135] Jefferson did not have unanimity among the faculty on discipline. One of his proteges, Robley Dunglison, disagreed with his patron's view that an appeal to a student's patriotism and honor will do more to preclude mischief than the threat of punishment. Dunglison cites cases of student disobedience and expulsion,[136] but notes also that, in nine years, no single act of insubordination took place at the university against foreign professors.[137] Major offenses were judged by the faculty; minor offenses were judged by a board of six censors drawn from the most discreet students. However, this attempt at student government was eliminated in 1827 when the faculty discovered that students detested informing on one another.

The first session at the university was hectic. Nightly disorders led to riots and chaos on the campus. Finally, the faculty summoned the

Visitors to the school for assistance. Jefferson and Madison addressed the students and were shocked at their indignant language. The ringleaders of the riots, including Jefferson's grand-nephew, were expelled, and a new discipline, liberal but firm, was hopefully introduced.[138]

A controversy over school vacations illustrates that Jefferson could bend. He initially rejected a students' petition for a July vacation. The rules of the university stated that "there shall be one vacation only in the year and that shall be from the 15th of December to the last day of January." Jefferson argued that "its object was to avoid the common abuse by which two or three months of the year are lost to the students, under the name of Vacations. The loss at their ages from 16, and upwards, is irreparable to them."[139] However, after a second student petitioning, Jefferson granted the midsummer vacation.

Much as he defended the right to freedom of inquiry, Jefferson's record on academic freedom is not completely consonant with his frequently stated belief on *lehrer freiheit*. At Virginia he granted freedom of inquiry in all disciplines but those chaired in ethics and law by Americans. He forbade the use of Federalist texts in political studies; only Republican writers earned royalties at Virginia.[140] Even his program of free electives had a hitch to it; to graduate, students had to master Latin.

Teachers did not escape Jefferson's censure. Convinced that many teachers are led astray by artificial rules, he wrote to his nephew that "a plowman is better prepared to decide a moral case than a professor because he has not been seduced into patterned and authoritative thinking."[141] Deploring the unhealthy eruption of petty academies run by one or two incompetents, he hoped instead for institutions "here, as in Europe, where every branch of learning, useful at this day, may be taught in the highest degree."[142] And worse yet, he would have to scour Europe for first-rate classical and mathematical scholars for the university since none could be found in the United States.[143] But happily, even though he could not lure talented George Ticknor from Harvard, Jefferson was bighearted enough to praise Cambridge's outstanding modern language scholar, and he "a Federalist to boot."[144]

If he resented poor teaching, he was always pleased to praise excellent teaching. Indebted to Professors Wythe and Small for inspiring him at William and Mary, and appreciative of the fine faculty he had assembled at Virginia, Jefferson believed, nevertheless, in the virtues of independent study. He admonished his daughter Martha to learn to study without teachers, advising her that overdependence on a master weakens a student's self-reliance.

Jefferson on Education of Blacks

Although Jefferson opposed slavery in principle, he never freed his slaves. At the time of the American Revolution he was in favor of abolishing slavery, believing that a nation founded on the premise that all men are created free could not endure while some men were enslaved. "I tremble for my country," he said, "when I reflect that God is just; that his justice cannot sleep forever."[145] Later, in his *Notes on Virginia,* he passionately arraigned the institution of slavery:

> The whole commerce between master and slave is a perpetual exercise of the most boisterous passions, the most unremitting despotism on the one part, and degrading submissions on the other. Our children see this, and learn to imitate it; for man is an imitative animal. . . . The parent storms, the child looks on, catches the lineaments of wrath, puts on the same airs in the circle of smaller slaves, gives a loose to the worst of passions, and thus nursed, educated, and daily exercised in tyranny, cannot but be stamped by it with odious peculiarities. The man must be a prodigy who can retain his manner and morals undepraved by such circumstances.[146]

But when would slaveholders learn that God's justice "cannot sleep forever"? Washington, Jefferson, Patrick Henry, and Benjamin Franklin had openly defied the political and religious canons supporting slavery, but the nation had not heeded their appeals. At best, those with uneasy consciences spoke vaguely of a natural gradualism toward abolition, but most Americans accepted the status quo and went about their business.

Jefferson wrote little on black education, but after examining an astronomical almanac written by Benjamin Bannecker, a self-educated free black, he wrote: "Nobody wishes more than I do to see such proofs as you exhibit that Nature has given to our black brethren talents equal to those of the other colors of men, and that the appearance of a want of them is owing only to the degraded condition of their existence both in Africa and America."[147]

Another farsighted plan was Jefferson's proposal to organize an evening school for technicians and craftsmen.[148] This proposal, like so many others, was never implemented, but Jefferson understood the need to satisfy the educational aspirations of workers. The first evening schools in the United States probably were founded in New York City about 1833, and the first evening high school was opened in Cincinnati in 1856.[149]

Jefferson on Education: A Summary

Jefferson learned soon after the defeat of his elementary education bill that education, after all, is a matter of money. The wealthy Virginians refused to subsidize the children of the poor. Besides, the dominant conservative classes could afford to have their sons tutored for college matriculation. In 1820, after the defeat of his second bill for public education, Jefferson criticized education in Virginia. At least twelve hundred schools were needed and it was not because of poverty that this dearth of schooling existed but because of the lack of an orderly system of education.[150] To help pay for education Jefferson favored imposts on foreign luxuries and the establishing of a state lottery.[151] In 1816 he wrote emotionally to his friend Colonel Yancy, exhorting him to support public education:

I am a great friend to the improvement of roads, canals, and schools . . . The literary fund is a solid provision, unless lost in the impending bankruptcy. If the legislature would add to a perpetual tax of a cent a head on the population of the State, it would be set a going at once, and forever maintain, a system of primary or ward schools and a university where might be taught in the highest degree, every branch of science useful in our time and country; and it would rescue us from the tax of toryism, fanticism, and indifferentism to their own State, which we now send our own youth to bring from those of New England. If a nation expects to be ignorant and free, in a state of civilization, it expects what never was and never will be.[152]

It was never Jefferson's intent to make education compulsory, but he hoped to encourage universal elementary education by making it free. When his efforts to have public education legalized had been twice defeated, however, he turned to higher education, convinced now that the state tax for elementary education enacted in 1818 had been a mistake.[153]

According to one student of Jefferson, each sees in him what he wills. In our own time the progressives John Dewey and Horace P. Kallen regarded him as their progenitor, whereas the humanists Robert Hutchins and Albert J. Nock minimized the supposedly extreme democratic bias in Jefferson's educational philosophy.[154] Nock, for example, criticized Jefferson's public school plans vehemently: "The scheme of public education which 'the great democrat' drew up for Virginia is more mercilessly selective than any that has ever been proposed for any public school system in this country";[155] but Merle Curti disagrees with Nock, seeing in Jefferson's search for an aristocracy of talent and virtue in the masses a "far more democratic idea than had previously existed."[156] To accuse Jefferson of betrayal of his democratic principles on the basis of his plan to subsidize the advanced education of only the talented children of the poor fails, since in the historical context of his age he was as democratic as one might dare to be.

Howard Mumford Jones attributes John Dewey's progressivism to his strong Jeffersonian leanings,[157] and Roy J. Honeywell cites Jefferson as the "foremost advocate of appropriate and progressive education for all, and of that cornerstone of democracy, the American public school."[158] But he was merely an advocate, for with the defeat of his bill for the more general diffusion of knowledge, Virginia went back to a system of free and charity schools, modified tutorial schools, and grammar schools.[159]

As President, Jefferson did not press strongly for free public education. In his sixth annual message (December, 1806) he recommended leaving ordinary branches of education in the hands of private enterprise.[160] He explained his attitude toward education as President in a letter to John Taylor, August 16, 1816: "But education not being a branch of municipal government, but like the other arts and sciences, an accident only — I did not plan it, with election, as a fundamental member of the structure of government."[161]

What of his own appraisal of his educational contributions? Jefferson confided to John Adams that had his bill been passed young people of "worth and genius would have been sought out from every condition of life; and completely prepared by education for defeating the competition of wealth and birth for public trusts."[162] Essentially optimistic, he wrote to Dr. Priestley that despite his defeat "we are not without a sufficient number of good country schools, where the languages, geography, and the first elements of mathematics are taught."[163] However, when his second bill for public education was proposed in 1818, he wrote to Albert Gallatin of its expected defeat: "But it has to encounter ignorance, malice, egoism, fanaticism, religious, political and local perversities."[164]

Attacked as he was frequently by the press when he was in office, Jefferson refused to take action against his detractors, believing strongly that a free press even with its excesses is a vital prop of democracy. He felt similarly about books, even though some are pernicious: "Permit the books to circulate freely, but encourage the most searching criticism of them and work vigorously to bring the criticism to public attention."[165]

After 1800, Jefferson turned to his project of a new university. The university was to be "based on the illimitable freedom of the human mind, for here we are not afraid to follow truth wherever it may lead, nor to tolerate any error so long as reason is free to combat it."[166] Here is Jefferson at his best — a champion of truth, a compassionate judge of error, and a pillar of freedom of thought. But he was aware that a college education does not necessarily endow a man with courage and vision. He often lamented the apathy of educated men in public affairs: "Of our college friends (and they are the dearest) how few have stood with us in the great political questions which have agitated our country; and these were of a nature to justify agitation. I did not believe the Lilliputian fetters of that day strong enough to have bound so many."[167]

Optimism does not negate realism; five months before his death Jefferson wrote: "I have long been sensible that while I was endeavoring to render my country the greatest of all services, that of regenerating the public education, . . . I was discharging the odious function of a physician pouring medicine down the throat of a patient insensible of needing it."[168]

His contributions to political and religious freedom have inspired Americans in all critical periods of the nation's history, and his educational writings have influenced the educational philosophies of countless teachers who believed in his dictum that an informed public is necessary in a republican government.

Conclusions

Although most of the Founding Fathers were philosophically committed to "the general diffusion of knowledge," the ravages of the recently ended war, the chaotic state of the nation's political and financial condition, and the business of uniting the weakened thirteen states consumed almost all the energies of the leaders of the country. At the Constitutional Convention educational problems were completely ignored. Later, the papers of Franklin, Washington, Jefferson, Madison, Rush, John Adams, Samuel Adams, Alexander Hamilton, and Patrick Henry would disclose their educational thinking, but none of these leaders wrote specific educational treatises. Franklin in Pennsylvania and Jefferson in Virginia fought more than ideological battles on education's behalf and Franklin's academy and Jefferson's university attest to their partial success.

The Founding Fathers wrestled with problems that still cause friction among Americans. In illustration, three presidents — Washington, Jefferson, and Madison — warned of the mischief that state aid to religious education might initiate, but Patrick Henry and Benjamin Rush saw no menace in public support of parochial schools. The education of blacks and of women were of little concern to the founders; it would be many decades before these problems would become significant national issues.

The colleges were the monopoly of the aristocrats. Few poor whites entered Harvard or William and Mary. The graduates carried on the traditions of their fathers; controversy in the universities was largely theological; few of the undergraduates supported the minor rebellions of the post-Revolutionary era. Fiery leaders of the Revolution, Patrick Henry for example, now saw the schools as the indoctrinators of reverence for authority and for the Constitution.

In a more universal sense it may be said that the Founding Fathers were the educators of mankind. In the conclusion of his essay "Washington, Franklin, Adams, Hamilton, Jefferson," Rupert Hughes honors the political creators of this Republic "whose writings have altered the whole course of human progress."[169]

CHAPTER 4

Pre-Jacksonian Writers on Education

E XCEPT in one neighboring province, nonsense and ignorance
wander unmolested at our colleges, examinations are dwindled
to meer form and ceremony, and after four years dozing there, no one is ever
refused the honours of a degree, on account of dulness and insufficiency.
[John Trumbull, "The Progress of Dulness."][1]

Trumbull Flays Teachers and Divines

Fifty years after Ben Franklin wrote "The Silence Dogood
Papers," John Trumbull, who matriculated, commenced and tutored
at Yale College, startled the academic and theological communities
with his satirical broadside against collegiate education in "The
Progress of Dulness." An intellectual prodigy, Trumbull learned to
read at two, read the Bible at four, wrote poetry at five, passed the
Yale entrance examinations at seven, but did not matriculate until he
was thirteen because of his father's compassionate refusal to promote
his genius at the expense of his sound emotional development. Later,
his brilliance was recognized by Noah Webster, who employed him
to read a sizable portion of his dictionary, and by his colleagues, who
asked him to assist Timothy Dwight in overhauling the state
curriculum.[2]

Trumbull read his master's oration, "An Essay on the Rise and Advantages of the Fine Arts," to a Yale convocation in 1770. To the
consternation of many traditionalists, young Trumbull
acknowledged the advantages of language, mathematics,
philosophy, and metaphysics to the intellectually gifted, but
questioned the value of these time-honored disciplines to most
students. Why not have them study fine arts and "polite literature"
which the seminaries of science neglected?[3] His oration, though,
manifested his faith in American learning: "America hath a fair
prospect in a few centuries of ruling both in arts and arms. It is uni-

versally allowed that we excell in the force of natural genius, and although but few among us are able to devote their whole lives to study, perhaps there is no nation in which a larger portion of learning is diffused through all ranks of the people."[4] Three years later, in 1774, he mocked the reactionaries at Yale who opposed his curricular reforms: "Justly should you under-value them [liberal studies] in comparison with that ancient learning which from experience you rightly term Solid, as your own wits were not able to penetrate."[5]

In 1772-1773, while he was a tutor at Yale, Trumbull composed his still readable satire in octosyllabic couplets, "The Progress of Dulness." This work is reminiscent of Milton's criticism of education at Cambridge. "The Progress of Dulness" is an educational classic that should be included in teacher-training courses as a reminder that some of the pedagogical inanities exposed by Trumbull in 1772 are still extant in many schools.

In the preface to "The Progress of Dulness" the young satirist stated that he had been "prompted to write by a hope that it might be of use to point out, in a clear and concise, and striking manner, these general errors that hinder the advantages of education and the growth of piety."[6] In addition, he denied the value of ancient languages, abstruse mathematics and "dark researches of metaphysics" to businessmen or professionals, an educational philosophy remarkably akin to Franklin's educational beliefs.

In "The Progress of Dulness" we follow the sorry educational, professional, and amatory adventures of Tom Brainless, Dick Hairbrain, and Miss Harriet Simper, three unsavory students taught worthless subjects by incompetent teachers. Tom's father, a farmer, knows his son well; since Tom hates hard work and "his genius is too much above it,"[8] his father decides to send him to college. Tom is pleased, for now he will escape rising ". . . by break of day / To drive home cows, or deal out hay." But first he will have to be tutored by a parson who

> . . . in his youth before
> Had run the same dull progress o'er:
> His sole concern to see with care
> His church and farm in good repair.
> His skill in tongues that once he knew
> Had bid him long, a last adieu;
> Away his Latin rules had fled,
> And Greek had vanished from his head.[9]

Tom spends a year with the parson in classical studies, but murders Virgil's verse, "construes Tully into farce," and blunders hopelessly through Greek. Nevertheless, the parson recommends Tom as "A genius of the first emission / With burning love for erudition" who needs no examination. He assures the college administration to

> Depend upon't he must do well,
> He knows much more than he can tell;
> Admit him and in a little space
> He'll beat his rivals in the race.[10]

At college Tom dislikes his studies, absents himself from class frequently, pleads illness during recitations, and plods through the classics which he cannot understand or appreciate. In a mood of hyperbolized sadness, the author deplores the sham learning that Tom apathetically attends to:

> O' might I live to see that day,
> When sense shall point to youths their way;
> Through every maze of science guide;
> O'er education's laws preside;
> The good retain; with just discerning
> Explode the fopperies of learning.[11]

Four years later, after having slept and played his way through college, Tom receives an unearned reward.

> A scholar see him now commence
> Without the aid of books or sense:
> For passing college cures the brain,
> Like mills to grind men young again.[12]

Tom now is awarded a "passport" to teaching. Trumbull, an excellent scholar himself, must have seen disheartening educational abuses at Yale to write so disparagingly of the Bachelor's degree:

> Our hero's wit and learning now may
> Be prov'd by token of *Diploma*,
> Of that *Diploma*, with which speed
> He learns to construe and to read;
> And stalks abroad with conscious stride,
> In all the airs of pedant-pride,

> With passport sign'd for wit and knowledge,
> And current under seal of college.[13]

His degree useless and unemployed three months after graduation, Tom's father advises him to "teach a school at first, and then to preach," since Tom is fit for nothing else. Hired by a rural district for forty pounds a year, Tom sits

> . . . thron'd aloft in elbow-chair,
> With solemn face and awful air˙
> He tries with ease and unconcern,
> To teach what ne'er himself could learn;
> Gives law and punishment alone,
> Judge, jury, bailiff, all in one;
> Holds all good learning must depend
> Upon his rod's extremest end.[14]

Fortunately for Tom and his students, his tenure is only for one year. At the year's end

> . . . he takes his leave;
> The children smile; the parents grieve;
> And seek again, their school to keep,
> One just as good, and just as cheap.[15]

His teaching days done, Tom retires from the world to prepare himself for preaching. He pores over "sermons to study and to steal," passes the clergy's licensing examination, and is ordained a preacher.

> What though his wits could ne'er dispense
> One page of grammar or of sense;
> What though his learning be so slight,
> He scarcely knows to spell or write
> What though his skull be cudgel-proof!
> He's orthodox, and that's enough.[16]

Now at sixty pounds a year, Tom settles down for life as preacher of a small town. His parishioners pay dearly for their pedant in boredom, for Tom

> On Sunday in his best array,
> Deals forth the dulness of the day;
> And while above he spends his breath,
> The yawning audience nod beneath.[17]

The second part of "The Progress of Dulness" follows the career of Dick Hairbrain, who is admitted to college after three years of grammar school where he studied "knav'ry more than Greek." College to Dick will be a lark:

> Let poor, dull rogues, with weary pains
> To college come to mend their brains,
> And drudge four years, with grave concern,
> How they may wiser grow and learn.[18]

No, Dick has a more glamorous curriculum in mind — gaming, wenching, drinking, and rioting. He has chosen a college

> Where kind instructors fix their price,
> In just degree on ev'ry vice,
> And fierce in zeal 'gainst wicked courses,
> Demand repentance — of their purses;
> Till sin, thus tax'd, produces clear
> A copious income ev'ry year,
> And the fair Schools thus free from scruples,
> Thrive by the knavery of their pupils.[19]

Dick swiftly loses his rustic manners; schooled by his fellow coxcombs at school in dress, free-thinking, and airs, he emerges as a sophisticated gentleman. Academically, he "prated much and studied none," and though he failed algebra and astronomy, "His talents prov'd of highest price / At all the arts of Cards and Dice."[20] Swearing, drinking, gaming, and rioting, Dick nevertheless repented easily and "*Pro Meritis* received degrees."[21] Conveniently, his father died and left him a fortune. The prince of coxcombs went abroad for the grand tour, "bent to gain all modern fashions"; returning to America he strove to

> Display his travell'd airs and fashions,
> And scoff at College-educations.
>   Whoe'er at College points his sneer
> Proves that himself learn'd nothing there.[22]

Trumbull gives his fop an inglorious future. In debt, prematurely aged, and replaced in society by younger fops, Dick "In lonely age . . . sinks forlorn / Of all, and ev'n himself the scorn."[23] Finally, the poet eulogizes Dick's opposite, the happy man ". . . whose early bloom / Provides for endless years to come" and whose persevering pursuit of knowledge "repays the course of studious pain."[24]

The Sad Career of Miss Harriet Simper

Trumbull did not neglect female education in "The Progress of Dulness." Poor Harriet Simper, trained in the false virtues of fashion, is smitten by Dick Hairbrain, who toys with her and leaves her. Desperate for a husband as her youth begins to fade, Harriet accepts Tom Brainless's offer of marriage and resigns herself to a secure but unglamorous clerical partnership. Trumbull attributed such marriages of convenience to the neglect of female education and "to the mistaken notions they imbibe in their youth."[25] He wrote the "Adventures of Harriet Simper" to encourage and advance female education, since "the sprightliness of Female genius, and the excellence of that Sex in their proper walks of science are by no means inferior to the accomplishments of men,"[26] an admirable aim for his age but one that would probably antagonize modern emancipated ladies because of the limiting phrase "in their proper walks of science."

Harriet's intellectual and social destinies were foreordained by the education she received in childhood. Her aunt scolded the child's mother for trying to interest six-year-old Harriet in reading and writing. Teach her social graces, charm, and the cultivation of beauty. That is all the truth Harriet knows! Harriet's aunt still speaks for legions of parents on female education:

> And what can mean your simple whim here
> To keep her poring on her primmer?
> 'Tis quite enough for girls to know,
> If she can read a billet-doux,
> Or write a line you'd understand
> Without an alphabet o' the hand.
> Why needs she learn to write, or spell?
> A pothook-scrawl is just as well;
> It ranks her with the better sort,
> For 'tis the reigning mode at court.
> And why should girls be learn'd or wise?
> Books only serve to spoil their eyes.
> The studious eye but faintly twinkles,
> And reading paves the way to wrinkles.
> In vain may learning fill the head full:
> 'Tis Beauty that's the one thing needful.[27]

Harriet is trained in the school of fashion, majoring in dress, vanity, coquettish arts, and cosmetic skill. Custom would have it so; ". . . by antient rule / The Fair are nurst in Folly's school," and she is taught that "dress and dancing are to women / Their education's mint and cummin."[28] Later, after a sojourn in the city for "finishing," she returns vainer than before. Admired by all the local coxcombs, she loses her heart to blackguard Hairbrain, who "own'd she'd charms for those who need 'em / But he, be sure, was all for freedom."[29] True to her love, she spurns all others who seek her hand, but when her charms begin to fade she is not too proud to wed humble Tom Brainless, and like the Guildsmen's wives in *The Canterbury Tales* she has precedence in social functions. The congregation "Greet her at church with rev'rence due / And next the pulpit fix her pew."[30]

Critical comment on "The Progress of Dulness" is generally favorable. William Cullen Bryant praised it as an original pleasing poem, not always pure in diction, but effective in its dialectal passages.[31] Vernon L. Parrington ranked the poem as "the cleverest bit of academic verse till then produced in America"[32] an opinion concurred in by the numerous readers in 1772.[33] Trumbull, however, did not go as far as he cared to in "The Progress of Dulness." Although his preface to part two of the poem is bold, he softened his criticism in the poem itself, fearing that a severe attack upon the college might harm his career.[34] But as an indictment of shabby teaching, compromising administrative standards, and public apathy toward education, "The Progress of Dulness" is a significant educational classic that merits more attention in educational literature.

Joel Barlow, An Outspoken Democrat on Education

Joel Barlow, like John Trumbull, was a Yale man, a poet, and one of the Hartford Wits, a name given to a group of conservative poets who imitated Pope and Addison, their literary gods. Timothy Dwight, Lemuel Hopkins, David Humphreys, Richard Alsop, and Theodore Dwight were also members of the group who contributed many patriotic poems during the Revolutionary period. Hopkins and Humphreys wrote "The Anarchiad," a Federalist diatribe against the "young democracy of hell" threatening to overturn the established order. Barlow, however, was not a conservative; a Jeffersonian democrat and a friend of Thomas Paine, he was one of the few intellectual supporters of the French Revolution who did not turn from the French Republic when its political excesses distressed many of its former American champions.[35] His pamphlet "Advice to the

Privileged Orders" angered many Connecticut conservatives since it subordinated property rights to human rights. Their hostility compelled him to leave the state and settle in Washington, D.C.[36]

In Washington, Jefferson encouraged him to write a history of the Revolution to counteract the Federalist bias of John Marshall's *Life of Washington*, but in 1811 Barlow was sent to Russia on a diplomatic mission which he did not survive, dying in a village near Cracow. His death ended Jefferson's hope for an anti-Federalist chronicle of his era; later nineteenth-century historians, with the exception of liberal George Bancroft, emphasized the viewpoints of the Federalists and their followers.

Barlow agreed fundamentally with Washington, Jefferson, Rush, and Madison that education is the most peaceful, energetic, and effectual way to ensure a nation's liberty and melioratively change the condition of man.[37] In his "Advice to the Privileged Orders" he wrote that "the state has no right to punish a man, to whom it has given no previous instruction" and that, in addition, the state had an obligation to instruct men in "the artificial laws by which property is secured, and in the artificial industry by which it is obtained."[38]

Barlow seconded Trumbull's criticism of Yale, finding fault with the school's inept teaching and musty curriculum. Discipline was at its breaking point in 1774, resulting in a wave of student hell-raising. The political unrest of the times infiltrated the campus, mention of which Barlow made in a letter to his mother, July 6, 1775:

The students are sensably affected with the unhappy situation of publick affairs, which is a great hindrance to their studies; and for that reason there has been talk of dismissing college; but whether they will tis uncertain.[39]

After serving in the army for two years, Barlow returned to Yale, joined student rebels who opposed the administration of President Daggett, and used his satirical pen to force the unpopular president to resign.[40]

Later, when Barlow's orphaned nephew, Thomas, was at Yale, he wrote a letter to Thomas's brother Stephan, cautioning him to steer Thomas away from the temptation to licentiousness and extravagance at the college.[41] Barlow wrote also of the ill effects resulting from bending over books too much, of the blessings of health, of the need for exercise, and of the value of cultivating good manners and clear, grammatical, and elegant speech.[42] An admirer of Homer and the classics, Barlow did not discount the value of practical education in college. Our institutions of higher learning are places

> Where homebred freemen seize the solid prize
> Fixt in small spheres with safer beams to shine.
> Found on its proper base, the social plan,
> The broad plain truths, the common sense of man.[43]

In book eight of *The Columbiad,* Barlow's almost forgotten attempt at an epic of America, the poet includes a stanza of praise for America's increasing number of colleges:

> Great without pomp the modest mansions rise;
> Harvard and Yale and Princeton greet the skies;
> Penn's ample walls oe'r Del'ware's spires ascend,
> On James's bank the royal spires ascend,
> Thy turrets, York, Columbia's walks command,
> Bosom'd in groves see growing Dartmouth stand;
> While, oe'r the realm reflecting solar fires,
> On yon tall hill Rhode-Island's seat aspires.[44]

Schools of education, always fair game for those who believe one cannot be taught to teach, have a friend in Barlow. He felt "that we lose the principal advantages of the little we know for want of proper methods of teaching it to our children." In his "Prospectus of A National Institution to be Established in the United States," Barlow joined Washington, Jefferson, and Madison in proposing the establishment of a national university. His institution would sponsor pure research, geographical and industrial exploration, the training of teachers, and the supervison of subordinate institutions.[45] In addition, the university would have museums, libraries, and conservatories of the arts.[46] Influenced by his own educational experiences, Barlow justified teacher-training courses because "there are so many useless things taught and so many useful ones omitted that it is difficult to say whether on the whole they are beneficial or detrimental to society."[47] But Barlow's dream of a national university was opposed by the Federalists, who feared that the school might become an instrument of political control. Jefferson tried vigorously to save the bill proposing the establishment of a national university, but it died in the Senate committee after a third reading.[48] Barlow's "Prospectus" was not written in vain; Johns Hopkins and other universities adopted many of the features Barlow had recommended, including research programs and separate professional schools.

"That Rascal Freneau" Views the Schools

Another of Jefferson's friends, Philip Freneau, was a classmate of Madison, Burr, and Brackenridge at Princeton. At college he already knew that "To write was my sad destiny, / The worst of trades, we all agree."[49] But in his romantic career, Freneau tried his hand at teaching, sailing, soldering, farming, pamphleteering, and writing. In Joseph Gostwick's *Hand-Book of American Literature* (1856), Freneau is mentioned briefly as the "most poetical" of the Revolutionary writers.[50] Henry Tuckerman (whose literary history was mentioned in Chapter Two) gives more space to Washington Allston, Richard H. Dana, James A. Hillhouse, and Charles Brockden Brown than to Freneau, but of the five poets only works by Freneau are found in today's literary anthologies.[51]

From college Freneau went into teaching, a profession that he thoroughly detested.[52] After thirteen days of schoolmastering in Flatbush, Long Island, he wrote to his classmate Madison:

> Long Island I have bid adieu
> With all its brutish, brainless crew,
> The youth of that detested place,
> Are void of reason and of grace
> From Flushing Hills to Flatbush plains,
> Deep ignorance unrivalled reigns.[53]

Apparently it was not Brooklyn's young Philistines alone that drove Freneau from teaching. His hair grown like a mop, and a huge tuft upon his chin, he complained to Madison again, this time about his new position at an academy near Princess Anne, Maryland, where "we have about thirty students . . . who prey upon us like leeches."[54] The year was 1772; at Yale Trumbull was exposing poor teaching, but Freneau damned the profession itself:

> A plague I say on such employment,
> Where's neither pleasure nor enjoyment,
> Who'er to such life is ty'd
> Was born the day he should have dy'd.[55]

Growing more suspicious of scholars who are mere "piddling orators" and learn and teach by rote, he warns inspirational writers to "avoid connexion with doctors of law and divinity, masters of arts, professors of colleges, and in general all those that wear black caps."[56] He has even more scorn for the servile teacher who hires himself out to instruct the children of fashionable families. In his satirical essay "The Private Tutor," Freneau narrates the fortune of a young man who responds to this ad: "Wanted: A Person capable of teaching not only the languages, but also Philosophy, Geography, Pneumatology, Metaphysics, Chemistry, Meteorology, Belles-Lettres, and other polite arts and sciences. He will be employed as private tutor in a family of consequence and if approved, may expect a handsome salary."[57] The poor lad, probably for want of better prospects, accepts the position that will net him thirty pounds annually for instructing three young gentlemen and two young ladies, attending the gentlemen at all times, at home and abroad, and employing games, marbles, and dice to make the learning experiences of his pupils more pleasant. He would dine with the family when no celebrities were invited.

The hapless tutor finds himself low man on the totem pole in the family's social hierarchy. He is snubbed by the servants, who pass the wine to him last and refuse to black his shoes. The daughters refuse to learn geography and find fault with the tutor. Naturally, the father heeds his pampered darlings and rebukes the defenseless teacher. At the end of the year, in troop the physician, the country lawyer, and the clergyman — a proper examining board for the seething tutor. He is found wanting. The angry father refuses to pay the just thirty pounds for unjust services rendered. The enraged tutor calls his host a swine and happily leaves teaching for basket-making.

In the person of Pedro Blanco, Freneau illustrates the type of academy schoolmaster whom he knew as a youth in pre-Revolutionary America. "The Silent Academy," written in 1775, is reminiscent of portions of "The Progress of Dulness." The couplets are amusing.

> Subjected to despotic sway
> Compelled all mandates to obey,
> Once in this dome I humbly bowed
> A member of the murmuring crowd,
> Where Pedro Blanco held his reign,
> The tyrant of a small domain.
> By him a numerous herd controuled

> The smart, the stupid, and the bold,
> Essayed some little share to gain
> Of the vast treasures of his brain.
> Some learned the Latin, some the Greek,
> And some in flowery style to speak;
> Some writ their themes, while others read,
> And some with Euclid stuffed the head,
> Some toiled in verse, and some in prose,
> And some in logick sought repose;
> Some learned to cypher, some to draw
> And some began to study law.[58]

Much went on in Blanco's school, and Freneau undoubtedly came away with some nuggets from his master. Freneau believed that "man in a state of simplicity, uncorrupted by the influence of bad education, bad examples, and bad governing, possesses a taste for all that is good and beautiful."[59] Schools like Blanco's and even colleges like Harvard taint the innate innocence of men, especially the innocence of Indians who are enticed by white men from their primitive but noble ways. After several months at Harvard, an Indian youth laments:

> "And why (he cried) did I forsake
> My native wood for gloomy walls;
> The silver stream, the limped lake,
> For musty books and college halls?"

He returns to his tribe, disillusioned with

> "The tedious hours of study spent
> The heavy-moulded lecture done."[60]

Freneau satirized politicians, educational administrators, teachers, students, and, to his credit, parents as well. He is more of a guidance counselor than a democrat in his admonition to parents in straitened circumstances who strain to have their children liberally educated. Of what avail are Hebrew, Greek, Latin, mathematics, geometry, ancient and modern history, and natural philosophy to a young man who will probably become an artisan of some kind? Liberally educated men in Europe starve unless they compromise with reality and elect to work in low professions.[61] He expresses compassion for those who waste their youth studying useless liberal arts in his poem "Epistle to a Student of Dead Languages":

I pity him, who, at no small expense,
Has studied sound instead of sense.
He, proud some antique gibberish to attain,
Of Hebrew, Greek, or Latin vain,
Devours the husk and leaves the grain.

In his own language Homer wrote and read,
Nor spent his life poring on the dead:
Why then your native language not pursue,
In which all ancient sense (that's worth review)
Glows in translation, fresh and new.[62]

It was Freneau's belief that genius will out in young people and that those not blessed with "that choicest gift of nature" will turn out to be arrogant, impudent, and vain, their educations notwithstanding.[63] Critical of the antics of the sons of the rich at college, he describes them as "a race of university blockheads who later possess diplomas and libraries but little else intellectually."[64] On the other hand, Freneau lauded the self-reliant innovator, who, like Franklin, rose to fame and fortune through self-discipline and independent study. A democrat politically, Freneau saw no conflict between rugged individualism and freedom of opportunity. He contrasts the unschooled inventor with the cautious scholar: "Many . . . great inventions have come from unlettered men. The illiterate man of inventions is a Columbus who, born to rely upon himself, boldly launches out into the immense ocean of ideas, and brings to light new worlds teeming with gold and diamonds before unknown; the scholar is the timorous and cautious pilot, who creeping along shores already discovered, by the help of his lead and line, makes shift in a bungling manner to get from port to port. . . ."[65] Freneau's caricature of the timorous scholar would later be perpetuated by Orestes Brownson, Ralph Waldo Emerson, Wendell Phillips, Thorstein Veblin, Upton Sinclair, and C. Wright Mills. Dependent upon private or public funds for his salary, the teacher cannot always be a Socrates, especially if he "hath given hostages to fortune."

Students in Freneau's times as in ours sometimes engaged in violent pastimes. On December 31, 1782, while Professor Ripley of Dartmouth College was boasting to a visitor of the mature behavior of the undergraduates, a band of one hundred students appeared and began to tear down the decrepit log-college then occupied by the college's servants. Embarrassed, Ripley implored them to disperse, but they refused and tore down the eyesore. Freneau memorialized this act of vandalism in a poem:

"Ah rogues, said he, ah whither do ye run,
Bent on the ruins of this antique pile —
That, all the war, has braved, both sword and gun?
Reflect, dear boys, some reverend rats are there,
That now will have to scamper many a mile,
For whom past time old Latin books did spare,
And Attic-Greek, and manuscripts most rare."

This appeal was useless. After felling the school

. . . Three huzzahs they gave, and fired a round
Then homeward trudged, half drunk — but safe and sound.[66]

Timothy Dwight's "Grave Preceptor" in "Greenfield Hill"

Timothy Dwight, another Hartford Wit, was president of Yale from 1805 to 1826. He destroyed all vestiges of the free regime initiated by his predecessor, Ezra Stiles, and forbade dancing, dramatics, and cakes and ale at the college.[67] In 1796, he warned that Harvard was too close to seductive Boston because the "bustle and splendor of a large commercial town are necessarily hostile to study."[68] Yet rigorous Federalist and Calvinist that he was, Dwight spoke out vigorously against slavery, favored higher education for women,[69] and advanced science at Yale by bringing the chemist Benjamin Silliman to New Haven.[70]

As a poet, Dwight imitated the long and didactic descriptive poem then fashionable in England. He damned all who differed from him in "The Triumph of Infidelity," gave sound practical advice as well as a few mildly pleasing descriptions of nature in "Greenfield Hill," aimed at grandeur and achieved empty pompousness in "The Conquest of Canaan."[71] Some excerpts from "Greenfield Hill" follow.

There is calm in Connecticut. Among its many virtues, especially in country districts, are its schools.

See, too, in every hamlet round me rose
A central schoolhouse, dress'd in modest guise
Where every child for useful life prepares,
To business moulded, ere he knows its cares.[72]

The teacher is neither an Ichabod Crane nor a Pestalozzi, but his benign mediocrity seems to serve his clients well.

A grave preceptor, there, her usher stands,
And rules, without a rod, his little bands.

Some half-grown sprigs of learning grac'd his brow,
Little he knew, though much he wish'd to know,
Inchanted hung o'er Virgil's honey'd lay,
And smil'd, to see desipient Horace play,
Glean'd scraps of Greek, and curious trac'd afar
Through Pope's clear glass, the bright Maeonian Star.[73]

But to his wondering disciples, the teacher was as learned as Faust.

Yet oft his students at his wisdom star'd
For many a student to his side repair'd,
Surprised they heard him Dilworth's knots untie,
And tell, what lands beyond the Atlantic lie.[74]

If what he taught was of small compass, yet the manner of his teaching was of great magnitude.

Many his faults, his virtues small and few,
Some little good he did, or strove to do;
Laborious still, he taught the early mind,
And urg'd to manners meek, and thoughts refin'd.
Truth he impres'd, and every virtue prais'd;
While infant eyes, in wondering silence gaz'd;
The worth of time would, day by day unfold,
And tell them every hour was made of gold.[75]

Irving Lampoons the Rural Teacher

One would wish that Dwight's "grave preceptor" was typical of the schoolmasters who "would gladly teach and gladly learn," but history tends to discount this. Washington Irving's pitiful Ichabod Crane, like Dwight's virtuous unscrambler of Dilworthean knots, is also "a product of Connecticut which sends forth yearly its legions of frontier woodsmen and country schoolmasters," but there the resemblance between the fictional teachers ends.[76] Crane teaches in a one-room log cabin, the windows of which are patched with copybooks. Crane is an authoritative birch-wielder, superstitious, presumed to be a scholar, and quite elegant with the girls. After flogging a mischief-maker, he would announce to the class that the victim "would remember it, and thank him for it the longest day he had to live." A conniver, he would convoy boys homeward who had pretty sisters or good cooks for mothers. His income was small; therefore, he lodged and boarded with the families of his pupils.

So poor was he that he carried all his worldy goods in a handkerchief. To supplement his paltry salary, he cut hay, drove cows, and instructed the parish in psalmody. Foremost in his mind was his desire to marry the fair Katrina, the daughter of an affluent farmer in the district. Then he would leave petty schoolmastering and show his disdain for the ignoble profession by "kicking any itinerant pedagogue out of doors that should dare to call him comrade." Meanwhile, he had to contend with obstinate parents like the Van Ripperts who refused to send their children to school because "nothing good could come from this reading and writing." Alas, after poor Ichabod was chased from Sleepy Hollow by the headless horseman, his worldly estate yielded only several shirts, a pair or two of worsted stockings, an old pair of corduroy small-clothes, a rusty razor, a book of psalms, and a broken pitchpipe.

Hugh Henry Brackenridge and Educational Know-Nothingism

Five years after his brief tenure as the troubleshooting master of the school in Gunpowder Falls, Maryland, Hugh Henry Brackenridge attended classes with his friends Freneau and Madison at the college of New Jersey, Princeton. There they learned from Dr. Witherspoon that "the function of government is the protection of liberty as far as it is a blessing."[77] In 1771, Brackenridge earned his B.A. degree and treated the assembled guests, graduates, and faculty to his impassioned rendering of the commencement ode, "The Rising Glory of America," which he and Freneau had written in imitation of Milton's grandest style.[78]

In 1772, he was a schoolmaster again. With Freneau as his assistant, he rejoiced, according to Freneau, in his communion with "the wealthy and highly polished society of the academy at Back Creek, Somerset County, Maryland."[79] In 1776, Brackenridge became an army chaplain, cleverly larding his sermons with moving accounts of British atrocities and patriotic and civic passions. When the British left Philadelphia in 1778, Brackenridge turned to writing as a career. After a brief sojourn in Philadelphia, he left for the wilder frontiers of Pittsburgh, unhappy with that large class "who inhabit the region of stupidity and cannot have the tranquility of their repose disturbed by the villainous jargon of a book."[80]

Even his major fictional work, *Modern Chivalry*, did not please the literary fancies of the Eastern Brahmins, who were "attuned to the accustomed sounds of England and the Continent." Volumes one and two of Brackenridge's great satire first left the presses in

1792; volume three emerged one year later and volume four delighted its readers in 1797. Part two of the novel appeared finally in 1804. In 1815, one year before he died, Brackenridge reworked and republished the entire work. Although he had given up formal schoolmastering for good, Brackenridge never lost his interest in education. In his essay "Observations on the Country at the Head of the Ohio River (1786)" he deplored the neglect of the literary education of youth in Pennsylvania, citing the need for a seminary of learning in western Pennsylvania for those citizens who could not afford to send their sons to the colleges at Philadelphia and Carlisle.[81]

In his novel *Modern Chivalry*, his Quixotic hero, Captain Farrago, a man of knowledge and temperate reason, inexorably exposes the sham, ostentation, and pretentiousness of the established classes in post-Revolutionary America. At the same time he reveals the shallowness, credibility, and materialism of the commoner in the pathetic person of Teague O'Regan, the captain's servant.[82]

In the novel the good captain discourses frequently on education; competition for honors among scholars is bad because ambition is the curse of the human mind. The young must be taught to love science for itself — not for the rewards it may bring them. Also, the unqualified must know their scope and not seek preferments beyond their reach. A principal of an academy harangues Captain Farrago; this administrative worthy holds that method in teaching is unimportant — that barbers and tumblers teach as well as wise masters because they amuse their students and, obviously, students want amusement, not learning. The principal agrees with Farrago that the graduates are not ripened for mature political and business life.

One of Farrago's haranguers thinks that seminaries are useful for keeping the young out of harm's way and that Latin will help them learn faster. But a correspondent of Farrago's complains that teaching Latin and Greek is wasteful. Why must a person learn all the languages from which English is derived? People learn new words without learning roots.

The captain criticizes colleges, too; some of them sell diplomas for half a crown. The philosophical societies publish picayune papers that rarely relate to science.

In one village visited by Farrago the inflamed residents are prepared to burn down the college with the professors inside. Farrago protests. Why burn down the college if learning is already put down? For example, a horse jockey can become a preacher in two weeks. Therefore, the college need not offer Latin, Greek, and Hebrew. All that is needed is a polyglot Bible, commentaries, treatises, and dissertations. Why indeed burn down the college? The building can be put to use. A citizen, impressed with Farrago's logic, agrees: "It is not every one that is born a genius, and can do without the help of education. I am, therefore, for continuing these crudities a little longer. When we can afford it better we can pull down the college."[83]

At the drop of a hat Teague, the captain's servant, will apply for a professorship, a congressman's seat, or a place in a philosophical society. Farrago once finds his errant servant holding forth as a professor of Greek at the university — "a common event in the country where boobs are hired by colleges."[84] The principal of the university admits to Farrago that Teague had not been examined because no one at the university was qualified to examine anyone in Greek.

So anti-intellectual are the citizens of this area that it is good policy for a politician to stress his lack of learning. A German from such a settlement says: "Larning isht goot for noting but to make men rogues."[85] But Farrago counters this know-nothing attitude: "Learning can't hurt you if you do not learn. Learning gives warning: the brick on the boy's back-side, the man's headache who pores over books."[86] Finally, the captain sums up his philosophy of education: "It is not the want of learning that I consider as a defect; but the contempt of it. A genius may not need learning — but a man of moderate intelligence should cultivate it."[87]

Daniel Marder, in his critical introduction to a *Hugh Henry Brackenridge Reader*, sees in Brackenridge's satires a consistent endeavor to educate the masses of men. If the unduly ambitious, the pretentiously educated, and the "monied asses" were not effectively opposed by the thoughtful man, exemplified by Captain Farrago in *Modern Chivalry*, democracy would fail.[88]

Brackenridge deserves more attention from literary critics and historians than he has received. Teacher, chaplain, editor, and judge, he participated fully in the nation's early development. A Jeffersonian democrat, he could defend the Constitution vigorously and yet encourage the Whiskey Rebels in their antitax revolt against the federal government. A disparager of the Indian, he nevertheless defended Indians indicted for murder. A foe of slavery, he saw the granting of Indian lands to liberated blacks as a panacea for the impending racial conflicts. A man of learning, he exposed the pedantry and ostentation of teachers, the hypocrisy of administrators, and the intellectual and physical poverty of academic institutions. *Modern Chivalry* is a book worthy of inclusion in modern interdisciplinary courses.

Hawthorne's Novel of College Life

One of the earliest books on American college life is Hawthorne's *Fanshawe* (1828). The young author was so distressed with this first novel that he destroyed most of the published copies. The book is unreadable to the modern reader, but Hawthorne's description of Harley College, possibly Bowdoin, has historical interest. Originating in the early eighteenth century, the college described in the novel was obscured by a multitude of rivals. The fictional school, in Hawthorne's setting a modest establishment and not sought out for honorary degrees by lawyers and divines, was never renowned; but situated away from the busy world, its location was favorable to the moral habits of students. Among its undergraduates were the sturdy, tanned sons of yeomen, the more polished upper classmen of paler cheek, bespectacled and somberly clad, and the sons of Indians, "recipients of an impracticable philanthropy." The President, Dr. Melmoth, ran a moral institution; a learned and orthodox divine, he ruled his obscure college paternally, taught efficiently, and gave to the country a set of men whose deficiency in theoretical knowledge did not imply a want of practical ability.

William Hill Brown, Susanna H. Rowson, and Charles Brockden Brown on Female Education

In the preface to his *Power of Sympathy* (1789), William Hill Brown assures us that "the dangerous consequences of seduction are exposed, and the Advantages of Female Education are set forth and recommended." He writes that women owe a great debt to writers of benevolence and morality; for example, Joel Barlow's "Vision of Columbus" and Timothy Dwight's "Conquest of Canaan" are admirable American epics which are entertaining and especially instructive for the female mind. In the novel Mrs. Holmes advises her young friend Myra to study Noah Webster's *Grammatical Institute* to facilitate her mastery of language. She praises the book because Webster "explains his meaning by examples which are calculated to inspire the female mind with a thirst for emulation, and a desire for virtue."[89]

Susanna H. Rowson, the successful author of *Charlotte Temple*, condemned the boarding schools of her time. In her "Essay on

Female Education" (1794), she portrays the graduate of a boarding school as one who jabbers bad French and worse English, neglects the old-fashioned needlework for modern "ill proportioned" figures in cloth, and misuses the harpsichord.[90] Her training makes her vain and superficial, but her parents see her as a cultured lady. Finally, when married, she is abused by her servants, denigrated by her friends, and censured by her husband. Her slovenly dress and careless manners drive her disappointed husband to drink and gaming. She is, alas, a sad product of a useless education.

Rowson considers the fine arts good for a married woman of independent fortune but not for a newly married girl who lacks time to engage in studies. A blend of the two disciplines, practical housewifery and the fine arts, is desirable for those who have time and money to cultivate them, but the domestic virtues are more important to most women.

However, the most impassioned plea for female education was written by a man. In 1798, Charles Brockden Brown published *Alcuin*, a strong brief for the liberalization of female education. A disciple of Rousseau and Voltaire, he also read the English radical writers enthusiastically, finding in William Godwin and Mary Wollstonecraft philosophical antecedents for his own beliefs. Possibly, it was Mary Wollstonecraft's *A Vindication of the Rights of Women* that influenced him to write *Alcuin*, an anticipation of "twentieth century ideas of feminism with respect to economic independence, political rights, and legal equality."[91]

His own educational experience probably also caused him to question existing educational philosophies. A student at the Friends' Latin School until sixteen, he disparaged the teaching of Latin and Greek and saw nothing but filth and immorality in ancient poetry. The value of this classical education was hardly worth the cost in time and money. Why study dead languages? Isn't it more sensible to master one's native tongue by reading English authors of merit? How could Latin and Greek "humanize the heart and polish the understanding?"[92] Were not Virgil, Juvenal, and Horace indelicate, licentious, and disgusting? Could more be said of Ovid and Propertius — poisonous and sensual immoralists? And the famed *Iliad* — what was it but a compendium of harrowing tales of revenge, cruelty, and slaughter? And who could fathom Plato's mysticism and Aristotle's subtleties? No, the classics were valueless, and even dangerous to the moral development of children. For students planning to enter business such studies were a total waste of time. In

England university men were usually failures in business because the college forms "habits of indolence, . . . inimical to mechanical processes of trade."[93]

Brown's contributions to educational progress lie not so much in his criticism of classical education as in his treatise on female education. In his treatise a priggish schoolmaster, Alcuin, and a Philadelphia bluestocking who subsidizes a salon for liberals, Mrs. Carter, engage in a dialogue on the natural rights of women. Mrs. Carter attacks male domination of the professions, attributing exclusion of women to writers like Swift and Defoe who relegate women to household drudgery, but Alcuin stubbornly questions the value of college coeducation. Are not certain classes unfavorable to moral development? For example, how could mixed classes in anatomy proceed without harm to the fair sex? Mrs. Carter is not impressed. Separation of the sexes tends to invite much mischief. Besides, the limited education that women receive is no more than a preparation for marriage, and marriage is a synonym for slavery.

Continuing in their dialogue, Mrs. Carter dispraises the alleged virtues of the needle and the piano, and Alcuin agrees moderately, tempering his concession with the sage observation that although society is ill, women should turn away from impractical schemes designed to liberate human beings. Alcuin is the eternal temporizer; he agrees with Mrs. Carter's call for equal rights for women and cites More, Plato, and Godwin to prove that women should be as eligible as men for all tasks, but "he fears that this is impracticable."[94] How convenient this rationalization has been to reluctant reformers throughout history! At any rate, *Alcuin* had little influence on public opinion, and Brown gave up dialectics for fiction.

Educational reform proceeds at caterpillar pace possibly because each generation is reluctant to concede that it has graduated from inferior schools. The halo of the glorious past, the memories of "the good old days," and the tendency to minimize the sorrows of youth create a conservatism in taxpayers that inhibits their outlook on change.

Ticknor Infuses Harvard with New Foreign Educational Practices

John Trumbull's moderate indictment of higher education did not incite the college community and the public to reform the colleges and universities. As late as 1807, when he was an undergraduate at Dartmouth College, George Ticknor, who was to publish his classic three-volume *History of Spanish Literature* in 1849, complained of the poor teaching at the college. A discerning young man, Ticknor felt that to prepare himself as a scholar he had to go abroad, especially to Germany, the enlightened land of better universities, teachers, and libraries. At Göttingen he was enthralled by the library of 200,000 volumes, compared to which Harvard's supposedly large library seemed like a closet full of books.[95] Even the famed German gymnasia — advanced secondary schools — were superior to the best American colleges. At Pforta he saw Jefferson's doctrine of natural aristocracy in practice; of 160 students enrolled at the school, 132 held full scholarships.[96]

Returning to the United States, he accepted a professorship at Harvard after declining Jefferson's offer of a similar position at the University of Virginia. Although he admired the college plant at Charlottesville, Ticknor feared that Jefferson's project might end dismally.[97] But later, he called the University of Virginia "the first truly liberal establishment for the highest branches of education that has been attempted in this country."[98] Earlier he had complained to Jefferson about the "indolence" of the Harvard faculty and the need for Harvard to have a rival in the university planned by Jefferson.[99]

Ticknor was honored with two professorships at Harvard. The new professor, influenced by the superior schooling on the Continent, immediately attacked Harvard's lecture system, which did not require students to take notes or examinations. The students were undisciplined, immoral, slothful, and extravagant,[100] and the college was no more than a degree factory offering subjects that would be useless to the graduates in future life.[101] In 1821, Ticknor wrote to the Harvard Corporation. In this letter he said Harvard was not even a good high school: "If we can ever have a University at Cambridge, which shall lead the intellectual character of the country, it can be I apprehend only when the present college shall have been settled into a thorough and well-disciplined high school . . . in which the knowledge preparatory to a professional education shall be taught thoroughly."[102]

Ticknor's proposed reforms for Harvard were too radical for the college's establishment, but many of his ideas are in practice today. He recommended a departmental system, a limited number of electives, grouping of students according to their proficiency, advancement relative to the student's will and talent, and the opening of the college to nonmatriculants.[103] He advocated also stricter entrance examinations, a one-term probationary period for the poor achiever, small classes, more dynamic teaching methods, rigorous examination, and invitations to visiting professors who would indirectly examine resident teachers.[104]

Ticknor was particularly displeased with the teaching techniques of Harvard's faculty. The traditional lecture was generally useless. Instead, the teacher should offer a thorough commentary on the lesson, using illustration and explanation to motivate the student's interest. But the ardent reformer did not attribute all of Harvard's deficiencies to the faculty. Above all, the college suffered from a lack of funds, which limited the purchase of adequate apparatus and the hiring of sufficient numbers of teachers.[105]

The faculty resented Ticknor's imputations of their mediocrity and his insistence upon change. Because the elective system in his department was successful, the Corporation permitted him to continue his progressive methodologies, but a quarter century later Henry Adams found little at Harvard that Ticknor had proposed. And the rowdyism continued; in 1823, of a class of seventy, forty-three students were expelled for battling on the Commons, vexing the teachers, setting off explosions, and sponsoring secret parties. Displeased with these antics, the Massachusetts General Court withdrew its $10,000 annual grant to the college.[106]

Noah Webster's Best-Selling Spellers and His Educational Views

Noah Webster wrote the *American Spelling Book* — over one hundred million copies were sold — but he also wrote treatises on medicine, history, and religion; and he mastered twenty-six languages, including Sanskrit. In 1828 he gave the world the ancestor of all the Websters of today, his *American Dictionary of the English Language*. His specific views on education were epitomized in the monograph "On the Education of Youth, in America" (Boston, 1790).

Webster believed ardently in universal elementary education as an instrument for the diffusion of knowledge and for the implanting of the principles of virtue, liberty, justice, and patriotism in the young.[107] This goal could not be attained in a nation that has unequal educational facilities in its states. In some states affluent men can educate their sons, but the poor cannot. Yet the franchise is given to every citizen harboring a few shillings in his pocket. Webster criticized this situation: "The constitutions are republican and the laws of education are monarchical. The former extend civil rights to every honest industrious man; the latter deprive a large proportion of the citizens of a most valuable privilege."[108] Webster, like Rush and Jefferson, felt that universal elementary education was more important to the nation than the higher education of an elite.[109]

Specifically, Webster recommended that every district in the land support a school for at least four months a year. These schools, staffed by excellent teachers, would educate the young in the general branches, inspire them to respect their superiors and the laws, and prepare them for citizenship.[110] To motivate students there would be varied curriculums in diverse fields; for example, the business curriculum would include foreign languages, chronology, geography, mathematics, history, international trade, insurance, and political science, a curriculum similar to the one proposed by Franklin for the Philadelphia Academy.

Webster's nationalism is illustrated by his rejection of foreign textbooks. He thought American schoolbooks should emphasize American history, geography, and political history to make the student conscious of his heritage. He objected to the Bible as a schoolbook because the immature reader might read it carelessly and lose its moral inspiration.

Webster deplored the lack of good teachers. He characterized the teacher of English as a bore who is responsible for much of the chaos in learning. The failure of a student to learn is presumptive evidence that the teacher lacks pedagogical acumen. Webster believed that it was the state's responsibility to hire good teachers in each discipline. But he warned the legislatures to avoid hiring foreign teachers and men of poor breeding who are bound to impart their vices to their students. When children cease to honor, love, and respect their teacher he should be instantly dismissed. Webster, then, was an advocate of student evaluation of their teachers, a practice that is being hotly debated by students, faculties, and administrators of many modern schools.

Jefferson viewed Noah Webster "as a mere pedagogue, of a very limited understanding," an appraisal which Adolphe E. Meyer speculates "is based no doubt more on Webster's Federalist predilections than on his orthographic bolshevism."[111]

Webster's notions on the education of women are amusing. Because women influence men they should be well educated. But Webster shrewdly assured his male readers that it would be unwise to educate a woman for duties above her station. Apparently Webster was willing to have American girls read and write elegantly, and explore belles lettres and poetry, but, like Jefferson, he frowned upon novels as trifling works, usually devoid of sense. On boarding schools for girls he anticipated Susanne Rowson's distaste for "finishing schools that are of little value to most girls, and instill in them a fondness for show, dress, and expense."

George Bancroft Tries Progressive Education

Another reluctant schoolteacher, the historian George Bancroft, published a book of poems in 1823, but turned thereafter to reporting the nation's origin and growth. He published the first volume of *The History of the United States* in 1834; after a half century of laborious study and writing he completed the final version of volume six. Although his history did not go beyond 1789, the work was an immediate success.[112] His mind alert to the end of his life, he published his last book, *History of the Battle of Lake Erie and Miscellaneous Papers*, at the age of ninety-one in 1891, the year of his death.

A prodigy, he entered Harvard at thirteen, charmed his dons with his precocity, and left for a European education at their expense. Returning in 1822, he formulated educational theories largely influenced by his European experiences. Schools, he believed, should offer courses in Greek and natural history, instill ideals of excellence in their students, operate without corporal punishment, and provide classes relevant to the character and capacities of each boy. The school should have an orphanage adjoining it to give apt students a chance to train as teachers.[113]

Bancroft failed as a teacher-tutor of Greek at Harvard because of his insistence upon factual responses, his undiplomatic airs, and his fondness for the German system of teaching. Ticknor, himself a disciple of German pedagogy, was the only professor at Cambridge who understood and defended Bancroft's unorthodoxy at Harvard, but even Ticknor could not save the young tutor's academic career. Undaunted, Bancroft opened the doors of the Round Hill School in 1823 "to educate not for an ideal world, but for the world as it is." He based his school on the plan of the French college and the German gymnasium, hoping persuasion and kindness would induce industry and obedience in his students. The curriculum offered nothing new; in his school boys would ponder the mysteries of English, the classics, modern language, history, geography, mathematics, reading, and composition. To maintain democratic ideals, pocket money was not allowed, one of the features of the school that endeared it to Jefferson.

To ensure a sound mind in a sound body, Round Hill encouraged hiking, field trips, and playground recreations. Students could maintain gardens and construct cabins. And to remind them of a Higher Proctor, the grounds boasted three chapels. Round Hill was truly an early prototype of progressive education.

Another sensible innovation introduced by Bancroft was to permit each student to advance at his own speed and recite when he was ready. Ticknor, too, had introduced this concept at Harvard, but the traditional-minded faculty preferred to think in rigid, chronological promotion patterns. Evidently, Bancroft's methods were successful; in 1826, the school boasted a complement of 135 students and ten teachers. To sustain the interests of this large group, Bancroft added elocution, bookkeeping, logic, horticulture, drawing, music, art, and dancing to the already broad curriculum. But a year later, he began to tire of teaching. He would fall asleep in class and frequently was the victim of student pranks. He wrote to a friend: "I sigh for the enjoyment of study and delight and pride of new acquaintances; a spirit within me repines that my early manhood should be employed in restraining the petulance and assisting the weaknesses of children when I am conscious of sufficient courage to sustain collision with men."

The history of academic freedom too often cites cases of men who are dismissed or resign under duress because they are critical of academic wrongs that honest men cannot abide. Bancroft reveals this side of his thinking in his unpublished essay "Of the Liberal Education of Boys." One of his educational aims was to instill moral courage in citizens — to have them act when common minds vacillate. But Round Hill School began to fold when Bancroft tired of teaching. Besides, it was too advanced for its age and not in harmony with neighboring schools and colleges. In 1831, the school closed its doors, and Bancroft then had sixty years to prove his manhood away from the confining walls of the academy.

Other Contemporary Critics

George Ripley, a leader in the Transcendentalist movement, praised the curricular regimen at Harvard under President Kirkland, but Emerson and Thoreau found the courses tedious. Of his stay at Harvard, Emerson wrote:

> I went to Cambridge when a boy
> To hear the gownsmen
> And found more sense
> On the way than in the hall.[114]

(Ripley, Emerson, and Thoreau's ideas on education are discussed in detail in Chapter Six.)

The tedious scholastic method of teaching, especially in science, was burlesqued by Francis Hopkinson in a satirical essay, "Modern Learning Exemplified by a Specimen of a Collegiate Examination" (1787). Perhaps this hyperbolized excerpt of a collegiate recitation illustrates the kind of teaching that Emerson, Thoreau, and Ticknor wanted to eliminate:

Professor: "What is the salt called with respect to the box?"
Student: "It is called its contents."
Professor: "Any why so?"
Student: "Because the cook is content *quo ad hoc*, to find plenty of salt there."
Professor: "You are quite right. Let us now proceed to Logic. How many parts are there in a salt-box?"
Student: "Three — bottom, top, and sides."
Professor: "How many modes are there in the salt-box?"
Student: "Four — the formal, the substantial, the accidental and the topsy-turvy."[115]

Royall Tyler Epitomizes Educational Criticism

Royall Tyler, dramatist and novelist, satirized education in his novel *The Algerian Captive*. Tyler, a Harvard graduate, was a contemporary of Brackenridge. The hero of Tyler's novel, Updike Underhill, begins his classical studies at twelve with the town's minister, a Harvard graduate who teaches Greek well. The author mocks the boy's college examiners, who consider the classics the source of all valuable knowledge: "One of them gravely observed that he was sure General Washington read Greek and that he never would have captured the Hessians at Trenton if he had not taken his plan of operation from that of Ulysses and Diomede seizing the horses of Rhesus, as described in the tenth book of the *Iliad*."[116] A Boston divine passing through the town tells Updike's father that Greek is of no other value than that of fitting one for college. This intelligence displeases Mr. Underhill, who presses the divine to clarify his position: "Do they not learn this Greek language at college? If so, why do such wise men as governors of colleges teach boys what is entirely useless? I thought that the sum of all good education was to teach youth those things which they were to practise in after life." The divine is not shaken by this question. He is a philosophical gradualist. Learning has its fashions and "like other fashions of this world, they pass away." But Mr. Underhill is persistent. He wants assurance that the study of the ancient tongues is valueless. The divine does not retreat; why study the originals if they are available in translation? Unfortunately, the governors of colleges are conservative and will teach only what they have been taught. Naively, Mr. Underhill asks: "Should not the legislature, as the father of the people, interfere?" The divine shrewdly responds that "we will not talk politics at this time."

His education complete, Updike turns to teaching. He is master of sixty pupils, including four overgrown boys of eighteen. He finds teaching irksome and depressing. Updike is not fond of his class, lamenting that "perhaps a more ragged, ill-bred, ignorant set never were collected, for the punishment of a poor pedagogue." The children are clamorous and Updike concludes that his students were sent to school "not to learn but to be kept out of harm's way." Parents are not cooperative. They call for discipline but will not tolerate beating of their unmannerly children. But his greatest humiliation is yet to come: "My request for present payment [four dollars per week] was received with astonishment. I found I was not to expect it until the next autumn, and then not in cash, but produce; to become my own collector, and pick up my dues, half a peck of corn or rye in a place."

Undaunted, the novel's hero attempts teaching again, this time in the South, but he does not expect a handsome salary because of the low estate of teachers in the region. Underhill learns that "the school-masters, before the war, had been usually collected from unfortunate European youth, of some school learning, sold for their passage into America: so that to purchase a schoolmaster and a Negro was almost synonymous."

Conclusions

Trumbull's three sorry educational failures are hyperbolized but still recognizable types in school and on campus. Tom Brainless, Dick Hairbrain, and Miss Harriet Simper amuse and sadden us as we follow their unhappy careers in "The Progress of Dulness," an educational satire that is remarkably relevant to our own age. Joel Barlow deplored the quality of post-Revolutionary teaching, but his dream of teacher-training institutes died when the Senate refused to consider a bill to establish a national university that would encourage the education of teachers. Philip Freneau, who disliked teaching, favored practical instruction for most students. The colleges were for the blockhead sons of the rich who wasted their parents' money in rioting, gaming, and wenching. A friend and classmate of Freneau, Hugh H. Brackenridge, anticipated much of contemporary criticism of education in his quixotic novel, *Modern Chivalry.* Students are mass-manufactured, the colleges have poor standards and even issue degrees for fees, and the nation is generally anti-intellectual. Royall Tyler complements Brackenridge's criticism in his novel *The Algerian Captive.*

Early American education had supporters in Timothy Dwight, poet and president of Yale. In the poem "Greenfield Hill" Dwight portrays the schoolmaster as a gentle imparter of learning to the children whom he loved. He is the antithesis of Irving's materialistic Ichabod Crane. Hawthorne, too, was a friend of the teacher; in his ill-fated novel *Fanshawe,* he depicts the president of Harley College as an honest scholar, a friend of the student, and an able administrator.

Although he was tied strongly to the past, Timothy Dwight sincerely advocated education for women and invited eminent scientists to teach at Yale. George Ticknor fought the lecture system, introduced electives and departments at Harvard, encouraged students to advance at their own wills, and commissioned distinguished visiting professors to evaluate Harvard's faculty. Noah Webster argued strenuously for a diversified curriculum in the lower schools and vigorously opposed the use of foreign textbooks in the schools. He advocated limited education for women. George Bancroft founded the progressive Round Hill School where students could advance at their own speed, where kindness superseded harsh discipline, and where play and field trips relieved the burden of formal studies.

Charles Brockden Brown wrote in defense of equal educational rights for women in *Alcuin,* but the main character argues that although women should have equal educational rights it is impracticable to initiate such reforms. Susanna H. Rowson condemned the female boarding school in her novel *Charlotte Temple.* Her unfortunate heroine is taught vain superficialities at school, and her diploma is of no value to her in her adult experiences. The novel was written in England, but Americans purchased thousands of copies of the book, which went into two hundred editions.

In brief, early American writers were not overly happy with the educational practices of their day. In his preface to *Lionel Lincoln* (1824), James Fenimore Cooper wittily sums up the influence that his college training had upon his writing: "Of the colleges it is necessary to speak with reverence, though truth possesses claims even superior to gratitude. He shall dispose of them by simply saying, that they are entirely innocent of all his blunders; the little they bestowed having long since been forgotten."[117] Emerson professed similar views, but one cannot read Emerson's college diaries and still be convinced that his writing was uninfluenced by his studies at Harvard. Sometimes, the writer protests too much.

CHAPTER 5

From "Old Hickory" to "Honest Abe"

BUSINESS is the very soul of an American; he pursues it, not as a means of procuring himself and his family the necessary comforts of life, but as the fountain of all facility. . . . It is as if all America were but one gigantic workshop, over the entrance of which there is the blazing inscription, "No admission here, except on business."[1]

The State of the Nation in Jackson's Age

The doctrine of social Darwinism had yet not been enunciated as a sacred dogma of Americanism when Andrew Jackson retired John Quincy Adams from the presidency in 1828. There were overt happenings in the land of rugged individualism and self-reliance that would later be canonized by Charles Sumner, the archpriest of antisocial welfare. Successful in two wars with England, a quasi-war with France, and an almost storybook mini-war with the Barbary pirates, the little giant of the western hemisphere turned to new adventures that would satisfy its voracious appetite for land and prestige. Not even Jefferson's bonanza acquired peacefully via the Louisiana Purchase and Jackson's gift of additional American real estate by his genocidal elimination of the Creek Indians satisfied the westering cravings of thousands of Americans, old and new. The still-debated Mexican War added Texas and California to the expanding empire, and the Oregon Compromise, if not a satisfactory solution to the Oregon question to rabid expansionists, served to calm the ruffled feathers of most war hawks.

Samuel Goodrich, the prolific author of the famed Peter Parley schoolbooks, portrayed the United States to the nation's children in romantic, inspiring, but unrealistic terms. (Goodrich is discussed in detail in Chapter Six.) In Peter Parley's *Common School History*, Goodrich advises the young American to traverse the nation:

If you are fond of traveling, cross Lake Erie in a steamboat and proceed through Ohio on the railroad. See there a country that has not been settled sixty years now studded over with thriving towns and villages. Go to Cincinnati, Louisville, Nashville, St. Louis, and proceed on the great bosom of the Mississippi to New Orleans.

If you are not satisfied with all this, cross to the Pacific; visit the gold mines of California; proceed to Oregon, and from this point of view consider the extent and resources of these United States.

When you have seen these interesting things, go home and reflect upon them. Sit quietly down, review the past, consider the present, and look forward to the future. What a glorious prospect for our country, if our present government continues, if the people are true to their own interests, and maintain the liberty their fathers left them.[2]

For most of the young scholars, education ended in grammar school. The dream of the Founding Fathers for a "general diffusion" of knowledge had not yet seeped into the consciousness of the American mass mind. Yet how would generations fed on such puerile pap cope with the great problems of industrialization, territorial expansion, slavery and abolition, labor and capital, education, social welfare, immigration, and religious strife that were distressing the nation?

For one-third of the nation of 4,000,000 souls in 1828 who dared settle on frontier land beyond the Appalachians, the problems of daily living exercised the bulk of their talents and energies. But these enterprising people knew that their votes would be prized by politicians North and South. The West now held the political balance of power and meant to use it to its advantage. Yet, the great tides of European immigrants were yet to come, for in 1830 only 1 percent of the nation's population were unnaturalized immigrants. Twenty years later 10 percent, or 2,210,000 American inhabitants, were unnaturalized immigrants. Interestingly, the nation's black population dropped from 18 percent in 1830 to less than 16 percent in 1850.

Politically, the nation was in ferment in 1830. Minor parties sprang up, and in the South the conservative opponents of the tariff rallied cohorts to a nullification convention in South Carolina. Also, this period marked the end of the Virginian dynasty. Jefferson died on July 4, 1826, within hours of the passing of John Adams; Monroe departed in 1831, John Randolph in 1833, and the eminent jurist John Marshall in 1835.[3]

Jackson, the First President of the "People"

Of the Presidents before Jackson, only Washington was not a college man. Jackson's parents were poor, and he had little formal education. A youthful volunteer in the Revolution, he bore scars inflicted upon him by a British officer whom he would not serve menially after his capture at Waxhaw, North Carolina. The young soldier survived wounds and smallpox to lead expeditions against the Creeks in 1813 - 1814 and against the Seminoles in 1818. In 1815, he inflicted a costly defeat upon the British, establishing himself as a stern but accomplished military leader. An emotional man, Jackson was wounded severely in two duels.

Perhaps his humble origins, plain manners, and simple speech endeared him to the common people who elected him. Obviously, his military record served him well at the balloting. Most likely, though, an aroused electorate were tired of their aristocratic leaders and saw Jackson as the leader who would give the people control of state legislatures, the right to elect state officials, and full manhood suffrage.

In office (1829 - 1837), Jackson fought against the privately chartered Bank of the United States, lashed out at the selfishness of wealthy individuals and corporations, and warned that rascally politicians would become the hirelings of the affluent. He feared sectionalism and factionalism, envisioning war as the final arbiter of the nation's disputes.[4] The period saw the beginnings of the labor, temperance, women's rights, and missionary movements. Crusades for public education intensified, and agitation for penal reform became significant. As the old leaders died, new blood entered the political mainstream, energizing the electorate to enlist in a struggle for more rights. In 1831, with William Lloyd Garrison spearheading the drive, abolitionists started an active campaign against slavery. The South, however, was adamant on the slavery question, an institution upon which its very life depended.[5] Franklin Pierce's assurance to planters in 1853 that he would not tamper with slavery probably won him the presidential election, although his service as a general in the Mexican War was undoubtedly of some help to him in the campaign.

Jackson rationalized that by moving the Creeks and Seminoles to the western plains he had saved them from extermination. Schoolbook writers piously perpetuated this myth. For example, Samuel Goodrich assured his Peter Parley readers that the Indians removed from Georgia, Alabama, and Mississippi in 1832 to new lands west of the Mississippi would benefit from the measures taken by the government "to promote their security, tranquility, and gradual civilization."⁶

Opposition to Jacksonian Democracy

The thought of a second term for Jackson was unpalatable to bankers, lawyers, merchants, businessmen, clerics, and college professors. Even Emerson regarded Jackson's election with misgivings. In a letter to Carlyle, March 14, 1834, he complained that government in America was becoming a "job" because "a most unfit person in the Presidency has been doing the worst things; and the worse he grew, the more popular!"⁷ Ironically, the emphasis upon individualism and self-reliance in Emerson's transcendentalism was seen as a rationalization for plunder by some. Did not the robber barons compensate for their rampant individualism by funding libraries, schools, and hospitals? Emerson, unlike his friend Thoreau, liked material comforts, invested in stocks, and seemed to be Hamiltonian in his aversion to the vulgarity of commoners. But he occasionally piped egalitarian tunes — given true education, the common people "might lay a hand on the sacred monuments of wealth itself and new distribute the land."⁸ Such doctrine anticipated the antiestablishment shibboleths of the late-nineteenth-century muckrakers who took from Emerson's seemingly contradictory social views only those that might advance their arguments against the social Darwinists.

While Emerson wavered, Charles Sumner of Yale, the academic apostle of social Darwinism to the intellectual classes, berated Jacksonian equalitarianism as a monstrous and unnatural denial of the doctrine of the survival of the fittest. Why perpetuate the unproductive? Why allow an "uneducated Indian fighter" to war against the Bank and imbue the people with the virus of agrarian radicalism?⁹ Sumner, however, seems to contradict his own thesis. Does not Jackson — an orphan, a self-schooled man, a military hero, an astute politician, and a watershed President — vindicate Sumner's doctrine of the survival of the fittest?

Emerson and Wendell Phillips Blast the Timid Scholar

In 1861, all the other major controversies initiated by Jacksonian politics paled before the more awesome battle that engulfed the land. Jackson's prophecy had come true. The sword alone would now resolve sectional differences. And in 1861, speaking before a college audience, Emerson indicted the intellectuals and scholars for their apathetic renunciation of their responsibilities in the stirring times leading up to the war.

Against the heroism of soldiers, I set the heroism of scholars. . . . These are giddy times. . . . Giddy times went before them and the new times are times of arraignment, times of trial, and times of judgment. 'Tis because the scholars did not learn to teach, because they were traders and left their altars and libraries and worship of truth, and played the sycophant to presidents and generals and members of Congress; and gave degrees and social honors to those whom they ought to have rebuked, incurring the contempt of those whom they ought to have put in fear.[10]

A college so ordered, said Emerson, could be only a "hospital for decayed tutors," a belief expressed decades earlier by John Quincy Adams, who had refused to be present at the conferring of a Doctor of Laws degree upon President Jackson. Jackson was unable to resist President Quincy's invitation to be honored at Harvard but he had turned down a similar invitation from the principal of an academy. Among Jackson's papers is an envelope wrapper recording his refusal to accept an honorary title from an academy: "Lebanon Academy have elected me an honorary member. I have been notified in many instances of the honor being conferred, but I never could accept an honorary title, where I had not claim to the honor, conferred, by some personal acts of my own. Therefore, this is not responded to."[11] Apparently, the thought of honoring his political enemy with his presence was too much for Adams to stomach. In his diary, Adams wrote that "as an affectionate child of Harvard . . . he would not be present to witness her disgrace in conferring the highest literary honors upon a barbarian who could not write a sentence of grammar and could hardly spell his name."[12] To Quincy's appeal that it was fitting to show respect to a President, Adams replied tersely: "I was not satisfied with these reasons; but it is college ratiocination and sentiment. Time-serving and sycophancy are qualities of all learned and scientific institutions."[13] Jackson did not miss Adams; he enjoyed himself famously at the proceedings, congratulating students and kissing the little daughters of Dr. Palfrey.

Wendell Phillips, a more fiery orator than Emerson, spoke out uncompromisingly against the timid intellectuals who did not take a stand against slavery. On March 12, 1860, he told an already turbulent assemblage of the Women's Rights Committee in New York City, "You know this: your Websters, your Clays, your Calhouns, your Douglases, however intellectually able they may have been, have never dared to touch that moral element of our moral life. Either the shallow and heartless trade of politics had eaten out their own moral being, or they feared to enter the unknown land of lofty right and wrong."[14]

Frederick Jackson Turner, an historian favorable to Jackson's democratic philosophy, applauds the advances made in the years 1830-1850: "Looking at the country and the era as a whole, whether we consider politics, invention, and industrial processes, social changes . . . or even literature and religion, the outstanding fact is that, in these years, the common man grew in power and confidence, the peculiarly American conditions and ideals gained strength and recognition."[15]

Horace Mann Campaigns for Public Education

The condition of the common schools in 1830 was deplorable. Education laws were not rigidly enforced, and as late as 1840, one of every twenty white Americans was illiterate. Sixty colleges, manned by four hundred teachers, and catering to five thousand undergraduates, many destined for the ministry, competed for patronage and recognition.[16] By 1847 this figure had doubled; one hundred and eighteen colleges hosting ten thousand students manifested the nation's growing interest in higher education, but from twelve to fifteen thousand other students were preparing themselves professionally in academies and preparatory schools.[17]

According to Horace Mann, the major deficiency of the schools was their tendency to "be satisfied with verbal memory of rules; instead of a comprehension of principles."[18] As for the colleges, few of them before the Civil War were interested in modifying their classical curriculums, probably because the sectarian-minded administrators viewed innovation with alarm. The census reported these interesting educational statistics for 1857.[19]

State	Children Between Five and Twenty	Children in Attendance	% Attending
Vermont	96,568	90,110	93.3
Massachusetts	283,000	203,031	71.7
Ohio	792,019	603,347	76.2
Georgia	275,316	77,015	35.2
Virginia	414,318	41,608	10.0
Mississippi	183,903	18,746	10.2

The compilers of the figures cited here did not indicate whether they include black children, free or slave. But the statistics are not reliable since they do not include the length of the terms that the individual states provided for their students. In 1847, 775,723 children attended school for some portion of the year. Their collective attendance record is charted below:[20]

Number of Students	Months of Attendance	% of Attendance
17,805	12	2.2
25,028	10 and less than 12	3.2
50,823	8 and less than 10	6.4
104,016	6 and less than 8	13.4
154,673	4 and less than 6	19.9
194,892	2 and less than 4	25.1
198,625	Less than 2	

Even if the large numbers of children taught by private tutors were subtracted from these astonishing figures, the number of undereducated children in the era would not be appreciably lowered. Yet, the nation prospered and expanded. Whether this growth would have been speedier and more altruistic had there been efficient educational systems in the country is now a matter of idle conjecture, but as late as the early twentieth century many still scoffed at mass education, especially the successful entrepreneurs, who like Franklin, but without his dedication to education, had risen from poverty to affluence by sheer pluck and common sense. Commodore Vanderbilt might boast with impunity that he had never read a book until he was seventy, but for most mortals a basic education is vital to their well-being. So thought Horace Mann, a pedagogical David who had to slay many Philistines before free public education would become a reality.

Mann did not lack strong political allies in his campaign for public education. Abraham Lincoln, as early as 1832, wrote in the *Sangaman* (Illinois) *Journal* that he viewed education "as the most important subject in which we as a people can be engaged in." Five years later, in an address at Madison, Wisconsin, Daniel Webster urged: "Open the doors of the schoolhouses to all children of the land. Let no man have the excuse of poverty for not educating his offspring. . . . On the diffusion of education rests the preservation of our free institutions."[21] From the South, however, came Calhoun's skeptical comments on education: "Neither religion nor education can counteract the strong tendency of the numerical majority to corrupt and debase the people."[22] Representatives of the numerical majority, namely, the workingmen of America, did not accept Calhoun's low regard for education's moral force. In 1829, workers in New York City and Philadelphia agitated for free schools since "no system of education, which a freeman can accept, has yet been established for the poor; whilst thousands of dollars of public money has been appropriated for building colleges and academies for the rich."[23] On March 6, 1830, *The Workingman's Advocate* charged editorially that "despotism garners talent and leaves the multitude in ignorance." To make wise and just laws the public must be educated.[24] But, said the *Advocate*, the children of the poor frequently are denied elementary education because they must work for their food and clothes instead of attending classes.

Professor Cubberley described the bitterness of the educational slugfest as a battle that transformed friends into enemies, fomented discord between pastor and parishioners, and neutralized politicians. Free-school opponents called their adversaries fanatics, and free-school advocates labeled their opponents conservatives.[25] In the South an anonymous letter (1829) to the North Carolina legislature proclaimed its author's distaste for free public education. The times were poor, and there was no money for education. Besides, existing schools were not filled, and, most likely, they taught little. Better that the young be sensibly employed "at the plow, in the corn patch" since "plain farmers and mechanics have no reason to read. And what prudent man cares to have his taxes increased?"[26]

But in the North, businessmen thought it wise to encourage their employees to read and to attend lectures. Merchants subsidized mercantile libraries for clerks and mechanics who had no other means of education, and in a sense these practical entrepreneurs salved their consciences by uplifting their operatives in a spirit of philanthropic self-reliance. Since 84 percent of the eminent businessmen listed in *Who's Who in America* (1900 edition) had not gone beyond high school, it is understandable why so few supported free public education.[27] An ambitious lad could climb to financial stardom without benefit of a coveted B.M.A., but the smattering of culture that he eked out of the library and lyceum gave him polish, and, better yet, his evening studies might keep him out of mischief after business hours.

Sectionally, New England boasted the best school systems in the land. In 1850 only 1.89 percent of the native white population was illiterate, although compulsory education was not strictly enforced and both the administration and the equipment of the schools were poor.[28] But dedicated men — James G. Carter, Horace Mann, and William Ellery Channing in Massachusetts and Henry Barnard in Connecticut — worked to introduce laws for tax-supported schools, for the reform of school district administration, and for founding free high schools and normal schools. To lure the prosperous but reluctant taxpayer into their fold, some public education advocates whispered it about that educated voters would become party-conscious bulwarks against the still rampant radicalism of Jacksonian democracy.

George Bancroft had given New Englanders a taste of progressive education that most of them could not savor. Bronson Alcott's progressive schools also came to grief. But as the battles for free public schools raged, the milder transcendentalists were dreaming up a model progressive school for their progeny at the Brook Farm utopia. The aims and characteristics of the Brook Farm School were clearly outlined in ads in *The Harbinger,* December 13, 1845, to June 6, 1846. In brief, the school offered the same curriculums as the academies and high schools of New England, but it emphasized modern European languages and literature, accepted students of both sexes and of different ages, provided friendly counseling, and imposed no arbitrary disciplinary restraints upon the students. The curriculum was both vocational and college preparatory. Also, free instruction was available in music, dancing, drawing, and painting.[29] Maternal care was a feature of the infant school; from this cradle school the child entered the primary school at six, and after four more years in basic studies he would be advanced to the preparatory school, which had won Harvard's stamp of approval. At sixteen the male graduate of the preparatory school was ready for college. Education took place everywhere at Brook Farm. The faculty and students lived and worked together. The barn, workshop, study, and parlor contributed to the student's learning. On any day distinguished visitors such as Ralph Waldo Emerson, Margaret Fuller, Horace Greeley, Amos Bronson Alcott, Orestes Augustus Brownson, Robert Owen, Theodore Parker, or Elizabeth Palmer Peabody might drop in on a class to dazzle the awestruck students with their genius.[30]

Public School Education in the Middle Atlantic States

The Middle Atlantic states saw many educational advances in the years 1830 - 1850. In New York, Governor De Witt Clinton urged the legislature to support public education because "a general diffusion of knowledge is a precursor and protector of republican institutions, and in it we must confide as the conservative power that will watch over our liberties and guard them against fraud, intrigue, corruption and violence."[31] In 1845, Horace Mann praised the state's county superintendents, normal school, and public zeal in promoting popular education. Labor and social idealists united to sponsor public education in New York, but Pennsylvania had to wait until 1839 for its first high school. The fiery Pennsylvanian Thaddeus Stevens strongly defended the Free School Law of 1834. His brief has exciting implications for our own times:

If an elective Republic is to endure for any length of time, every elector must have sufficient information not only to accumulate wealth and take care of his pecuniary concerns, but to direct wisely the legislature, the ambassadors, and the Executive of the Nation — for some part of all these things, some agency in approving or disapproving them, falls to every free man.[32]

Public Education in the West

The West did not encourage free elementary schools and high schools until the late 1850's. The new western states, especially, used school laws they did not enforce to attract immigrants. Consequently, federal lands given to the states to encourage education were sacrificed to increase their populations. An early supporter of education in the West, the Reverend W.G. Eliot, Jr., grandfather of T.S. Eliot, prayed for an educated West to offset the greed and immorality of its settlers. A champion of lyceums, he predicted that if they were erected throughout the West they would "exert a purifying influence upon public morals and tastes, and serve to remind many who are engrossed in money-getting that they have an intellectual treasure within them which ought not to be entirely forgotten."[33]

Wherever New Englanders settled in the West they supported school building. Between 1830 and 1850, thirty new denominational colleges were founded in the West, including pioneering Oberlin. This unique college admitted black students, a breakthrough for educational integration more than a century before the word became significant in American academic mores.[34]

The South Epitomizes Class Education in Early America

Southerners, though, had harsh words for the New England teachers. Censuring northern textbook writers who depicted plantation owners as bestial despots, John B. Thompson, an editor of the *Southern Literary Messenger*, wrote that southern opinion of the North could be judged only by the swarms of "half-educated teachers and peripatetic vendors of clocks" who invade the South. Editor Thompson disliked the poor specimens of intellectual talent that New England sent to his region: "For one real scholar that comes to us from the colleges (and it is remarkable that all of them are graduates of Harvard University), we have a score who cannot speak their own language correctly. . . . "[35]

But the South did not care to import competent teachers for its lower schools. In 1830, teachers were paid parsimoniously. Thomas Jefferson had learned how adamantly Southerners opposed taxation for schools. Consequently, the lower schools were commandeered by apathetic teachers who taught spelling, declamation, and arithmetic. Simple visual aids such as maps and globes were not available to students who studied geography by rote. Illiteracy was alarmingly prevalent in both the South Atlantic and the South Central states; in 1850, the illiteracy rate of the South was five times that of New England. Poor whites in the South Central states were almost un-taught, and in Mississippi, as late as the mid-1840's, at least seven counties lacked a schoolhouse.[36]

The planter who could afford tutors for his children had little reason to support free public education. His ideal cultivated man was one who could ride, hunt, and dance with distinction. In addition, he should have a practical knowledge of law, agriculture, and material science. He should also converse well and know Greek and Latin, languages stressed by tutors, academies, and colleges. Usually, the planter's children were taught by competent tutors from New England who came South to earn money before establishing themselves professionally in the North. For example, William Ellery Channing and William Seward served as tutors on southern plantations, and, unlike poor Ichabod Crane's unhappy "boardin' round" in New York, these contented New Englanders dined with the family and were waited upon by slaves. In illustration, James B. Hammond, a rich North Carolina planter, requested Professor Gibbs of the College of Charleston to provide him with a tutor for the education of his six children. He would pay four hundred dollars a year for a classical teacher or five hundred dollars a year for a teacher of French for his six children and four of his neighbor's. To lure a talented teacher, the planter offered fringe benefits — board, laundry, a horse, and a month's vacation. Gibbs chose a Yale man for this desirable position. Another Connecticut man declined a position to teach at a subscription school in Greensborough, Alabama, when he learned that he would be paid twenty-five dollars a head for sixteen students in a district whose teachers were known to be dunces and blockheads.[37]

But the South was signally rich in secondary schools. There were twenty-seven hundred of these academies, the highest number sectionally in the nation. The academies varied from poor to very good. In addition to the standard high-school curriculums, they offered courses in public speaking to inspire patriotism and moral virtue, practical subjects, and education for girls. At Moses Waddell's academy in Wellington, South Carolina, the boys lived in log cabins, arose at daylight, and made their own fires. To encourage diligence, both prayer and whipping were intermittently employed, and apparently these contrasting teaching aids were not detrimental to the academic and political success of many of the academy's alumni.

The teaching career of Samuel B. Sweat illustrates the hazards of teaching in a poor southern academy. Appointed in 1843 to the Lightwood Knot Ridge Academy in South Carolina, schoolmaster Sweat taught sixteen scholars, half of whom absented themselves in bad weather. At the end of the term he was let go without pay because the school fund was empty. Undaunted, he took up the ferrule again — this time at the Pebble Hill Academy. Here he taught fourteen pupils for three months and was actually paid twenty-five dollars per month. In 1852, he was teaching thirty-four pupils ranging in age from six to twenty-two. Finally, in 1867, he forsook teaching for the more satisfying positions of timber factor and country preacher.

The upper classes were taught well. The 1850 census listed Virginia as having 12 colleges, 1,343 students, and 73 teachers. Massachusetts, with 100,000 more people than Virginia, had fewer college students enrolled, and South Carolina College, under the administration of Dr. Thomas Cooper (1820 - 1834), was the most liberal institution of higher learning in America.[38]

Higher Learning Has Its Lows

In 1850, the graduates of New England's high schools and academies had twenty colleges to choose from. An elite body of three thousand young men, these favored lads were taught in small classes; even famed Harvard had only twenty-four instructors and 236 undergraduates. To the Democrats, Harvard was a center of aristocracy; even middle-class parents found it burdensome to pay the two-hundred dollar annual board and tuition fee. Harriet Martineau reported in her account of Harvard the advice of a "jolly" lady to Harvard's dons that they should strike for higher wages since their annual salaries ranged from five hundred dollars to fifteen hundred dollars annually.[39] Miss Martineau disliked Harvard's aristocratic airs, wealthy students, weak attainments, and indolent, careless, and ill-paid professors who did nothing more than lecture and test their students.[40] Edward Everett, president of Harvard (1846 - 1849), wrote: "I supposed I was to be at the head of the largest and most famous institution of learning in America. . . . I find myself the submaster of an ill-disciplined school."[41] His lamentation is reminiscent of Ticknor's earlier admonition to the Harvard establishment — before one can think of Harvard as a university the college must first attain the rank of a good high school.

The number of colleges in the Middle Atlantic states had grown from thirteen in 1830 to forty-four in 1850. The colleges were really nothing more than high schools and seminaries, but the professors influenced their students well. Columbia College, for example, had only nine instructors. This small faculty introduced courses in architecture, maritime arts, and business administration, but the trustees censured the faculty's innovative curriculum.[42] An eminent alumnus of Columbia College, Samuel Ward, entered the school at fourteen and recalled in later years how easily he had won his degree: "The duties of the students were light, of the professors still lighter, of the President lightest of all. . . . We were boys of leisure, as at Eton. . . . The truth is, the country was under educated." His memories of his studies were not complimentary to Columbia: "I remember only having improved my Latin, added nothing to my Greek, picked up a pinch of chemistry and having found myself home at mathematics — this thanks to the training of Timothy Walker."[43]

In 1830, a convention of "literary and scientific gentlemen" met in the Common Council of the City of New York to recommend plans for the founding of the University of the City of New York, a tentative name for New York University.[44] The distinguished clergymen, educators, and statesmen left an admirable record of their proceedings, which included debates on topics ranging from the fate of the classical languages to the advisability of open enrollment. For example, Albert Gallatin, who had served as Jefferson's secretary of the treasury, opposed the inclusion of the classical

languages as an entrance requirement on the grounds that such requisites are discriminatory. Gallatin believed that the academies
should teach useful and practical arts, and he proposed that an
English college be instituted on an equal basis with the classical
college. Why should Greek and Latin be the measure of an educated
man?

An educational prophet at the convention, Dr. Jonathan
Wainwright, argued at length for the admission of qualified students
to nondegree programs within the university — a program which
New York University has successfully administered for many
decades. In addition, he defended the rights of mature students to
follow their own elective inclinations. But Dr. Wainwright's greatest
philosophical contribution at the convention was his bold advocacy
of open admissions. His proposals were 130 years premature, but his
plea for an open admissions system is significant historically.

The only plausible arguments, if they deserve that name, that I have seen
adduced against the introduction of the open proposed university system,
which asks of the candidate for admission, no other qualifications (besides of
course a fair moral character) but that he be qualified by his age and
previous education to attend with advantage to himself, the course or
courses of instruction on the subjects he is desirous of becoming acquainted
with, are, in the first place that this system would act as a discouragement to
the acquisition of classical literature, — secondly that the several courses of
instruction would necessarily degenerate into more popular courses; by popular courses being here understood, an instruction divested of precision,
and, therefore, communicating only a superficial acquaintance with the
topics treated of, — and lastly, that the object of education is not so much to
make good scholars in any particular branch of literature or science, as to
present to the student a culture of the whole range of knowledge, and to subject his mind to that preparatory discipline which may afterwards fit him for
vigorous and useful exercise in his future pursuits in life.[45]

In the appendix to the journal of the convention's proceedings, a
strong plea is made for educating the children of the poor. The state
and the wealthy are asked to subsidize the schools because

the public good also imperiously demands, that some system be adopted, by
which the chief source and strong hold of ignorance and vice, should be con-
tinually assailed. For this object the lowest level of society should never be
left out of view. There first are laid the foundations of ignorance, crime, and
disorder. And as there also lies a large portion of the political power of the
country, there is an imperious demand on good men, to devise means, and
adopt measures, for its being purified and ennobled.[46]

The Low Estate of the Teaching Profession

But how were the lower classes to be "purified and ennobled" when the children of the poor were taught by incompetents? An outspoken critic of the teaching profession, Lieutenant Mahan, asked the delegates convened in New York: "Why do all professionals earn more than the teacher? Why is he little respected?" Mahan answered his rhetorical question with a cutting truism: "Any man can be a school-master, and no man whose talents will command a higher market will bring them into this."[47]

In 1837 Francis Joseph Grund, a naturalized Austrian, supported Mahan's criticisms in his analysis of the culture of his adopted land, *The Americans in Their Moral, Social, and Political Relations.* Grund saw the poor pay of teachers "as too sordid to enable them to live as gentlemen," and he deplored the large turnover in the profession by men who viewed teaching as a temporary job on their ascent to more esteemed professions.[48] He agreed wholeheartedly with the sorry findings in the *Annual Report of the Superintendent of Common Schools of the State of New York* for the year 1835. The document is a noteworthy epitomization of the historical attitude of the public toward teachers:

The incompetency of teachers is the great evil of the common school system of this State, and it may, indeed, be said to be the source of the only other material defect which pertains to it, — a low standard of education in most of the schools. The evil, however, is by no means universal. There are many teachers of ample qualifications, and many schools of high standing, both as regards the nature and extent of their acquirements. The principal obstacle to improvement is the low wages of teachers; and as this is left altogether to be regulated by contract between them and their employers, there would seem to be no effectual remedy for the evil, but to inspire the latter with more just conceptions of the nature of the vocation, and its high responsibilities, and of the necessity of awarding to those who pursue it, a compensation in some degree suited to its arduous duties and requirements. . . . The practice of paying "low wages" has, as might be expected, introduced into the common schools, teachers wholly incompetent to execute their trusts, who have brought in bad methods of teaching, and kept down the standards of requirements for their pupils on a level with that by which their employers have measured their qualifications.[49]

The tendency of professionals in law, medicine, and preaching in Grund's time to look down upon teaching as a mere steppingstone to their respective fields has, with the substitution of science for preaching, continued to this day. For example, the medical faculty of the University of the State of New York has insisted upon contractual salaries that are competitive with the incomes of experienced physicians in private practice. The education professor must settle for half the salary of his medical colleagues and regardless of the merits of the physician's brief for nobler salaries, the lower-paid professor of pedagogy will understandably lament his inferior honorariums. Grund saw this educational dilemma clearly in his classical exposition of one of the major problems in education. Since he who remains a low-paid teacher will not rise in social and economic status, those who have taught "as a sort of relief from the most pressing necessities" and as an end to honorable destinations, look down upon him after they leave teaching for more prestigious professions. This professional contempt for the teacher, continues Grund, "has communicated itself to all ranks of society," and he predicts that "as long as this opinion of instructors is entertained in the United States, the schoolmaster's task will be degraded."[50]

Horace Mann Attempts to Raise the Status of Teaching

Horace Mann worked assiduously to elevate the teaching profession by instituting teacher-training programs, dignifying teacher qualifications, and humanizing the practice of teaching. He hoped to inspire young people planning to teach to master their disciplines and techniques for communicating knowledge to the young.[51]

To elevate teaching from a little-respected craft to a respectable profession was Mann's lifetime aspiration. But how could he conciliate economy-minded taxpayers and their agents, the trustees and board members? Was it possible to deny school boards their time-honored practice of selecting academy graduates, college sophomores, and frustrated schoolmarms to wield the ferrule in town and country schools? Few gifted teachers can withstand the drudgery of classroom chores indefinitely. Mann knew this and hoped to entice creative young people by encouraging the state to found normal schools that would transform teaching into a creative art. Normal or teacher-training schools were introduced in France in 1808 as part of Napoleon's reorganization of French higher education. The *Ecole Normale Supérieure* (higher normal school) was the forerunner of thirty new normal schools in France between 1831 and 1833. American educators who visited these schools praised them highly in their reports, and somehow the term "normal school," a school "which set the norm or standard for the teaching practice," became widely used in the United States to designate a teacher-training institution. The State of Massachusetts was loath to support normal schools, but in 1845 a weary legislature recognized the normal school founded by James G. Carter in 1839 at Lexington as a state normal school, the forerunner of a dozen similar institutions established before the 1850's.[52]

Undaunted by the strong opposition to his plans for public education, Mann persisted in his crusade. His barbs were aimed at businessmen and politicians who resented his repeated admonitions that teachers are more important than rulers because "he who forms is better than he who commands."[53] Theoretically, a teacher can form minds if he is not himself subservient to the ruler's commands. But kings, dictators, and school boards give commands, and discreet teachers often find refuge in Bacon's rationalization for intellectual timidity: "He who hath a wife and child hath given hostage to fortune."

To reform education one must be prepared to reform school boards, trustees, and legislatures. But if trustees are scoundrels, what of the governmental agencies that support them? A report in 1847 on education in the State of New York cited "instances in the state of trustees who are unable to read and write, intemperate, averse to schools and education; of town superintendents incompetent and dishonest; of districts quarrelsome and blind to their true interests": but fortunately the report concludes that "these are exceptions to the rule."[54] Mann, however, must have felt differently. In setting up the qualifications for trustees and school committees, he urged that they have integrity to refuse bribes, common sense to judge the fitness of teaching candidates, and a thorough knowledge of educational principles.[55]

As the number of professionally trained teachers increased, teachers' associations were formed. George Ripley and Charles Dana, editors of the *New American Encyclopedia*, wrote in the 1865 edition on the function of teaching associations: "In view of the recent origin and rapid increase of normal schools, an association for professional improvement was deemed essential by their instructors. Many fundamental points in reference to the distinctive character and specific aim of normal schools, the science of education, methods of instruction, terms of admission, curriculum of study, length of the course, prominence to be given to the theory and act of teaching, still demand investigation."[56]

On the Education of Blacks

Although educational debate was occupying much of the public's attention in this period, very little of the debate concerned itself with education of the blacks. The English commentator on American affairs Thomas Hamilton observed in 1833 that American scholars believed blacks learned as well as whites, but blacks could not attain their potential because of the prejudice of whites. Try as they might, the best of the black students would never become marine officers; they might become cooks and stewards, but white sailors were not yet ready to serve under black officers.[57] For a time blacks had monopolized the domestic services, but now hungry Irish immigrants were replacing them. Masters would not accept free blacks as apprentices. Education was for the privileged well-to-do white. Few blacks could make Poor Richard's formula work for them. Chattels in the South and menials in the North, blacks could not easily enter the mainstream of American life.

But there were exceptions. Every history of black life in America proudly lists hundreds of blacks who have "made it." But for pre-Civil War blacks the road to status and comfortable living was almost impassable. Yet deacons and elders in small towns and rural areas taught young blacks to whom all schools were barred,[58] and in large cities black teachers taught considerable numbers of black children competently.[59] In New York City, for example, there were 3,399 black children in school ten years before the Civil War broke out — a number proportionate to the white school population.

In 1853, Frederick Douglass wrote to Harriet Beecher Stowe of the poverty, ignorance, and degradation of the free black people in the United States. Believing that his people were not yet prepared for high school and college, he advocated instead a period of gradualism in education to bridge the gap. To help them earn respectable incomes, he recommended that young blacks study agricultural and technical arts since even black college graduates could not find employment in the more elite trades and professions.[60] Douglass knew that white mechanics would resent black competition, but he proposed nevertheless the establishment of an industrial college that would prepare black youth for positions in the mechanical arts.[61]

Idealistic and militant whites fought vigorously for the educational rights of blacks. William Lloyd Garrison planned to build a Negro College in New Haven, Connecticut, because he erroneously supposed that there was minimal antiblack prejudice in the town that hosted old Eli. To raise funds for the project fifteen free blacks from five states met in convention to plan a fund-raising campaign among blacks and whites. But Garrison had to contend with a hostile city government that opposed the erection of the Negro College on the grounds that "it would be an unwarrantable and dangerous interference with the internal concerns of other states," and that it would be incompatible with the prosperity of Yale and other educational institutions operating in the city.[62]

Noble New England! A tiny Negro College a threat to Yale's prosperity! Perhaps it was such rank hypocrisy that enraged Southerners when Northerners depicted them as heartless and insufferable masters. But at least one Northerner would not be silenced. Incensed because black children in Boston's schools were not integrated with their white peers, Wendell Phillips petitioned the school committee. The committee summarily dismissed his petition. Obstinately, he petitioned the committee again, and in 1846 the committee tired of battling the adamant abolitionist and relented. At the annual meeting of the Massachusetts Anti-Slavery Society Phillips wrote: "Resolved, that this society rejoice in the abolition of separate colored schools in the city of Boston, as the triumph of justice over the pride of caste and wealth."[63]

In 1860 nine out of ten blacks were illiterate, but at Oberlin College one-third of the student body was black, thanks to Asa Mahan's acceptance of the college's presidency on condition that blacks be accepted.[64]

The Education of Girls Proceeds Slowly

The education of girls before the Civil War was generally limited to the elementary level. Affluent parents hired tutors or sent their daughters to female academies and seminaries for "finishing." Not much progress toward equal educational rights for women would be noted until the male voters enfranchised the female 50 percent of the population. But there was a determined "women's liberation" movement operating in the antebellum days of the republic; brave ladies startled respectability with their reform programs in education, penology, and slavery. Though scorned and minimized by society as social innovators, these early feminists influenced society appreciably. As early as 1821, Emma Hart Willard opened the doors of the Troy Female Academy to young ladies who desired a more substantial education than that offered at superficially taught "charm" schools. At Troy, her girls would learn to be intelligent wives by studying science, mathematics, geography, metaphysics, and scientific housewifery.

In 1837, Mary Lyon invited young ladies to attend her famous Mount Holyoke Seminary. Here, as at Troy, young ladies would be taught solid fare. Charm was out, but domestic economy, the source of marital harmony, was strongly accented.[65] Catherine Beecher endorsed housewifery as a dignified profession in 1842. She also recommended teaching and nursing as legitimate female professions. Although her Female Seminary at Hartford failed in 1828, her propaganda for innovative female schools was very successful.

Lucy Stone's rise to fame was very dramatic. At sixteen, as a teacher she earned one dollar per week — hardly a legitimate profession — and by diligence worked up to a handsome sixteen-dollar weekly salary. A student at Mount Holyoke and Oberlin, she taught preparatory black students for twenty-five cents a day and lectured against slavery at Oberlin to a coeducational, interracial audience. Another feminist, Lucretia Mott, deplored the fact that women teachers were paid half the salary of men and were ignominiously ranked by every state institution with "idiots, lunatics, criminals, and minors."[66]

In the West a female seminary was founded near Transylvania College to teach girls reading, writing, arithmetic, spelling, grammar, elocution, rhetoric, philosophy, history, music, drawing, painting, and sewing. These edified ladies would sometimes marry untutored husbands in backward regions, and then the good wife would instruct her illiterate spouse and her stalwart children.

In 1836, Georgia Female College, the first of its kind in the United States, tried to compete with the better seminaries for matriculants. But its curriculum was poor, its male professors dull, and its degrees unhonored. Not until Vassar started in 1861 was there a good college for girls in the country.[67]

The Moral Training of Youth

In an age of sectarian influence in the schools, much attention was given to the student's moral education. Daniel Bryan, a southern poet, included a triplet on moral education in his Presbyterian discourse in verse that condemned war, dueling, intemperance, avarice, profanity, factionalism, and party rage:

'Tis Education's promise then, no less
With Moral treasures to enrich the heart,
Than with its mental gems to store the head.[68]

Secular educators could not easily eliminate religious influence from the schools, but they tried to convince divines that moral education might be administered to students without benefit of a particular sect's offices. Stephen Girard's experiment with nonsectarian education at his Orphan College in Philadelphia proved successful. In 1831, delegates meeting in New York City to plan a new university for the city were advised by George Bancroft to avoid religious entanglements: "God forbid," he wrote in his letter, "that the day should arrive, when there should be a separation of pure morality and deep religious conviction from our public places of education; but the character of a University requires that it should subordinate no religious party, be subservient to no religious sect. It must be established independently, on its own merits."[69] A delegate to the convention, M. F. Hasler, warned that ill-prepared professors might use religion to curb dissenting students having legitimate independent opinions, proof that some of the spirit of the Enlightenment still persisted in the thinking of American intellectuals.[70]

Although Mann embraced Unitarianism in his young manhood, he was never completely free from the pessimistic Calvinism his parents had nurtured him on in his childhood. At Brown he began to feel the call of humanitarianism, and at commencement he addressed the assemblage on "The General Advancement of the Human Species in Dignity and Happiness," a theme he would advance throughout his life. If man is evil, he need not be so forever. Properly administered education would enable men to resist their propensity for selfishness and assist them to understand and correct evil in others.[71] Specifically, he attacked the vague, casuistical, and intricate books on moral problems that abounded in his time. He advised educators to concentrate on books and monographs that have "specific directions and practical aids for training children in daily domestic and social studies on which their own welfare, and the happiness of society depend. . . . "[72]

Foreign Criticisms of American Education

Alexis de Tocqueville praised both American public education and American desire for independent rule as essential to the development of American democracy. Democracy will grow "where the instruction [that] teaches the mind is not separated from the education which is responsible for mores." But education alone does not make good citizens since "true enlightenment is in the main born of experience, and if the Americans had not gradually grown accustomed to rule themselves, their literary attainments would not now help them toward success."[73]

Alexis de Tocqueville admired the independent spirit of American girls, who "rarely suffer from shyness or childish ignorance." Aware of evil, "her morals are pure rather than her mind chaste."[74]

English critics of American education were plentiful. Perhaps some Englishmen could never forgive the upstart colonies for turning on their mother country. Frances Trollope toured America in 1837 and found the citizens woefully deficient in taste and learning. Specifically, American education was inadequate since it rarely went beyond reading, writing, and bookkeeping. For most American youth, education ended at sixteen because the American goal was money making, not learning. Few Americans sacrificed themselves for learning.[75] This charge would later be made by Americans themselves. Another caustic critic of American education, Thomas Hamilton, discovered no great scholars and no great colleges in America. Like Mrs. Trollope, he saw the Americans as a business-oriented people lacking cultural aspirations: "Even to this day [1831], the value of education in the United States is estimated, not by its result on the mind of the student, in strengthening his faculties, purifying his taste, and enlarging and elevating the sphere of thought and consciousness but by the amount of available knowledge which it enables him to bring to the common business of life."[76]

A German student of American life, Frederick Von Raumer, professor of history at the University of Berlin, applauded Americans for being so critical of their schools and for striving to extend the scope of education.[77] His brief digest of American educational ills, culled from Mann's annual reports, reads like a sorry condemnation of American pedagogy in the 1840's:

Americans complain of the indifference of parents; the incapacity, too frequent change, or extreme youthfulness of the teachers; the short period allotted to schooling; negligent attendance; defective schoolbooks; bad methods of instruction; lax discipline; improper efforts to gain popularity, dependence on contributions; squandering of money; useless architectural display in buildings; appeals to false ambition; the erroneous importance attached to mere outward worldly objects; the excessive variety of subjects of instruction; and consequent superficial treatment; the injurious influence of political feelings.[78]

But Von Raumer found much virtue in American education. Eventually, the West would be the foundation for the inevitable American empire, but in America's sparsely settled state "her youthful forces are yet employed in subduing nature and establishing governments." Yet, even in its infancy America "brought forth authors who would dispute the palm with the most fertile poets of Europe." Could Europe boast of authors whose works were read with as much pleasure as those of Cooper and Irving?[79]

Alexis de Tocqueville, although a friendly critic of American education, correctly reminded historians that since Anglo-Americans brought their English education and culture with them and gradually spread their learning westward, society in the United States "had no infancy, being born adult." But he found no district anywhere in the United States "sunk in complete ignorance."[80] Finally, he praised the young country as the first in the world to found "so many schools and such efficient ones."[81]

Conclusions

Sparked by educators like Mann and Barnard, by writers of the Transcendentalist school, and by alert politicians, American education advanced steadily. The advance was slow and sometimes interrupted by regression, but as the wilderness was tamed and cities sprang up, public education gained impetus. Education for blacks was negligible, but abolitionists succeeded in establishing schools for blacks in large cities. Education for girls was limited, but feminists opened innovative seminaries for young ladies that equaled the best of the academies for boys. Many new colleges were erected, but their curriculums adhered to the classical tradition.

In the period 1820 - 1865, American statesmen, save for Lincoln, did not equal their predecessors in writing state papers, although in the papers of Clay and Calhoun there is comparable writing. It is in the works of essayists, novelists, and poets that the bulk of educational allusions in the literature of this period is sequestered. This literature is still conditioned by its English ancestry, but American writers show unequivocal evidence of weaning themselves away from the mother culture that nurtured them.

CHAPTER 6

Mostly New Englanders

A TREATISE on education, a convention for education, a lecture, a system, affects us with a slight paralysis and a certain yawning of the jaws. [Ralph Waldo Emerson][1]

Journalists, authors, and scholars have rarely been kind to the schoolmaster. From colonial times to the present, the intellectual classes as well as the general public have been loath to accord the teacher true professional status. Perhaps the teaching craft has not truly earned ascension to professionalism. The historical image of the teacher vindicates Irving's realistic caricature of the pedagogue in the person of hapless Ichabod Crane.

The writer-once-teacher, liberated by literary success from the drudgery of teaching chores, tends to highlight his unpleasant teaching experiences in his stories, poems, and essays. Undoubtedly, teaching is a poor choice of profession for a person who must write or explode. Each recitation keeps him from his flying pen; each paper he grades keeps him from adding a page to his burgeoning book. How often teachers have lamented to unsympathetic listeners: "If only I had time to finish my book!"

In the thirty-five years between 1830 and 1865 a plenitude of books were written. Save, perhaps, for the thirty-five years beginning about 1915, no other period in American literary history has seen the publication of so many well-written books. New England's golden age gave the works of Emerson, Hawthorne, Thoreau, Longfellow, Lowell, Holmes, and Whittier to a receptive America; New York offered the best of Whitman and Melville; and the South contributed the writings of Simms, Kennedy, the Cookes, Hayne, and Timrod. The South claims Poe, a Virginian, but because he wrote his major works in the North, Poe is claimed also by northern critics.

Emerson Hates Schoolmastering

Sectionally, New England dominated American letters and education. Harvard is chastised frequently in the books of some of its most eminent alumni. What did Emerson's mentors think of their prodigy when he wrote: "One of the benefits of a college education is to show the boys its little avail?"[2] As an undergraduate he had read prolifically; his notebooks attest to his extraordinary interest in history, philosophy, and literature for one so young. Perhaps his dissatisfaction with the professions of teaching and theology prompted him to disparage the practical value of a college degree. As a novice teacher in a "hot-steaming, stoved, stinking, dirty ABC spelling school" in the winter of 1820, Emerson, a Harvard senior, began to have doubts about teaching. A year later, although reinforced in spirit as a B.A., he continued to feel sorry for himself as a teacher, complaining that he was a "hopeless schoolmaster, just entering upon years of trade . . . toiling through this miserable employment without even the poor satisfaction of doing it well."[3] But Richard Henry Dana, Jr., a student at a Cambridge boarding school, praised young Emerson as "a very pleasant instructor, . . . although he had not system or discipline enough to ensure regular and vigorous study."[4]

Although Emerson's teaching career was brief, he was associated with teaching throughout his life. A popular lyceum lecturer, he brought learning to thousands of adults whose formal education had ended in the one-room schoolhouse. In his lectures and writing he anticipated many of the progressive principles of education canonized by John Dewey. Never contemptuous of the proper use of formal drill in the classroom, he saw a compatibility between enthusiasm and drill since "accuracy is essential to beauty,"[5] a concept immortalized in Edna St. Vincent Millay's sonnet, "Euclid Looked on Beauty Bare." But education has even loftier aims than swelling the child's inflatable mind with knowledge, for the great object of education should be a moral one — to teach the child self-reliance and to excite the young man with a passion to know himself and to understand the resources of his mind.

Emerson Supports Student Independence

A prolific reader himself, Emerson at twenty-five cautioned scholars to eschew pedantry. A sincere teacher will speak to the people in terms they can understand, and stimulate the students' individualities by inviting them to speak on the special knowledge they may possess.[6] An admirable man, said Emerson, is one who "likes to see a fine barn as well as a good tragedy."[7] Empathizing with the problems of youth, he wrote: "I suffer whenever I see that common sight of a parent or senior imposing his opinion and way of thinking on a young soul to which they are totally unfit. Cannot we let people be themselves and enjoy life in their own way?"[8] Besides, Emerson tells us, students will soon detect fraud and incompetence: "They know truth from counterfeit as quick as the chemist does. They detect weakness in your eye and behavior a week before you open your mouth and have given you the benefit of their opinion quick as a wink. They make no mistakes, have no pedantry. . . ."[9]

There is no great philosophical wisdom in Emerson's pronouncement that "the school, the college, society, make the difference between men,"[10] unless, of course, he believed that the doctrine of innate ideas was still favored by the generality of mankind. Yet, even educated Americans who lacked self-culture were only superficially educated; else, why were they drawn in hordes to foreign lands, mesmerized by "the superstition of Travelling . . . to Italy, England, Egypt. . .?"[11] Later, Mark Twain took up this theme in *The Innocents Abroad*, a prototype for many fictional works lampooning the American Babbitt abroad.

One of Emerson's loftiest hopes was for education to supersede politics and become the panacea for war, slavery, gambling, and intemperance.[12] Alas, his hopes have been unrealized in each category. Ironically, it was not education but a bloody war that set the black man nominally free. To lure the female into reform of mankind it was first incumbent upon whoever educated society to "improve and refine the men,"[13] an Emersonian notion that today's militant order of women's liberation would undoubtedly hoot down as asinine masculine chauvinism, since the "liberated" woman does not accept the Emersonian doctrine that males must have precedence over females in education and reform.

The paradox is that the child who is sincere, earnest, and beautiful is frequently educated by people and systems who are insincere, opportunistic, and ugly in soul. In brief, Emerson insisted that "the whole theory of the school is on the mother's knee" and "that the child is as hot to learn as the mother is to impart."[14] Theoretically, a child should be aflame to learn and the mother eager to teach.

Emerson's Good Teacher

Respect the child, admonished Emerson. Do not be overprotective and do not rob him of his needed solitude.[15] The teacher, as well as the parent, must respect the child. He must be a giver, the child a receiver, but teaching cannot take place until both teacher and pupil are in the same state, united, as it were, by a transfusion of feeling that facilitates learning.[16]

Emerson's scholar is not an Ichabod Crane. Speaking at Waterville College in Maine on August 11, 1841, Emerson said: "Whilst the multitude of men degrade each other, and give currency to desponding doctrines, the scholar must be a bringer of hope, and must reinforce man against himself."[17] In addition, the scholar must accept martyrdom graciously. In his passion for truth, he must deny himself the vanities of the laity.[18]

The virtuous teacher holds his own tongue, does not snarl or chide, and governs by the eye.[19] He learns from every man he meets. Yet some things cannot be taught. For example, "where is the Master who could have taught Shakespeare?"[20]

Emerson on the Classics, Sports, and Games

Regarding the classics, Emerson shared Franklin's utilitarian ideas. Few college graduates ever read Greek, and professionals who didn't study Latin and Greek are as successful as those who did.[21] The tormented student passes Latin and Greek for "four, or six, or ten years . . . and as soon as he leaves the University, as it is ludicrously called, he shuts these books for the last time."[22] On the reading of books, Emerson wrote: "Never read any book that is not a year old; never read any but famed books; never read any but what you like or, in Shakespeare's phrase, —

No profit goes where is no pleasure ta'en
In brief, Sir, study what you most affect."[23]

As Franklin and Rush before him, Emerson believed in the educational value of games and sports. What if the child endures a few bruises or scratches? Let the boy participate in gymnastic training, archery, cricket, fishing, hunting, riding, and boating. Also, to put him at ease socially, let him learn to dance, dress, and speak gracefully.[24] He will only too soon begin "to dress like collegians and sing in serenades and make polite calls"; while he is young let him learn life by doing, by experimenting, by suffering.[25]

Emerson also disapproved of oversized classes. "To maintain discipline in schools [with large classes] something must be done; and in this distress the wisest are tempted to adopt violent means, to

proclaim martial law, corporal punishment, mechanical arrange-
ment, bribes, spies, wrath . . . and ignorance, in lieu of that wise,
general providential influence that they had hoped, and yet hope at
some future day to adopt."[26] The consequences of poor discipline in
the school are many: the teacher becomes a hopeless clock-watcher,
catering to the whims of dunces and rogues.

Emerson — A Genteel Muckraker of Higher Education

As a critic of education, Emerson almost joins the muckraking
school of Upton Sinclair, a modern writer who admired Emerson.
Schools are planned foolishly and without regard for cultural
differences;[27] the students are indolent and unenthusiastic;[28] and the
regular course of study in academy and college is no more useful
than "some idle books under the bench at the Latin School."[29]

Emerson depicted the college as the repository for a multitude of
indifferent students taught by ardent and inventive dons who could
not cope with large classes. The brilliant student, eccentric, irritable,
explosive, solitary, and worldly, would not conform to the
mechanical methodologies employed by overworked professors.
Consequently, education meant dull students, routine teaching,
militarylike discipline and campus police.[30]

And what becomes of the graduates of these colleges? Unhappily,
they are immediately inflicted with a paralysis that attenuates their
manly aspirations and converts their enthusiasms into conformist
quiescence.[31] Emerson's lampooning of the homecoming alumnus
has a contemporary tone: "I have seen finely endowed men at
college festivals ten, twenty years after they had left the halls,
returning, as it seemed, the same boys they went away. The same
jokes pleased, the same straws tickled; the manhood and offices
brought thither at this return seemed mere ornamental masks; underneath they were boys yet."[32] Unfortunately, the schools teach
mere words. After ten or fifteen years of schooling, students enter
the world without having learned more than a memory of words.[33]

Why had the university failed in its noble mission? Emerson
charged that an unenlightened conservatism had made the university its tool.[34] The attractions of trade lured young people away from
learning. Although he did not exculpate American radicalism for its
part in deadening the spirit of inquiry in the university, Emerson
reserved most of his diatribes for the conservative class that deifies
property, opposes reform, discourages the arts, pays lip service to
religion, and ignores the plight of the needy, the Indians, the slaves,

and the immigrants.[35] Himself a propertied man, Emerson spoke out forcefully against his own class. In "Self-Reliance," he sorrows that men have looked away from themselves and at things so long that they have come to esteem the religious, learned, and civil institutions as guards of property, and they deprecate assaults on these, because they feel them to be assaults on property. They measure their esteem of each other "by what each has, and not by what each is."[36]

Emerson even called Harvard College a tool of the Boston countinghouse,[37] and in a paragraph foreshadowing Upton Sinclair's indictment of the schools and colleges as creatures of predatory capitalism he set forth the purported educational aims of the establishment of his day:

The cause of education is urged in this country with utmost earnestness — on what ground? Why, on this, that the people have the power, and if they are not instructed to sympathize with the intelligent, reading, trading and governing class, inspired with a taste for some competition and prizes, they will upset the fair pageant of Judicature and perhaps lay a hand on the muniments of wealth itself and new distribute the land.[38]

Education in this sense is prostituted to the preservation of a conservatism that will tolerate a minimal admission of the masses to its precincts of affluence. Emerson repeatedly scored the administrators of universities for their timidity, for their refusal to leave "the ruts of the last generation," and for their fear of arousing the young to a "just and heroic life."[39] He understood the inertia of the generation gap well:

It is very certain that the coming age and the departing age seldom understand each other. The old man thinks the young man has no distinct purpose, for he could never get anything intelligible and earnest out of him. Perhaps the young man does not think it worth his while to explain himself to so hard and inapprehensive a confessor.[40]

If Emerson was merely a skeptic who loved to discuss ideas and not a reformer, he nevertheless motivated men to reexamine themselves, to question the traditional values of conformity, and to embrace idealism at the time of great obeisance to materialism. Not all men can bring themselves to demonstrate, picket, and agitate verbally to advance their particular ideologies. Emerson wrote as he pleased but in his criticisms of conservatism he was the man thinking, not acting.

But the power of the pen is unfathomable. Oliver Wendell Holmes praised Emerson's "American Scholar Address" as our "intellectual Declaration of Independence . . . that startled grave professors and sedate clergymen." The young left Harvard's halls after listening in awe to the orator "as if a prophet had been proclaiming to them, 'Thus saith the Lord.' "[41] Emerson was indeed an educational prophet in the Old Testament tradition, but he asked too much of the security-minded men who teach. Perhaps each teacher should nail a copy of this excerpt from "The American Scholar" to his desk.

Free should the scholar be — free and brave. . . . It is a shame to him if his tranquillity, amid dangerous times, arise from the presumption that like children and women his is a protected class; or if he seek a temporary peace by the diversion of his thoughts from politics or vexed questions, hiding his head like an ostrich in the flowering bushes, peeping into microscopes, and turning rhymes, as a boy whistles to keep his courage up.[42]

In summarizing Emerson's educational influence, Frederick Ives Carpenter notes that many educators have pointed out the vagueness of Emerson's educational observations. But these criticisms pale before the mighty accolades of Horace Mann, Charles W. Eliot, John Dewey, and Edwin C. Mead.[43] Can it be said that a man's ideas are vague when they are usefully incorporated in the practical philosophies of his followers? Charles W. Eliot acknowledged his debt to Emerson in "Four American Leaders," and in Emerson's "American Scholar Address" Eliot found motifs that inspired him to quicken Harvard's declining spirit, to introduce free electives for undergraduates, and to rebuild the university's libraries.

Negatively, Emerson's ideas have been subjected to the same criticisms as Dewey's. Free electives are wasted upon the immature students who tend to choose easy courses; self-reliance is an admirable trait in geniuses, but a difficult trait to impose upon the average; and the child converts freedom into license if he is unrestrained.[44]

Amos Bronson Alcott's Educational Woes

Amos Bronson Alcott never heeded Voltaire's advice in *Candide* to visionaries — first, it is necessary to cultivate one's own garden. A mystic and social reformer, he neglected his family in his whirlwind and quixotic attempts to impose justice upon a world that seemed content without it. Jailed in January, 1843, for refusing on principle to pay taxes, Alcott set the example for Thoreau's voluntary imprisonment in July, 1846.

Alcott, a schoolteacher who dared to innovate and speak his mind, lost several positions because of his educational progressivism. An unlettered man, he peddled wares in Virginia, read avidly in planters' libraries, became a peripatetic philosopher, lectured on divinity, human nature, ethics, dietetics, and education, and founded the Temple School in Boston, immortalized in Elizabeth Peabody's *A Record of a School*.[45] He praised peddling as a better educator than a college — for what could college have taught him about slaves, planters, women, and children?[46] Alcott practiced what Emerson taught in "Self-Reliance." Guided later in his reading by William Russell and William Ellery Channing, and influenced by his daughter Anna, he accepted transcendentalism as his philosophic creed,[47] yet insisted upon method as "everything in teaching."[48] His educational idols, Pythagoras, Plato, Aristotle, Jesus, and Paul were all methodologists, and although Jesus taught intuitively, Alcott saw no dichotomy between Christ's "logic of heart" and philosophical logic and dialectic.[49]

From Robert Owen, the practicing utopian, Alcott acquired a lifelong sense of social consciousness and optimistically saw the imminent supplanting of competition by cooperation.[50] Owen's influence was reflected in Alcott's teaching. Man could be regenerated since he was not inherently depraved. Education, if altruistically applied, would shape men ethically.[51] When he met Josiah Holbrook, father of the American Lyceum and spiritual drummer for the Sunday School movement, Alcott listened enthusiastically to Holbrook's gospel and became an apostle of the movement himself.[52]

Alcott Believes in Social Progress via Education

Alcott's educational philosophy was drawn from his readings, his intellectual association, and his experiences. His emphasis was upon intuition and ethics; the good teacher recognizes the natural gifts of the child and guides him to use these wisely and easily in the vocation for which they were designed.[53] The sympathetic teacher lends his mind to the pupil temporarily, enabling the borrower to see prospects he had never previously envisioned "become present and memorable forever."[54] Kind and lovable as he was to his students, Alcott insisted that the teacher always be in command of his class. He praised his daughter Anna for her "strictness on decision in the management of the scholars"[55] and her successful application of original, persuasive teaching.[56]

Alcott's teaching career was hectic from the start. He labored at the Centre District School, Cheshire, Connecticut, for eighteen dollars a month and even bought school supplies with part of his salary. Alcott immediately abolished corporal punishment, introduced comfortable seats, bedecked the colorless classroom with scented bouquets, and ordered lively textbooks.[57] His students kept journals — even as their master did — and evaluated themselves, their classmates, and their teachers.[58] To phonetics he added meaning, and he abolished spelling lists as an unnatural learning device. He visualized arithmetic problems; beans and blocks of wood served as catalysts to the students in their trials with numbers. He disliked parsing; to the regret of the formal grammarians he celebrated the virtues of functional grammar. To make geography a reality to his lads and lassies, he had them map the schoolyard and later, when their cartographic art would flower, they would even map the city's streets.[59]

Obviously, these innovations added to the taxpayer's expense. Already disenchanted with Alcott's "no whipping" policy and his questionable social evenings with students, the good citizens of Cheshire cried "enough!" Alcott was sacked, and of his former patrons he wrote:[60]

Wretched indeed is the publick sentiment in reference to Education in this village. . . . The publick sentiment needs enlightening, the prejudices of men dissipated; intelligence diffused; precedent rendered ridiculous; and what is worse than all to effect, avarice liberalized. This is the work which requires the talent and temper of a true Reformer to accomplish. I am not that one.[61]

His fortunes were no better at Bristol. There, in addition to inviting opposition by his unorthodox educational methodology, he denounced the locals' Calvinistic creed and called for the application of what he called true Christianity in the family, school, and government.[62] If he was not a reformer, he was undoubtedly a gadfly. Unfortunately for Alcott, he was always being banished for his unorthodox views.

The Temple School and Elizabeth Peabody

In the mid-1830's Alcott administered the famous Temple School in Boston. He applied his intuitive arts to teaching without let. The child at Temple was pressed to turn inward to find his divinity. Once found, this precious spark would flame throughout his being and guide him morally through life.[63] Happily for Alcott, Elizabeth Peabody encouraged eminent Bostonians to entrust their children to his transcendental meanderings, and for a time the proper Bostonians gazed upon Alcott's experiments with their children with fondness and sympathy. In this singular school the children were the decision-makers. Evildoers were judged and punished by their peers. Ostracism from the congenial company of his peers was the ultimate doom of the convicted student, a penalty possibly introduced by Alcott in imitation of the ancient Greeks whom he admired.[64]

As in his earlier teaching, Alcott emphasized thought before style. Grammar was secondary in literature; let the novices master substance by analyzing their readings in groups. Grammatical accuracy and individuality in style would emerge gradually as the little minds read, probed, and questioned their readings. In biographical and journal writing the children would have many motivated opportunities to develop their talents.[65]

Elizabeth Peabody, who taught at Alcott's school, was charmed by his conversations with children. Her good sense inspired her to record some of these conversations, which appeared in 1835 as a book, *Record of a School Exemplifying the Principles and Methods of Moral Culture*. Today, many elementary school teachers might hesitate to puzzle their little ones with such awesome questions as: "Is it aspiration to seek knowledge for our own good alone?" "Which of you have gone inward and viewed yourselves?"[66]

Although the book was praised by Emerson and brought recognition to Alcott, his good fortune was ephemeral. The orthodox in Boston who hated Alcott's reforms branded his "Conversations with Children on Gospels" heretical, since it denied Jesus's special divinity.[67] Emerson and the Unitarians rose to Alcott's defense, but the depression of 1837 and the continued attack upon Alcott's supposed obscenities and heresies killed the school. When Alcott admitted a black child to the foundering school his patrons left for good. The gadfly had stung too hard.[68]

Not that he didn't deserve some of his humiliation. Elizabeth Peabody, one of Alcott's friends and disciples, reluctantly exposed one of her master's unreasonable traits:

Alcott subjects everything to the test of his talismanic words, and as they answer to them in his predisposed ear, they take their places — nor does he do anything more, at the utmost of his liberality, than to endure the sugges-

tion of a contrary view. It seems no part of his plan to search the thoughts
and views of other minds in any faith that they will help his own. He only
seems to look in books for what agrees with his own thoughts.[69]

Disappointed in Bostonians, Alcott resolved now to become a missionary to parents. In a letter to his mother dated June 21, 1840, he
wrote: "I left Boston, finding that the people were not ready to support a man who like myself would reform not only their children but
themselves, by my teaching and life . . . but I shall hope to return to
my teaching again in school when the public have opened their eyes
a little to what I can do for them."[70]

Despite his setbacks, Alcott was named superintendent of the
Concord schools in 1859, a post he held until 1864. His salary was
nominal, but he probably enjoyed this opportunity to guide young
teachers. He permitted teachers to visit one another one day a month
and to take their classes to other schools for new learning experiences. His school report (1860-1861) epitomizes his educational
views and gives a minute description of the Concord schools.[71]

Alcott, an educational prophet, was not overly honored in his own
time, and critics of the present age who blindly condemn all
progressivism because of the foibles of some of its eccentrics should
closely reexamine his concepts. He saw in the conversational
methods of Jesus, Socrates, and Pythagoras models for his own
teaching and was not deterred because this method martyred Jesus
and Socrates. Despising cunning as the commonplace driving force
in most schools, he sought to replace it with love and understanding.
Books too frequently impress us because of their eminent authors, he
thought, but people should be self-reliant in thought and rebel
against imposed authority. Alcott often said that cities do little for
books and college less.[72] Colleges sometimes defile the students'
speech and writing. Rural boys and girls, on the other hand, "not
vexed with their grammar and school tasks," speak with purity and
simplicity.[73] Although teachers of teachers are necessary, Alcott
praises Horace Mann's Teachers' Institute reservedly: "But I
learned little from teachers, or the teachers' teachers, on
education."[74]

Alcott Pioneers in Child Psychology

Alcott believed that the child is innocent and closer to God than
adults are. It is incumbent upon thinking man to preserve the child's
innate goodness; even the acquisition of knowledge must be made

subservient to this goal.[75] These ideas were challenged by William Ellery Channing, who denied that experience and intuition are incompatible.[76]

The child should be awakened and directed, not coerced to dwell upon "prescribed and exclusive courses."[77] He is basically good, and schoolmasters, presuming that they are good themselves, could refashion the world by molding the child decently.[78] In his monograph "Observations on the Principles and Methods of Infant Instruction," Alcott hypothesizes:

Infant education . . . is founded on the great principle, that every infant is already in possession of the faculties and apparatus required for instruction, and, that, by a law of his constitution, he uses these to a great extent himself; that the office of instruction is chiefly to facilitate this process, and to accompany the child in his progress, rather than to drive on or even to lead him.[79]

Whether or not contemporary educational psychologists agree with Alcott's stress on intuition, they must surely acknowledge the debt that all educators owe to his unwavering insistence upon the study of the mind's functions as a requisite for applying psychology to educational progress. In *Concord Days*, Alcott epitomizes his philosophy of educational psychology clearly:

The Dialectic, or Method of the Mind, constitutes the basis of all culture. Without a thorough discipline in this, our schools and universities give but a showy and superficial training. The knowledge of Mind is the beginning of all knowledge; without this a theology is baseless, the knowledge of God impossible. Modern education has not dealt with these deeper questions of life and being.[80]

Orestes Brownson on Truth in Education

The men and women who met informally at one another's house in Boston or Concord for sessions of intellectual communion were serious, each in his own way, concerning the melioration of man's lot on earth and, to a lesser degree, his prospects for postmortem immortality. Alcott, Emerson, Thoreau, Theodore Parker, Brownson, Margaret Fuller, and Elizabeth Peabody were the most eminent of the Transcendental Club's charter members, and perhaps the most interesting of these celebrities was Orestes Augustus Brownson, who sought God through four churches before he found Him in the Mother Church. In his search for the true faith, Brownson preached as a Presbyterian in 1821, a Universalist in 1825, a Unitarian in 1832, a minister of the Society for Christian Union and Progress in 1836, and, finally, as a Roman Catholic in 1844.[81]

A controversial man all his life, Brownson asked teachers to dedicate themselves unselfishly for man's betterment. He wrote: "Ask not what your age wants, but what it needs; not what it will reward, but what, without which it cannot be saved; and then go and do."[82] From Emerson, who influenced him greatly, he adopted his views of self-reliance. Books alone do not educate; the truly educated man is a self-educated man who learns from observing man and nature.[83] Like Alcott, he warned that slavish book learning is harmful. Existing systems of education tend to stifle the child's natural inductive proclivities, associating learning with "the most disagreeable chores and processes."[84] How, then, should the child be educated? First, advised Brownson, have him study nature; second, let him be trained in the use of words, letters, and books and the realm of thought; third, "let him be a discerning reader before he learns to read and let him be an authentic and judging reader in order not to become a servile fawner upon authority."[85] He approved the Brook Farm School, which was "half a charming adventure, half solemn experiment."[86]

Brownson saw the key to education in the scholar's willingness to defy public opinion. In his "Oration on the Scholar's Mission," he called upon scholars to identify themselves with the social and personal needs of the people[87] and, if so dictated to by their consciences, to defy authority because "the only equality of men exists in their accountability to God; and no one is bound to obey any merely human authority."[88] Here, Brownson and Thoreau are at one. John Brown marched to Harper's Ferry at God's behest and he could justify his civil disobedience since God's law supersedes man-made law.

Having made God the ultimate judge to whom man may appeal for guidance, Brownson made it difficult for his critics to question his practical vision. In illustration, Arthur M. Schlesinger, Jr., commends Brownson for advocating education as the means of rescuing the underprivileged, but accuses him of failing "to see that the privileged are reluctant to elevate the workers when the price would be the loss of some of their own privileges."[89] But Brownson was not so naive. The following passage shows that he saw only too well that educators and priests generally reflect the attitudes of the established classes:

For our part we yield to none in our reverence for science and religion; but we confess that we look not for the regeneration of the race from priests and pedagogues. They have had a fair trial. They cannot construct the Temple of God. . . . In a word they always league with the people's masters, and seek to reform without disturbing the social arrangements which render reform necessary. They would change the consequents without changing the antecedents, secure to men the rewards of holiness while they continue their allegiance to the devil. We have no faith in priests and pedagogues. They merely cry peace, peace, and that too when there is no peace, and can be none.[90]

Furthermore, even the practical man must not dread change in society, and his education should prepare him for more than vocational aims, namely, for participation in a society in which "each man is essentially and inalienably free, and the brother and equal of every man."[91] Brownson opposed state boards of education because he feared they menaced individual liberty.

Brownson Defends Public Education Against Catholic Attacks

A dissenter all his life, Brownson finally sought peace of mind in the structured conformity of Catholic doctrine. But he did not withdraw from the social battles raging outside the Church. He never forsook his new church — he died a Catholic — and involved himself fully in the open and clandestine warfare raging between native Americans and the large number of Catholic immigrants. However, the Church hierarchy was disturbed when Brownson defended the public schools against Catholic charges that they encouraged immorality and irreligion in America. Where in Europe, he asked, have Catholic schools always effectively inhibited corruption and irreligion?[93]

Catholic education is not infallible even if the bishops so proclaim it; indeed, they should be under scrutiny themselves to ensure that they maintain their true Catholicism.[94] To operate more sincerely they should educate their pupils to appreciate their own age and nation and humanize the pupil's life to fit him for religious and practical life.[95]

Brownson had some barbs for Catholic scholars and colleges as well. Few Catholic scholars courageously take sides on issues as do their peers in non-Catholic colleges. Those who take determined stands on social issues find themselves thinking differently from their more cloistered brethren. The Catholic college reveres the past unduly, and the Church acts as if there were no future for mankind on earth.[96] A reform of Catholic collegiate education would result in the graduation of living men — men broadened by liberal studies and endowed with generous aims.[97]

Undoubtedly, Brownson was torn between his liberalism and his duty to abide by the canon of the Catholic Church. What he criticized in the Catholic schools was also open to censure in the public schools and non-Catholic colleges; to demonstrate his objectivity, a teacher will punish a pet pupil inordinately.

Thoreau's Early Views on Teaching

It is likely that Thoreau's social views were influenced by Brownson. In 1835, Thoreau dropped out of Harvard for several months to teach school in Canton, Massachusetts. Brownson, then pastor of the Universal Church in Canton, examined young Thoreau for the position and found him satisfactory. Two critics of Thoreau, Christian C. Gruber and Wendell Glick, attribute much of Thoreau's social thinking to Brownson's tutelage. Yet later Thoreau wrote: "I have lived some thirty years on this planet, and I have yet to hear the first syllable of valuable or even earnest advice from my seniors. They have told me nothing, and probably cannot tell me anything to the purpose."[98]

Ingratitude? Cynicism? Egotism? Mere literary hyperbolization? Or vindication? For on December 30, 1837, in times of severe economic depression, Thoreau wrote to Brownson for a recommendation for a teaching position. Brownson did nothing for him, but the letter is a candid exposition of Thoreau's early educational philosophy, resembling much of Alcott's and Emerson's thinking:

I seek a situation as teacher of a small school, or assistant in a large one, or, what is more desirable, as private tutor in a gentleman's family.

Perhaps I should give some account of myself. I would make education a pleasant thing both to the teacher and to the scholar. This discipline, which we allow to be the end of life, should not be one thing in the classroom, and another in the street. We should seek to be fellow students with the pupil, and we should learn as well with him, if we would be most helpful to him. But I am not blind to the difficulties of the case; it supposes a degree of freedom which rarely exists. It hath not entered into the head of man to conceive the full import of that word — Freedom — not a paltry Republican freedom with a *posse comitatus* at his heels to administer it in doses as to a sick child — but a freedom proportionate to the dignity of his nature — a freedom that shall make him feel that he is a man among men, and responsible only to that reason, of which he is a particle, for his thoughts and actions.

I have even been disposed to regard the cowhide as a nonconductor. Methinks, that, unlike the electric wire, not a single spark of truth is ever transmitted through its agency to the slumbering intellect it would address. I suspect it may teach a truth in physics, but never a truth in morals.[99]

Thoreau did not deviate from these principles of education. The child is innately good; therefore, all educational philosophy must be geared to have the child develop in an earthly paradise.[100] The cost of education should be charged to the government, since the best education obtainable will benefit both the child and the community.[101]

Thoreau Has Little Praise for Harvard

Of his own education, Thoreau wrote: "I was fitted, or rather made unfit, for College, at Concord Academy and elsewhere, mainly by myself, with the countenance of Phineas Allen, Preceptor."[102] He entered Harvard in 1833. Conditioned in Greek, Latin, and mathematics, he did not enjoy the pre-Revolutionary curriculum, but praised Edward Tyrell Channing as inspirer of his literary art.[103] To Emerson, who boasted that Harvard taught most of the branches of learning, Thoreau replied: "Yes, indeed, all the branches and none of the roots."[104]

As a senior he wrote that his presence at Harvard had been merely physical. "Heart and soul I have been far away among the scenes of my childhood. Those hours that should have been devoted to study have been spent in scouring the woods, and exploring the lakes and streams of my native village."[105]

College should be more than play or study, though. Students should experiment in living while at school. Why not have students build their own living quarters at college and so learn mechanics, construction, and economy?[106] Colleges tend to teach subjects, not living. The lad who reads Adam Smith and Ricardo may nevertheless run his father into debt.[107]

When asked for biographical data to be included in the record of the tenth anniversary of the class of 1837, Thoreau responded: "I confess that I have very little class spirit, and have almost forgotten that I ever spent four years at Cambridge. . . . It is difficult to realize that the old routine is still kept up."[108] Christian P. Gruber, however, discounts much of Thoreau's minimization of Harvard. Despite its limitations in 1833, Harvard had on its faculty cosmopolitan Europeans, some of them exiles from monarchical despotism. Many of the faculty wrote, edited, and translated important works; Harvard's library was the richest in America; and the student body included boys of diverse backgrounds, many of them with professional and literary ambitions.[109]

Thoreau's Brief Career as a Teacher

As is the case with so many other writers, Thoreau did not care to make a career of teaching. He believed himself to be a good teacher at Canton, but some local citizens thought otherwise.[110] In 1837, he taught at Concord for five hundred dollars a year. But after flogging six students at the command of Deacon Nehemiah Ball, a school committeeman, he resigned rather than flog more students. Then he and his brother went into schoolmastering on their own. On September 15, 1838, when Concord Academy opened its doors to students of both sexes, twenty-five children of well-known families trooped in to test Thoreauvian pedagogy. The brothers let it be known that they would not tolerate idlers, but that their innovations at Concord Academy were designed to satisfy the play-instincts of all young people. Stressing learning by doing, the faculty of two escorted their classes on field trips to nature's haunts, to the shops of compositors and gunsmiths, and to the fields and barns of farmers. Half-hour recesses charmed the busy scholars and the classrooms were airy.[111]

Edmund Sewall, a pupil at the academy in 1840, recalled that once a fortnight he was permitted to write a letter home instead of writing a formal composition, that Thoreau read aloud to his students, and that the brothers were more like comrades to the students than they were teachers.[112] In brief, the school was an early example of Dewey's progressivism.

Thoreau had contempt for the general run of teachers, but he spared neither great scholars nor great thinkers. "They make shift to live merely by conformity; practically as their fathers did, and are in no sense the progenitors of a nobler race of men."[113] Too often, scholars cannot express themselves clearly; if they lived more earnestly, "we should not witness those lame conclusions to their ill-sown discourses, but their sentences would pass over the ground like loaded rollers, and not mere hollow and wooden ones, to press in the seed and make it germinate."[114] More generally, Thoreau noted that it is almost impossible to teach truths, that readiness in the child is requisite before he can be taught, that drill rarely benefits the child, and that young men accept the history lecturer's "poetic pablum" uncritically.[115] Perhaps his progressivism and satirical pen inhibited college authorities from offering him a professorial chair or an honorary degree. Could the author of "Civil Disobedience" have been happy at faculty meetings or Honors Day commencements?

Thoreau's Belief in Continuing Education

After Concord Academy closed, Thoreau left schoolmastering forever. He fought courageously to allow controversial speakers to lecture at the lyceums. He also proposed that Concord hire artists, philosophers, writers, and scientists to give adult education courses in the town. "Deploring that we spend more on almost any article of bodily aliment or ailment than on our mental aliment," he advocated schools not unlike our community colleges: "It is time that we had uncommon schools, that we did not leave off our education when we begin to be men and women."[116] In his journal for 1852, he was more specific. Men should have continuing education. Each village should be a university where people may study the liberal arts for life.[117] Edward Bellamy, almost a half century later, championed a system of community colleges throughout the land, an idea he possibly borrowed from Thoreau.

Like Emerson, Thoreau praised the college library as the only part of his college training which gave him "passing pleasure and lasting good."[118] In 1849, he wrote to President Sparks of Harvard for permission to use the Harvard library. At first the startled president was adamant; then, unknown to Thoreau, he relented. Meanwhile, Thoreau wrote another strong appeal to Sparks that highlights his belief in continuing education:

I ask only that the University may help to finish the education whose foundation she has helped to lay. I was not ripe then for higher courses and now that I am riper I trust that I am not too far away to be instructed by her. Indeed, I see not how her children can more properly or effectively keep up a living connexion with their Alma Mater, than by continuing to draw from her intellectual nutriment is some such way as this.[119]

George Ripley at Brook Farm School

In volume XV of the *New American Encyclopedia* (1865) edited by George Ripley and Charles A. Dana, only eleven uncritical lines appear to note that Thoreau lived, dreamed, wrote, and died, an oversight that is puzzling in view of Ripley's awareness of Thoreau's talents. True, Ripley had denounced Thoreau as a pantheist in his review of *A Week on the Concord and Merrimack Rivers* for the *New York Tribune*,[120] and he probably misinterpreted him because he failed to read Thoreau's humor accurately.[121] Still, Ripley, a Brook Farm founder, should have accorded his fellow Concordian greater homage than eleven skeletal lines in his encyclopedia. At Brook Farm, Ripley applied Pestalozzi's progressive ideas in the practical administration of the school. The child would develop into maturity through self-culture. Guided by a loving teacher who would cultivate his instincts, the child would gain confidence, embrace democracy, and live optimistically.[122] Unhindered by formal discipline and official hours of study, the Brook Farmer ranged far afield in curriculum, did not scorn the industrial arts, and enjoyed visits to shop and field. Science was advanced from book to laboratory, shop, and field, and the boys did not hesitate to assist the girls in their work and studies.[123]

Obviously, the school functioned well because "progressive" parents supported its aims. Students came from as far away as the Philippines, but it is questionable whether any of Boston's slum children attended. Ripley, though, believed strongly that education of the masses was the only road to world progress. The teacher and the journalist had a mission to join with the scholar to grasp the control of education from the hands of aristocrats.[124]

Richard Henry Dana Learns More at Sea than at School

Richard Henry Dana's poor eyesight led him to leave Harvard for adventure on the high seas aboard the *Pilgrim* bound for California.[125] Happily, his tour of duty afloat gave us *Two Years Before the Mast*, a narrative that helped ease the hardships of men brutalized in the merchant marine. Possibly, his educational recollections inspired him to expose flogging of sailors; at fourteen, while enrolled at a highly regarded preparatory school in Cambridge, he endured the agonies of a curriculum of Latin, Greek, French, history, mathematics, and flogging. The school was gloomy and unsanitary and its intellectual regimen rarely prepared a boy adequately for college. His third teacher at the prep school, Horatio Wood, called Dana a shammer and a truant, inflicted eighteen blows with a ferrule on each of the boy's hands, but refrained from harming young Dana further when the audible hostility of the class chastened his sadistic penchant.[126]

At Harvard Dana studied under Josiah Quincy's perplexing

overlordship. On the one hand, Quincy fostered religious and academic freedom; tolerated all sects and abolished the forced chapel; demanded no religious tests of the faculty; supported faculty abolitionists; and strove to rid science and learning of sectarian and political bias. On the other hand, Quincy was tyrannical toward the students. By enforcing a weekly grading system, abolishing the elective system, and prohibiting town visits, he alienated the students. The sophomore class rioted in the spring of 1834, smashing windows and breaking furniture to show their displeasure. Quincy swiftly turned suspicious students over to a grand jury for grilling and dismissed the entire sophomore class. For showing sympathy with an accused student, compassionate schoolmates were suspended for six months.[127]

Longfellow Prefers Göttingen to Bowdoin and Harvard

Henry Wadsworth Longfellow, himself a Harvard graduate and a Harvard don, considered Harvard and Bowdoin mere secondary schools when compared to the German universities, a belief shared by his predecessor, Ticknor.[128] Longfellow toured Germany in 1829, and his long letter to Stephen Longfellow probably includes the basis for his later criticisms of Bowdoin and Harvard:

What has heretofore been the idea of an University with us? The answer is a simple one. Two or three large buildings with a chapel, and a President to pray in it. I say University, because with us University and College have till now been almost synonymous terms. Mr. Jefferson it is true made a bold attempt — but it failed — if not totally — at least in part if failed — and why? Because with all due respect he does not seem to have begun right. He began where everybody else in our country would have begun — by building college halls and trying to stock them with students. But that is not the way to found an University. European Universities were never founded in this manner. Indeed, as far as regards University buildings — one might live in Göttingen from one year's end to the other without having the slightest idea of its being the seat of an University.

No it was by collecting together professors in whom "the spirit moved" who were well enough known to attract students to themselves — and after they had assembled them capable of teaching them something they did not know before. It was so with the Italian, Spanish, German and French Universities and when there is an American University, it must and will be so with that. Then, instead of seeing a new College ushered into existence every winter by a petition to the Legislature for funds to put up a parcel of Wooden-Factory buildings for students — we should see capital better

employed in enriching the libraries of the country and making them public!
And instead of seeing the youth of our country chained together like galley
slaves and "scourged to their dungeons," as it were, our eyes would be
cheered by the grateful spectacle of mind throwing its fetters off — and
education freed from its chains and shackles.[129]

Longfellow was not unaware, however, of the drawbacks in the
European university system. Paul Flemming, the enthusiastic young
hero of Longfellow's novel *Hyperion*, praises the University of
Heidelberg where the cloistered professors study sixteen hours daily
to "feed undying lamps of thought."[130] His host, the learned Baron
Hohenfels, reminds Flemming that excessive seclusion is harmful to
a scholar. How can he learn about the world, removed as he is from
the arena of men acting?[131]

Longfellow was only twenty-two when he was studying at Göttingen, but he saw clearly in his educational meditations that
teachers are generally ignorant of the immaturity of their students.
The youthful mind must be pleasurably excited to learn.[132]
Churchill, the fictional character in Longfellow's novel *Kavanagh*,
sees poetry in mathematics, but acknowledges that "it is our way of
teaching that makes it so prosaic."[133] To illustrate his point, he cites
a poetic arithmetic problem from the *Lilawati* of Bhascara Acharya,
a Sanscrit author:

One fifth of a hive of bees flew to the Kadamba flower; one third flew to the
Silandhara; three times the difference of these two numbers flew to an ar-
bor; and one bee continued flying about, attracted on each side by the
fragrant Ketaki and the Malati. What was the number of the bees?[134]

His unhappiness with the college did not deter Longfellow from
applying for a professorship at Bowdoin. After many discouraging
postal exchanges with the college's administration, he was finally
granted the coveted professorship.[135] On Inaugural Day, the young
professor of modern languages spoke eloquently on the scholars'
mission:

I regard the profession of teacher in a far more noble point of view than
many do. I cannot help believing that he who bends in a right direction the
pliant disposition of the young, and trains up the ductile mind to a vigorous
and healthy growth, does something for the welfare of country and
something for the great interests of humanity.[136]

Longfellow Tires of Teaching

But Longfellow found teaching at Bowdoin frustrating, drudgerous, and ill-paid. The conservatism of the faculty and the administration stultified meaningful learning.[137] Depressed and disillusioned, he sought unsuccessfully to interest William Cullen Bryant, then editor of the *New York Evening Post*, in his plan for the establishment of a female academy in New York City.[138] Two years earlier, Longfellow had noted that America was concerned mainly with gain, amusement, expansion of territory and population, commerce, agriculture, cities and plantations, "but the true glory of a nation consists in . . . what nature and education have given to the mind. . . . But still the main current of education runs in the wide and not well defined channel of immediate and practical utility."[139]

As Smith Professor of Modern Languages at Harvard, Longfellow was as unhappy as he had been at Bowdoin. In addition to his teaching chores, he was a department chairman who intensely disliked supervising teachers. He had little use for the pageantry of ritualistic academic exercises. When faced with the inevitable academic red tape, he courageously confronted the Harvard Corporation with some unpleasant facts. How could he teach 115 French students, thirty German students, and still supervise his department, prepare his lessons, and write?[140] Later, he argued against a miserly policy that increased the number of students in French classes from twelve to twenty and, finally, to thirty.

There are conflicting commentaries on his teaching effectiveness. Edward Wagenknecht praises Longfellow as a master of his subject who avoided the pitfalls of abstraction and speculation. He lectured simply and translated expertly.[141] He patronized the students, with whom he would sit, walk, and talk, and his urbanity drew undergraduates closer to him. But he was unhappy. The minds of boys are unchallenging. He needed to commune and grapple with men's minds.

Longfellow complained that education is a "tread mill" and that teachers lead a "dog's life." Waxing poetic in his lamentations, he wrote, "The college work is like a great hand laid on all the strings of my lyre, stopping their vibrations." Undoubtedly, his reason for remaining at Harvard was partly economic; in five years, 1840-1844, Longfellow earned only two thousand dollars from his book and periodical royalties. Although he frequently had thoughts of resigning, he could not renounce his fifteen-hundred dollar annual salary at Harvard until 1854 when his literary reputation seemed to ensure him a satisfactory income.[142]

Churchill, Longfellow's Fictional Counterpart

Churchill, the village schoolmaster in *Kavanagh*, reflects Longfellow's attitude toward teaching. "Nature had made Mr. Churchill a poet, but destiny had made him a schoolmaster. This produced a discord between his outward and his inward existence."[143] To his friend, Kavanagh, Churchill rationalizes his failure to write in a pathetic plea for understanding familiar in spirit to all procrastinating teachers who would be creative: "I now despair of writing anything excellent. . . . My life is given to others, and to this destiny I submit without a murmur; for I have the satisfaction of having labored faithfully in my calling, and of having perhaps, incited others to do what I shall never do."[144] But Churchill's virtues are not valued by the townsfolk:

To the people in the village he was the schoolmaster, and nothing more. They beheld in his form and countenance no outward sign of the divinity within. They saw him daily moiling and delving in the common path, like a beetle, and little thought that underneath that hard and cold exterior lay folded delicate golden wings, wherewith when the heat of day was over, he soared and revelled in the pleasant evening air.[145]

From 1854 to his death Longfellow was emancipated from the demands of students, faculty, and administrators. He chose not to become a self-sacrificing Churchill for his remaining years, but his contributions to education were considerable. With George Ticknor he established modern languages as a course of study at Harvard; he helped advance modern language studies beyond their limited level of easy grammar and elementary readings; and he facilitated the establishment of graduate study in modern language and literature when he chaired the department.[146] As early as 1829, he drew up a prospectus for a girls' high school. Several months later, the school opened as the Female High School of Portland.[147] He envisioned a university for Portland founded without legislative funds; the students would collect fees, pay the professors, and regulate their own discipline.[148] But this university, modeled on Göttingen, remained only a vision, even as his still poignant, idealistic lines:

> Were half the power that fills the world with terror,
> Were half the wealth bestowed on camps and courts,

> Given to redeem the human mind from error,
> There were no need of arsenals or forts.

James Russell Lowell as Student and Teacher

When the seven representatives from Massachusetts voted in favor of the war with Mexico, James Russell Lowell responded to what he believed was a betrayal by Massachusetts of its antislavery position with his "Bigelow Papers," censuring his home state severely in this stanza:

> Massachusetts, God forgive her,
> She's akneelin' with the rest,
> She, they ough' to ha' clung ferever
> In her grand old eagle nest;
> W'ile the wracks are round her hurled,
> Holdin' up a beacon peerless
> To the oppressed of all the world!

Lowell was a precocious child, entering Miss Whitney's kindergarten and elementary school at two. His father spared him the hidings and thrashings of the common school teachers by sending him in 1828 to a "civilized" Latin school.[149] Here, under the tutelage of William Wells, Lowell prepared himself for Harvard. Richard Henry Dana, Jr., Lowell's classmate, recalls that the school's thirty students slept seven to a room under Spartan conditions. The rooms were cold and unlit and floggings were administered freely. But Wells was a fine classical scholar, and many of his students were accepted by Harvard.[150]

In 1886, Lowell reviewed Harvard's history; unfortunately the reforms introduced by Everett, Ticknor, and Bancroft were short-lived. Harvard's frivolous students were mere schoolboys, preferring music and dancing to learning.[151] At Harvard Lowell rarely touched a textbook — "he was too well prepared" — and cared little for his apathetic teachers and their dull exercises. The best teachers refused to teach freshman courses, but Professor Pierce, Lowell's mathematics teacher, helped students generously and allowed them to progress at their own pace.[152] Only three other teachers won Lowell's praise — Tyrrel Channing, Longfellow, and Machi.

Returning to Harvard as Longfellow's successor, Lowell was not always happy in class. Listening to routine grammar recitations bored him, yet a visiting committee that examined his classes reported back to the Overseers that Lowell actually instructed his students, "an uncommon thing. Few . . . teachers consider it their duty to teach. . . . They simply regard it as their business to act as examiners."[153] Edward Everett Hale is more critical of Lowell's teaching. Lowell's scholarship and friendliness to students did not compensate for his weak class teaching. When a student read with difficulty Lowell "would break in, do most of the reading, and ruin the correction because of his muffled articulation."[154]

Lowell Deplores Mediocre Teaching

Lowell's eminent students, among them Henry Adams and Barrett Wendell, enjoyed his friendly and sympathetic teaching. Lowell insisted that people know what things mean. Judgment, not memory, is the basis for true scholarship.[155] As critical of collegiate education as Emerson, Lowell praised the students of the eighteenth and early nineteenth centuries for their willingness to study and learn independently, but he scorned the spoiled children of rich parents. In "A Fable for Critics," his celebrated satire on his literary contemporaries, Lowell lampoons college education in verse reminiscent of Trumbull's "The Progress of Dulness":

> In this way our Hero got safely to College,
> Where he bolted alike both his commons and knowledge;
> A reading-machine, always wound up and going,
> He mastered whatever was not worth the knowing,
> Appeared in a gown, with black waistcoat of satin,
> To spout such a Gothic oration in Latin,
> That Tully could never have made out a word on it,
> (Though himself was the model the author preferred in it,)
> And grasping the parchment which gave him in fee
> All the mystics and so-forths contained in A.B.,
> He was launched (life is always compared to a sea)
> With just enough learning, and skill for the using it,
> To prove he'd a brain, by forever confusing it.[156]

Much of Lowell's educational philosophy is recapitulated in his "Harvard Anniversary Address." The fame and usefulness of all institutions of learning are contingent upon their teachers, but "great teachers are almost rarer than great poets."[157] Above all let the humanities be taught, for the liberal arts inflame the imagination and liberate the mind.[158] The teacher's power of intellect is heightened in proportion as it is made gracious by measure and symmetry. He should teach only that science that dignifies life and makes it generous, a truly Baconian precept; and he should foster a curriculum unshackled by specialism.[159] The elective system is a significant innovation, but who will choose the courses — parents, teachers, or the students themselves?

Like Longfellow, he asked for the reduction of the teacher's work load: "Our professors have been compelled by the necessities of the case . . . to do too much work not properly theirs, and that of a kind so exacting as to consume the energy that might have been ample for higher service."[160] The rich, he agreed, should pay for public schools, but "to furnish their [the schools'] students with textbooks and slates is to make them paupers and will advance State socialism,"[161] a strange *non sequitur* to a liberal public-education philosophy. Mediocre teachers abound in the schools because "ideal teachers can't be had . . . for the price offered."[162]

Lowell joined Emerson in ridiculing Southern education. In the "Second Bigelow Papers," Birdofredum Sawin writes to his wife in New England on learning below the Mason-Dixon line:

> For folks in Dixie th't read and rite, onless it is by jarks,
> Is skurce ez wut they wuz among th' oridgenle patriarchs;
> To fit a feller F'wut they calle the soshle higherarchy,
> All thet yo've gut to know is jes' beyund an evrage darky;
> Schoolin's wut they can't seem to stan' . . . [163]

In an article carried by the *North American Review*, October, 1866, Lowell writes of the South: "There were no public libraries, no colleges worthy of the name; there was no art, no science, — still worse, no literature but Simms; there was no desire for them."[164] Lowell even denied Poe to the South, probably because Poe was in the North for most of the late thirties and forties.

Professor Woodberry praises Lowell as "probably the most memorable figure in the minds of several Harvard generations,"[165] a significant accolade since Lowell both taught competently and wrote masterfully during his Harvard tenure.

Oliver Wendell Holmes on Prenatal Influence

In 1857, Lowell asked his friend Oliver Wendell Holmes to contribute to the newly formed *Atlantic Monthly*, which he edited. Not known to intellectual circles outside Boston, Holmes surprised the literary world with *The Autocrat of the Breakfast Table*, a work which simultaneously made him famous and brought the *Atlantic* to the nation's attention.[166] A versatile man, Holmes "could talk with any man on any man's topic, be it medicine and anatomy, the eighteenth century, New England dialect, the statistics of trotting horses, pugilism, photography and rowing, rattlesnakes, elm trees, heredity, the Harvard Class of 1829, microscopes, and prenatal influence."[167]

Holmes wrote three novels dealing with heredity and psychiatry, but of the three "medicated" novels *Elsie Venner* alone deals significantly with education. In the second preface to *Elsie Venner* (1883) Holmes states: "The real aim of the story was to test the doctrine of 'original sin' and human responsibility for the disordered volition coming under that technical denomination."[168] Elsie was born several months after her mother was fatally bitten by a rattlesnake. Three weeks after Elsie's birth her mother died. Throughout her limited life span of eighteen years, Elsie displays ophidian (snakelike) traits. Holmes was aware of the criticisms his theory of prenatal influence would elicit from his colleagues. He acknowledged that his theory of transmission of prenatal influences was not based on any well-ascertained physiological fact, but he defended his use of prenatal influences to "form the starting point of an imaginative composition," since there existed a body of curious facts on the subject.[169] In 1891 a new edition of *Elsie Venner* carried Holmes's third preface to his controversial theme. Somewhat agitated by continuing criticism of his now popular "snake-bite" theory, Holmes asked: "But what difference does it make in the child's responsibility whether his inherited tendencies come from a snake-bite or some other source which he knew nothing about and could not have prevented from acting?"[170] Holmes even suggests that the serpent might have bitten Eve in Eden, a plausible hypothesis for Cain's murderous instincts!

In his study of Holmes's psychiatric novels, Clarence B. Oberndorf, himself a psychiatrist, dismisses Holmes's premises as unpsychoanalytical. But Dr. Oberndorf cites the increasing knowledge being gleaned clinically about the influence of prenatal damage on later anxiety states on the growing child.[171] In *Elsie Venner*, Helen Darley, a dedicated teacher who is disturbed by Elsie's abnormal behavior, questions Bernard Langdon, a medical student, and now a colleague of hers at the Apollinean Female Institute, on the transmission of tendencies. Langdon's reply reassures her that her guilts as a teacher are unjustified: "No doubt there are people born with impulses at every possible angle to the parallels of Nature, as you call them. If they happen to cut there at right angles, of course they are beyond the reach of common influences. Slight obliquities are what we have to do with in education. Penitentiaries and insane asylums take care of the rest."[172]

Holmes on Lower and Secondary Education

If asylums and penitentiaries take care of the abnormal members of society, colleges take care of talented individuals whose aptitudes for learning "are congenital and hereditary."[173] Rural readers of *Elsie Venner*, if there were any, could not have enjoyed Holmes's characterization of their sons who left the farm for college. These awkward sheepskin seekers were robust, but inelegant in movement; they displayed uncouth faces, marked by coarse features and unsympathetic eyes; their voices were rough and unmusical, and, alas, they were slow at learning, unscholarly, and successful only in practical life. The New England Brahmin, on the other hand, sent young Apollos to Yale and Harvard. These handsome lads were slender and boasted smooth, pallid faces having regular features and bright eyes. They were the spawn of congenital scholars whose names always appeared in college catalogues. But Holmes does allow for occasional hereditary surprises: "Our scholars come chiefly from a privileged order just as our best fruits come from well-known grafts, — though now and then a seedling apple, like the Northern Spy . . . springs from a nameless ancestry and grows to be the pride of all the gardens in the land."[174]

Bernard Langdon, the aforementioned medical student and teacher, is a Brahmin ancestrally, but unfortunately, an impoverished Brahmin. Because of his family's genteel poverty he decides to leave medical school for teaching and self-sufficiency. His professor protests — Langdon is his most promising student — but the lad is adamant. Proud of his heritage and social standing, he refuses to accept his mentor's recommendation that he apply for financial assistance. Armed with his professor's certificate attesting to his competency to teach both sexes in common and secondary schools, Langdon sets forth on his pedagogical itinerary, but not without promising his saddened teacher that he would continue his studies and eventually return for his M.D. sheepskin. His teacher has an afterthought; Bernard is very handsome and undoubtedly scores of pretty young ladies would set their lures for him.

But first Langdon is tested at a poor, grim, red, one-story school situated on the bare rock apex of a hill. Its unpainted desks, hacked

by generations of jackknife artists, attested to the school's poverty
and to the community's low regard for schooling. Successor to
Master Weeks, a weak, slender youth from a country college,
Langdon proved himself by ousting the class bully from the school.
Having won his educational spurs, Langdon resigned his post and
rode out in search of more satisfying adventures.

Soon Mr. Peckham, principal of the Apollinean Female Institute,
hired the young Adonis to help teach the one hundred attractive
girls who dabbled in English, modern languages, Latin, if desired,
natural philosophy, metaphysics, and music, for a fee. The
Peckhams were interested in profits, not education. Their
overworked staff of four teachers and one assistant tried vainly to
teach the various curriculums. Ignorant and miserly, Peckham was
more of a quartermaster than a principal; his wife, equally un-
cultured, resembled a housekeeper more than she did a matron.

Helen Darley, the daughter of a poor clergyman, now dead, took
up schoolteaching at the Peckham school. She speaks for her
teaching sisters and herself when she contemplates the drudgery of
grading scores of mediocre themes:

How she dreaded this most forlorn of all a teacher's tasks! She was con-
scientious in her duties, and would insist on reading every sentence, — there
was no saying where she might find faults of grammar or bad spelling. Of
course she knew pretty well the leading sentiments they could contain: that
beauty was subject to the accidents of time; that wealth was inconstant, and
existence uncertain; that virtue was its own reward; that youth exhaled, like
the dewdrop from the flower, ere the sun had reached its meridian; that life
was o'ershadowed with trials; that the lessons of virtue instilled by our
beloved teachers were to be our guides through all our future career. . . . Yet
every now and then one is liable to be surprised with strange clairvoyant
flashes, that can hardly be explained, except by the mysterious inspiration
which every now and then seizes a young girl and exalts her intelligence, just
as hysteria in other instances exalts the sensibility.[175]

One composition, Elsie's, disturbs Helen. It is a strange paper,
hinting of vague longings and undefinable places. It induces hysteria
in Helen and on the next day, as the class enters, she confides in Bernard that she is afraid of Elsie. As they talk, Elsie enters. She is a tall,
slender, and rounded girl of seventeen. Her piercing eyes, black,
braided hair, and elaborate dress set her off from the others. A splen-
did scowling beauty, she comes to class as she pleases. She lives in an
isolated mansion with her father and Sophy, a devoted black

housekeeper. Her father cannot communicate with her. Frequently, Elsie wanders away from the house and sleeps somewhere on the mountain cliff overlooking the valley. She is unapproachable and her hand is cold to the touch.

But she succumbs to Bernard Langdon's charms. She tells Sophy that nobody loves her and that she cannot love anybody. At the Sproule party, Bernard had not even noticed her. One day, she asks Bernard to walk with her toward her house. When he professes to be her friend as they walk, she suddenly turns to him and commands, "Love me!" But Bernard cannot feel for her reciprocally; he offers her the unsatisfactory substitute of brotherly love. Rejected, Elsie falls sick and dies soon after. Denied love, her serpentine inheritance consumes her. Only love might have saved her.

If the tale is fanciful and unscientific, it does nevertheless stress the need for understanding in education and love in human affairs. The Peckhams reflect the opportunistic materialists in education, while the Darleys and the Langdons are the idealists. Helen finally finds her reward in the love of Dudley Venner and Bernard returns to medicine, marries well, and rejoices when his wife consents to wear Elsie's bracelet, which the dying girl gave to Bernard.

Although the Peckhams are finally ousted from their reign of misrule and better prospects are in store for the "Institoot," as the natives called the academy, Holmes is not entirely negative about the good that even a Peckhamian school might initiate, for even "the least perfect of these schools may stimulate the higher tastes and partially instruct them."[176] The graduates will soon be wives of men whose practical bents have need of cultural tempering. But for strange temperaments like Elsie's there seems to be only death, isolation, or incarceration in prison or asylum.

Henry Adams Is Unhappy With Harvard

Henry Adams was also educated at Harvard and returned there to teach. Educated at home and abroad he rarely had kind words for schools and teaching, and if one reads Adams's letters closely he will detect few generous references to anybody save his close coterie of genteel aristocrats. That he detested his elementary and secondary education is not unusual. What is there to cheer about rote learning, mass-production techniques, and time-harried schoolmasters? School from ten to sixteen was a waste; he could profit more by reading half an hour at home with his father: "The American boy of 1854, in concepts of science, in essentials like religion, ethics, philosophy, literature, art, stood nearer the year one than 1900."[177]

If Harvard taught little, it at least left the mind free from bias and receptive to knowledge from other sources. Specifically, in his "four wasted years," Adams complains that he was never taught mathematics, "a universal language he needed most." Political economy was an antiquated maze of incoherent theories of free trade and protection that neglected to mention Marx or Comte. His chemistry course befogged his mind for life, but he admired Louis Agassiz's lectures on paleontology. In brief, he could have negotiated the four-year course in four months later in life.[178]

Harvard was not a total loss. It offered social advantages and endowed its students with a sense of calm.[179] But Adams was critical of foreign universities as well, failing to see the superiority of the German university as Ticknor and Longfellow had. In a letter from Berlin in 1858, Adams wrote sarcastically about the "donkey-like" students he saw at the university.[180]

Adams also saw little virtue in the German high school that stressed arbitrary memory training, discouraged reasoning, and polarized the child's thought.[181] The schools themselves were poorly ventilated, the children were poorly fed, and recreation was negligible because playgrounds were lacking.[182] Methodology at the Berlin Law School was no better. The medieval system of lectures encouraged mediocre teaching. The professor mumbled, the students affected to take notes, and he could learn in a day more than the professor could teach in a month.[183]

When he taught Anglo-Saxon history at Harvard, Adams spoke out against the lecture system — the average student gets little from a scholarly lecture.[184] Adams's views on class size should delight every teacher. "Any large body of students stifles the students. No man can instruct more than half-a-dozen students at once. The whole problem of education is one of its cost in money."[185]

Whittier Praises the Rural Teacher

John Greenleaf Whittier, who taught school in West Amesbury, Massachusetts, for twelve weeks, always regretted his lack of a college education, but he respected self-educated men who had an ardor for learning. To a youth who solicited the poet's assistance for schooling, Whittier answered: "Poverty is ill but if one uses leisure in educating himself school is really not needed if he reads and studies daily."[186] Of his schooling at Haverhill Academy, Whittier recalled only two teachers who were "fit for the not very exacting position they filled."[187] One of them, Joshua Coffin, was a kind, genial, and learned teacher who influenced the poet's antislavery thinking.[188] Whittier pays homage in "To My Old Schoolmaster" to Coffin, who

> Luring us by stories old,
> With a comic unction told,
> More than by the eloquence
> Of terse birchen arguments.[189]

In "Snowbound," however, the schoolmaster is a "brisk wielder of the birch and rule." What's more he could "doff at ease his scholar's gown / to peddle wares from town to town," a rare combination of intellectual and financial virtuosity. To young America, he is an idol to be revered:

> Large-brained, clear-eyed, of such as he
> Shall Freedom's young apostles be,
> Who, following in war's bloody trail,
> Shall every lingering wrong assail.[190]

Judge David Pierce Thompson's Ideal Teacher

For every Joshua Coffin, there are, unhappily, scores of Ichabod Cranes, the conclusion of Judge David Pierce Thompson in his novel *Locke Amsden*, "frequently praised for its account of education in early Vermont" but so filled with clichés and stereotypes that "it has little meaning as a record of local manners."[191] But *Locke Amsden* is a lively book, and if it fails to equal the author's more famed *Green Mountain Boys* it is nevertheless a meaningful contribution to American educational fiction. Horace Greeley thought the book's educational message so important that he devoted five columns to it on the front page of the November 13, 1847 edition of *The Tribune*.[192]

The problems of Thompson's character, Locke Amsden, schoolmaster in the Green Mountains of Vermont, are not so remote from those of today's sophisticated, urban teacher. Captain Hill Bunker, an illiterate storekeeper who serves on the school committee, asks the young candidate: "Will you be equal to managing our rough boys in the mountains here?"[193] Bunker is not impressed with Locke's academic certificate, contending that "not one in three candidates are fit to teach."[194] In chapter three of the novel, Bunker submits the beleagured Locke to an exhaustive teaching test that includes questions in mental arithmetic, geography, physics, geology, and meteorology.

Socially, poor Locke was ostracized from all fashionable parties. The people placed a schoolteacher on the social level of a servant or groom. Generally, people could not associate socially with a person who would settle for fifty dollars a month and "boarding round."

Locke is not particularly desirous of going to college. His friend Seaver tries to convince him that, in addition to certifying him to teach in an academy, the college would allow him to test his mind in communion with all kinds of intellects. The company of scholars with whom he mingles will represent many viewpoints. A loner couldn't possibly acquire all this "sifted knowledge."[195]

Locke will not teach in a high school because the faltering elementary schools need better teachers; they radiate knowledge to the masses, and the youngest must be educated best.[196] His friend, Dr. Lincoln, feels similarly; people build comfortable homes, stables, and sties, but schools are always neglected.

By the end of Thompson's book, Locke is a wealthy and liberal congressman. He gives Cartersville a good public school taught by well-paid teachers. Locke Amsden is indeed the ideal philanthropist.

Samuel Goodrich Gives America "Peter Parley"

Poets, essayists, and fictional writers may influence the public considerably, but the authors of "best-selling" textbooks have captive audiences waiting to be proselytized. Samuel Goodrich was the author of the tens of thousands of "Peter Parley" schoolbooks that were mentioned in Chapter Five. He fed the young of America with such elevating spiritual manna as "the Chinese are ignorant and superstitious — their religion like Mahomet's is false."[197] The British resented the harsh anti-English bias in his textbooks. An editorial in the *London and Westminster Review* assailed Goodrich's careless historical assumptions: "Peter Parley is a bad dealer in slip-slop on many subjects, and however voluminous and however amusing an author may be, we have a right to insist that he shall know what he is talking about."[198]

Undoubtedly, Goodrich helped advance American education. His books were charmingly illustrated and well written, but he wrote with a paternalistic tone that would repel today's schoolchildren. His philosophical educational aims were progressive; an uneducated man is a savage "but by means of education he may be exalted to a rank but a little lower than the angels." Probably it did not occur to the pious Mr. Goodrich that man cannot ascend to near angeldom by looking down upon his "heathen" brethren in distant lands. Locally, though, he flayed the public for building schools without regard for the student's welfare. In "Fireside Education" (1838) he asks: "Is it not a reproach to human nature that school committees, teachers, and fathers often select a site for a seminary for children with less regard to comfort of position than if they were mere animals?"[200]

Three other New England writers, all female and all lacking a college degree, helped influence education in this country. Margaret Fuller, Emily Dickinson, and Louisa May Alcott, all self-reliant and well motivated, read considerably more than their teachers required of them. Margaret, the critic, Emily, the poetess, and Louisa, the novelist, demonstrated to American men of letters that the field was not entirely theirs.

Margaret Fuller and Amos Bronson Alcott

Margaret Fuller, associate of transcendentalists, was an editor of *The Dial*. She was an unhappy, guilt-ridden, and sick girl at the Misses Prescott's school in Groton, but she was helped by a kind teacher who had herself experienced similar traumas. When she was twenty-one she became a schoolteacher, the natural refuge "for a young American woman who wishes to support herself and educate her younger brothers and sisters."[202] In 1837, Amos Bronson Alcott hired her to teach in his ill-fated Temple Street School. She defended him as a noble man, a philosopher akin to Socrates, and a disinterested warrior aiming to redeem mankind from error.[203] But she did not hesitate to criticize him for lacking an understanding of the nature of genius. She was very blunt in her criticism: "You are too impatient of the complex, and not enjoying a variety in unity, you become lost in distraction and cannot illustrate your principles."[204]

Alcott, though, admired his young disciple: "She takes large and generous views of things and her dispositions are singularly catholic and liberal."[205] She courageously defended Alcott when his "Record of a School" was attacked in *The Courier* as "one third . . . absurd, one third . . . blasphemous, and one third . . . obscene."[206]

In 1837 the young schoolmistress left the Temple Street School for a position in the Greene Street School in Providence, Rhode Island. Her students there were docile and miserably prepared.[207] However, the building and grounds were new and the work was not difficult. Her superiors gave her full rein to experiment with those ideas of Alcott that she admired. Her educational philosophy was progressive. To her brother Arthur, also a teacher, she offered this advice:

> The most important rule is, in all relations with our fellow creatures never forget that if they are imperfect persons they are immortal souls, and treat them as you would wish to be treated by the light of that thought. Beware of over-great exposure in being popular, even beloved. As far as an amiable disposition and powers of entertainment make you so, it is a happiness, but if there is one grain of plausibility, it is a poison.[208]

Finding writing and social reform more congenial, Margaret Fuller reluctantly left teaching. In 1838, she wrote to the Reverend W. H. Channing: "I do not wish to teach again at all. If I consult my own wishes, I shall employ the remainder of my life in quite a different manner."[209]

And so she did. Accepted as an equal in the Transcendental circle of Emerson, Theodore Parker, Bronson M. Alcott, and Thoreau, she found a forum for her feminist notions at Brook Farm, an experiment which, on the whole, repelled her. In her bible of women's rights, *The Great Law Suit*, she adamantly demanded political and sexual freedom for women. Finally, vindicating Emerson's analysis that "behind the poet was the woman, fond and relying," she had an affair in Rome with Angelo Ossoli, and married him after the birth of their child. Tragedy struck the family when their ship was wrecked off Fire Island. The child's body was recovered but no trace was found of Margaret and Angelo.[210]

Emily Dickinson at Amherst Academy and Mount Holyoke Seminary

Unlike flamboyant Margaret Fuller, Emily Elizabeth Dickinson believed that "publication is the auction of the human mind," an unfortunate maxim that kept her poetic vignettes from the public eye. Educated at Amherst Institute and briefly at Mount Holyoke Seminary, she wrote to Thomas W. Higginson, with whom she corresponded frequently, on her schooling: "I went to school — but in your manner of the phrase — had no education."[211] She delighted in her lexicon, and attended many lectures at the lyceum. At Amherst Institute, an academy housing sixty-three scholars, she studied mental philosophy, geology, Latin, and botany, noting in a letter to Abiah Roat, "How large they sound, don't they?"

After passing the severe entrance examinations for Mount Holyoke Seminary, Mary Lyon's famous school, Emily spent a rigorous year under the tutelage of kind and affectionate teachers, who, at the same time, maintained the strict discipline decreed by Miss Lyon. Emily admired the awesome prexy, but was too independent to be dominated by her.[212]

In her seminary hall lectures, Mary Lyon stressed good habits, discipline, and the student's obligation to uphold the school's name in all she does.[213] Perhaps the energetic Miss Lyon was overly concerned with the school's reputation. George F. Whicher, in *This Was a Poet*, credits Emily with taking from school "what she needed without being dominated by the process."[214]

Louisa M. Alcott Enshrines Her Father's Educational Thought

Today, only graduate literature majors read Margaret Fuller. Emily Dickinson is read by mandate on all school levels and is brought to the public's attention frequently by her many biographers. But Louisa Alcott's *Little Women* is a perennial favorite in print, in the cinema, and on television. Few readers realize, though, that Louisa's fictional Plumfield School, originating in *Little Women* and maturing in *Little Men*, is based on her father's educational concepts. In a sense, then, Amos Bronson Alcott's rejected progressivism saw practical fruition in the royalties Louisa earned from books bearing some of his educational notions.

Louisa was an impatient kindergarten teacher for a brief period. She preferred writing, and when her stories began to sell, she gave up teaching forever.[215] Meg, one of the four March sisters in *Little Women*, dislikes teaching tiresome children all day; and Amy, the youngest sister, agrees gladly with her. Schoolgirls are impertinent, snobbish, insulting, and disrespectful to indigent fathers.[216] Interestingly, Louisa protested to Mr. Thomas Niles, a publisher, that she was not interested in girls and did not understand them when he asked her to write a book for girls. But she dreaded poverty more than she feared the vicissitudes of writing. The resolution of her conflict culminated in the publication of *Little Women*.[217]

Toward the end of *Little Women* the March family plans a school for orphan boys. Plumfield School would be a kind of cooperative venture; in return for their education and board the boys would work in the garden and the orchard. After some debate, the family decides on a plan to put the school on a sound financial basis by admitting rich boys first, then the sons of the poor. But Plumfield would never become a fashionable school; it would always be "a happy, homelike place for boys who needed teachers, care, and kindness."[218]

In *Little Men*, Plumfield is a reality. The school is in a large square house in which boys of all sizes play and rest. One of the boys, unused to kindness, engages Mrs. Bhaer's attention:

"What a very nice school this is," observed Nat in a burst of admiration. "It's an odd one," laughed Mrs. Bhaer, "but you see we don't believe in making children miserable by too many rules, and too much study."[219]

Plumfield was quite the opposite of the wretched school described by the young March children in *Little Women*. Mr. Davis, their teacher, who found girls trying as pupils, declared pickled limes a contraband, forbade gum chewing, incinerated novels and newspapers, and prohibited facial distortions, nicknames, and caricatures. Amy, who secreted pickled limes in her desk, was apprehended by the vigilant Mr. Davis, who punished her by striking the palms of her hands several times and ordering her to stand on the platform until recess. To Amy, this was an incomprehensible punishment. For twelve years love alone had guided her life, and now this cruel vindictiveness of Mr. Davis! Mrs. March indignantly took Amy out of the school, but firmly scolded her for manifesting conceit and disobedience.

There was no beating at Plumfield and no humiliation of children. Plumfield is a pedagogical paradise:

There were the boys, and they live together as twelve lads could, studying and playing, working and squabbling, fighting faults and cultivating virtues in the good old-fashioned way. Boys at other schools probably learned more from books, but less of that better wisdom which makes good men. Latin, Greek, and mathematics were all very well, but in Professor Bhaer's opinion self-knowledge, self-help and self-control were more important, and he tried to teach them carefully. People shook their heads sometimes at his ideas even when they owned that the boys improved wonderfully in manners and morals.[220]

To poor Nat who complains that others know more, Professor Bhaer gently replies, "You have other virtues — control, desire to learn, music."[221] The professor urged: "Give a boy a trade and he is independent. Work is wholesome, and whatever talents these lads possess, be it for poetry or ploughing, it shall be cultivated and made useful to them if possible" — an Emersonian principle that parents, teachers, and guidance counselors still find useful.

In a sense, *Little Men* includes educational precepts that epitomize the progressive thought of Amos Bronson Alcott, Elizabeth Peabody, Emerson, and Thoreau. Professor Bhaer's respect for the innately good child, his repudiation of corporal punishment, his emphasis upon the value of play and experience in child development, and his enthusiasm for vocational education competently sum up the pedagogical beliefs of New England's Transcendentalists. The book, popular for more than a century, must have affected the educational thinking of many readers. If Amos Bronson Alcott was not taken seriously by his contemporaries, his theories, at least, have been given prominence by his more famous daughter.

Melville Goes to Sea from Teaching

Born and educated in New York, Herman Melville taught for a time in Pittsfield, Massachusetts. He knew the port of New Bedford well, immortalizing its strange seagoing types, its industry, and its mores in *Moby Dick*.

Fathers are sometimes fatally blind to the beautiful souls that they conceive. Melville's father was not happy with Herman's progress as a student.[222] Melville's science teacher at the Albany Classical School, Charles E. West, remembered his pupil as a distinguished writer of "themes" or "compositions."[223]

Four years before he set sail on his memorable whaling odyssey aboard the *Acushnet*, young Melville wrote to Peter Gansevoort of his initial teaching experiences:

But now, having become somewhat acquainted with the routine of business, having established a system in my mode of instruction, and being familiar with the charactars and disposition of my schollars: in short, having brought my school under a proper organization — a few intervals of time are afforded me, which I improve by occasional writting and reading.[224]

The eighteen-year-old schoolmaster taught thirty pupils of all ages, ranks, and sizes. Some of the eighteen-year-olds could not add and others had been taught too rapidly and insufficiently.[225] The young schoolmaster saw almost immediately the dichotomy that exists between the theory and the practice of education. His four concluding words in the following passage are charitable:

Our orators may declaim concerning the universally-diffused blessings of education in our Country, and Essayists may exhaust their magazine of adjectives in extolling our system of common-school instruction, but when reduced to practice, the high and sanguine hopes excited by its imposing appearance in theory are a little dashed.[226]

In his *Journal of a Visit to London and the Continent,* Melville appended two notes after the term "schoolmaster" that reveals some of his antipathy toward teaching. The first, "could have killed his scholars sometimes," is from Rousseau's *Confessions;* the other, "intolerable," refers to Samuel Johnson's irksome duties as a school-usher in Leicestershire. The schoolmaster nevertheless is a king, especially if he can lord it over the tallest boys, and the transition from a teacher to a sailor "is a keen one . . . and requires a strong decoction of 'Seneca and the Stoics' to enable him to grin and bear it."[227] A whaler, especially, is a hard school of learning, and from its decks the teacher turned sailor makes amusing but instructive analogies:

The forty-barrel-bull schools are larger than the harem schools; like a mob of young collegians, they are full of fight, fun, and wickedness, tumbling around the world at such a rollicking rate, that no prudent underwriter would insure them any more than he would a riotous lad at Yale or Harvard.[228]

The Educational Itineraries of the Brothers James

Born in New York City, William and Henry James were educated in three schools in New York State before 1855, and in European schools at Geneva, London, Paris, and Boulogne between 1855 and 1858. They were exposed to this unusual eclectic system of education by their father, Henry James, Sr., who hoped that these learning opportunities would endow them with cosmopolitan tastes and insights.

Henry James is a virtuoso with words, but were it not for literature professors, few Americans would know of his high position in the hierarchy of American letters. The cinema has popularized *The Turn of the Screw* and *Washington Square,* and the paperback *Daisy Miller* sells well to the undergraduates who tend to weigh a book before reading it for a report. Perhaps Leon Edel's definitive critical biography of James will inspire more people to read James, but the best-seller clients will undoubtedly read on and continue to ignore the sophisticated plots and intricate rhetorical devices in *The Ambassadors*, *The Portrait of a Lady*, and *The Golden Bowl*. Happily, James has recorded his educational thoughts and experiences in his *Autobiography*, itself a book that one does not read at the extravagant speeds promised to students of rapid-reading schools by their teachers. Looking backward, James has dim memories of his first school — a dame's school in Albany, New York, which was "a mere medium for small piping, shuffling sound, and suffered heat." William and he had a hectic educational youth: "We were day boys . . . at dispensaries of learning the number of which today excite my wonder." Of his female instructors he recalls Miss Rogers, who "beat time with a long black ferrule to some species of droning chant or chorus in which we spent most of our hours." James remembers another female instructor, Miss Daly, in the following passage:

They [small red houses on Waverly Street in New York City] carry mine [memories] to a stout red-faced lady with grey hair and a large apron, the latter conveniences somehow suggesting, as she stood about with a resolute air, that she viewed her pupils as so many small slices cut from a loaf of life on which she was to dab the butter of arithmetic and spelling, accompanied by a way of jam with a light application of the practice of prize-giving.[229]

The delightful metaphor unfolds gracefully before the reader's vision. But so much of James meanders elusively, leading the reader into rhetorical mazes that confound his search for passageways to lucidity.

As the brothers continued their itinerary from one unusual school to another, they paused for a while at the Institution Vergnes on Bond and Fourth Streets in New York City. Here, among a host of Cuban and Mexican students, they were treated to an exhibition of shrill teaching, possibly because of the unfamiliarity of the foreign students with English. The school had one merit — it forbade flogging.

From the Institution Vergnes to the academy of Mr. Richard Pulling Jenks on Broadway and First Street was a short walk downtown. The boys paid homage to Mr. Coe, the drawing master, and Mr. Dolmidge, the writing master — the only good educational influences they had in years of pupilage.[230]

Of Mr. Jenks, the principal of the school, James wrote: "Clearly the good man was a civilizer — whacks and all."[231] In a reflective mood, James evaluated his early educational adventures: "It is beyond measure, and doubtless, that my main association with my 'studies' whether of the infant or adolescent order, should be with almost anything but the fact of learning — of learning, I mean, what I was supposed to learn."[232]

His transfer to a school operated by Masters Forest and Quackenboss was an unhappy change. The classroom was crowded, smelly, and smoky. The students were sociable and gay, but the dreadful blight of arithmetic was as depressing as the polluted air.

The boys were in Europe again in 1859-1860, but until 1862 their father isolated them in Newport, Rhode Island. James then made his only attempt at formal education, in the Harvard Law School, an experience from which he apparently did not profit. He saw college as an impediment to his great aim — writing. However, Professor F. J. Child, the great folklorist, taught the humanities with humor and passion, compensating young James somewhat for the dearth of inspired teaching in his uneventful Harvard experience.

In 1865, when it was in vogue for literary critics to hurl rhetorical broadsides at Walt Whitman, Henry James, then only twenty-two, fired his pip-squeak missiles at the burly poet, hoping to demolish *Drum-Taps* and Whitman's reputation in one attack. Carried anonymously in the *Nation* (November 15, 1865), his vitriolic review lived to haunt him in later years.

The maturer James had more regard for Whitman; in May, 1886, his name was on the contributor's list of eighty Englishmen who had donated a sum of eight hundred fifty dollars to the indigent poet.[233] But Whitman would have been more delighted with James's disavowal of his *Nation* review in an unpublished letter dated October 10, 1903. Ashamed of his youthful arrogance, James wrote that he had not seen the detestable article for more than thirty years, and that he destroyed the "abominations" of his youth whenever he spied them.[234]

Whitman "Boards Round" on Long Island

Young Whitman, not blessed with affluent parents who could send him off on foreign tours and to Harvard if he so desired, took up schoolmastering shortly after his eighteenth birthday. He "boarded round" on each position he held in country schools on Long Island, New York, later praising that practice as "one of my best experiences and deepest lessons in human nature behind the scenes, and in the masses."[235] In his rarely reprinted short story "The Shadow and the Light of a Young Man's Soul," Archie Dean, a young man disillusioned with life in New York City, accepts a poorly paid teaching position in the country. Dean is soon shorn of his illusions, about teaching, for teachers, too, "are born into the world merely to eat and sleep, and run the same, dull monotonous round."[236] His poor salary, his unromantic work, and the lack of respect of the people for teachers depress him; he is comforted, however, "by his country life, by his long walks over the hills, and by his rides on horseback every Saturday."[237]

From 1836 to 1841 Whitman taught in the country schools of Babylon, Long Swamp, Smithtown, Woodbury, Little Bayside, Whitestone, and Dix Hills — all on Long Island, New York. In an article, "Long Island Schools and Schooling," Whitman discusses his teaching experiences in Smithtown, 1837-1838. The classroom was unpainted and poorly heated, and the curriculum included the usual courses in reading, writing, arithmetic, geography, elocution, grammar, and surveying. For the more astute scholar, Latin, French, and algebra were offered. In this unattractive, cold, and uninspiring classroom, the teacher was king. He assigned students to do sweeping and woodcutting, probably a relief to those selected, for the benches were uncommonly hard. For his services, Whitman received a handsome $72.50 monthly stipend, but his salary contract stipulated that in addition to teaching six days a week without holidays, he was required to rule foolscap, sharpen quills, and, strange to relate, sit up with corpses.[238]

A biographer describes Whitman as an unorthodox teacher who did not care for textbooks and who would punish wrongdoers by narrating their crimes anonymously.[239] He taught mental arithmetic to stimulate quick thinking, used educational games to motivate learning, and encouraged poetry memorization to give students lasting impressions of good literature.[240] Later, when he was an editor for the *Brooklyn Evening Star,* he wrote critically of the schools in Brooklyn. His article "The Whip in the School" (October 23, 1845) condemned flogging, appealed to the public to reduce overcrowding in the classrooms, and censured the prevailing techniques in grammatical usage.[241]

The public contempt for teachers in this period is admirably illustrated in a Whitman editorial written in 1847 for *The Brooklyn Daily Eagle. The Evening Star* had disparaged Whitman's teaching background.

The *Star* seems to think that it demolishes us skin and bone by calling us "country schoolmaster." We are rather pleased with the title, if given sincerely; a proper schoolmaster is one who is an honor and a benefit to his race. And many a more famous man don't do half as much good. Our ancient neighbor also talks of the "true scurrility" of our character as a schoolmaster, by which we are to suppose, not only that teachers are generally scurrillous persons, but that there is also such a thing as false scurrility.[242]

Whitman uses the royal, plural first person in his chastisement of his competitor, and he can not resist correcting his opponent's shabby usage. But elsewhere he seems to recognize the teacher's limitations. In "The Song of the Open Road," he proclaims: "Let the school stand! Mind not the cry of the teacher." The public's image of the teacher may be distorted, but was this unflattering picture of the teacher so prevalent? Whitman writes:

As things are, the word schoolteacher is identified with a dozen unpleasant and ridiculous associations — a sour face, a whip, hard knuckles snapped on tender heads, no gentle fatherly kindness, no inciting of young ambition in its noble phases, none of the beauties of authority, but all that is small and in after life productive of indignation.[243]

The whip and the ferrule are odious to Whitman. He illustrates this in a short story, "Death in the Afternoon." Master Lugare, the "low thick set" tyrant in the story, insists upon silence when he speaks to his tormented pupils.[244] A sadist, he convicts students of alleged crimes before ascertaining their guilt or innocence. For instance, he accuses young Tim Barker of stealing fruit from Mrs. Nichol's garden and refuses to heed the boy's protestations of innocence. Later, after vainly beckoning the boy — who had apparently fallen asleep — to come to the platform for a flogging, he attacks the lad furiously, ceasing from his waves of whipping frenzy only when he tires. Alas for poor Lugare; his joy was all in vain, for he had been beating a corpse. The wrongly accused boy had died of a strange malady. In a brief aside in the story, Whitman sums up his arraignment of the bestial schoolmaster: "We are waxing toward that consummation when one of the old fashion'd schoolmasters, with his cowhide, his heavy birch-rod, and his many ingenious methods of torture will be gazed upon as a scorn'd momento of an ignorant, cruel, and exploded doctrine. May propitious gales speed that day!"

The practical and the transcendental are both valuable in Whitman's educational philosophy. He gave his support to normal schools, recommending that teachers attend these centers of learning all their lives. Reading and writing are tools to "polish and invigorate the mind," to endow it with self-reliance and a love for knowledge.[245] A public-school education is sufficient for women. Girls should be educated at home since boarding schools teach superficially and lead girls astray. Given enough learning to have them practice self-cultivation, they will become good, intelligent mothers.[246] Parents and teachers should cooperate, for parental abuse of teachers undermines the child's trust.[247]

Education in Whitman's Poems

But beyond the tangible, the reachable, and the demonstrable in man's consciousness there is an intuitive, and almost undefinable, awareness of a higher wisdom. In "Song of the Open Road," Whitman contrasts practical wisdom with wisdom of the soul:

> Here is the best of wisdom,
> Wisdom is not finally tested in schools,
> Wisdom cannot be pass'd from one having it to
> another not having it,
> Wisdom is of the soul, is not susceptible of proof,
> is its own proof.

The lecture hall is not the true proving ground of knowledge:

> Now I re-examined philosophies and religions,
> They may prove well in lecture rooms
> Yet not prove at all under the spacious clouds and along
> the landscape and flowing currents.[248]

Again, he turns from the lecture hall to nature for deepest insights into wisdom:

> When I heard the learn'd astronomer,
> When the proofs, the figures, were ranged in columns before me,
> When I was shown the charts and diagrams to add, divide, and
> measure them.
> When I sitting heard the astronomer where he lectured with much
> applause in the lecture room,
> How soon unaccountable I became tired and sick
> Till rising and gliding out I wonder'd off by myself.[249]

The university, almost totally committed to an examination of the material world, must teach the student that there is something beyond matter in the universe — that there is an ideal beauty in the immaterial world to discover and revel in.[250] In "The Base of All Metaphysics" an old professor, after having taught ancient and modern systems, including the wisdom of Kant, Fichte, Hegel, Plato, Socrates, and Christ, gives his students a final metaphysic:

Yet underneath Socrates clearly I see, and under Christ divine I see,
The dear love of man for his comrade, the attraction of friend to friend.
Of the well married husband and wife of children and parents,
Of city for land and land for land.[251]

In 1872, Whitman was asked to recite an original poem at the inauguration of a public school in Camden, New Jersey. His poem "An Old Man's Thoughts of School" is his reaffirmation of his belief in progressive public education.

An old man's thought of school,
An old man gathering youthful memories
    and blooms that youth itself cannot.

Now only do I know you
O fair auroral skies — O morning dew upon the grass!
And these I see, these sparkling eyes
These stores of mystic meaning, these young lives,
Soon to sail out over the measureless seas,
On the soul's voyage.

Only a lot of boys and girls?
Only the tiresome spelling, writing, ciphering classes?
Only a public school?
(As George Fox rais'd his warning cry "Is it this pile of
    brick and mortar, these dead floors, windows, rails,
    you call the church?
Why, this is not the church at all —
The church is living, ever living souls.")

And you America
Cast you the real reckoning for your present?
The lights and shadows of your future, good or evil?
To girlhood, boyhood look, the teacher and the school.[252]

Educational history does not record that governments and taxpayers really look to the child, the teacher, and the school for the ad-

vancement of the nation's welfare. School boards frequently represent the established constituencies in the communities that elect
them. In the battle for the minds of their children, factionalism in a
community creates walls of intolerance between the contending
groups. The child's welfare is frequently sacrificed by the vindictive
votes of taxpayers against a program that they emotionally resent.
Whitman writes idealistically, but when tax dollars become the major issue in educational debates, idealism is overwhelmed in the
deluge of economy votes against the so-called frills in education.

New England Sends Teachers to the South and the West

From New England and the Middle Atlantic states, itinerant
teachers swept into the South in quest of teaching positions. Fitz-
Greene Halleck, a Connecticut poet, satirizes the New England
teacher in Virginia:

> Wandering through the Southern countries teaching
> The ABC from Webster's Spelling Book;
> Gallant and godly, making love and preaching,
> And gaining by what they call "hook and crook,"
> And what the moralists call overreaching,
> A decent living. The Virginians look
> Upon them with favorable eyes,
> As Gabriel on the devil in Paradise.[253]

In James Robert Gilmore's novel *My Southern Friends*, Mr. Kirke
places an ad for a teacher in a New England newspaper: "Wanted, a
suitable person to go South, as governess in a planter's family. She
must be thoroughly educated, and competent to instruct a boy of
twelve."[254] He receives a quick response from Catherine Walley of
New Hampshire. In his interview with Miss Walley, Kirke notes that
she is self-possessed, plain, but neat, and stooped in the shoulders
because of her study habits. To his surprise, she is ready to leave at
once: "We Yankee girls are accustomed to taking care of ourselves."

Some Southern Writers on Education

Many Southern planters sent their children to private academies.
William A. Caruthers describes a flourishing female seminary in his
epistolary novel, *The Kentuckian in New York*. Located in a town of
German religionists, the school operates on a utilitarian plan. Each
girl receives a turn at menial labor, an admirable plan according to

Beverley Randolph in her letter to her friend V. Chevielere in Salem, North Carolina.[255] Perhaps it was an academy similar to this that the novelist Mary Noailles Murfree attended in Nashville in 1856. As a persistent tyke of six, Mary followed her older sister Fanny to school, knocked on the classroom door, and was admitted to the same grade as Fanny. The precocious miss soon led the class, a tribute to the teacher that admitted and encouraged her. The Nashville Female Academy hosted five hundred girls on a campus of five acres, and offered French and Spanish as electives in addition to the courses in Latin and the classics.[256]

From an educational viewpoint the most interesting passage in *The Kentuckian in New York* is the long and detailed catalogue of ills suffered by collegians. B. Randolph contrasts the carefree life of a girl in a seminary with the life of a harassed collegian:

How happy a life is that of a girl at a boarding school, exempt from all the pains and penalties of collegians — the hair-breadth scapes — the formal trials for riding other people's horses — ringing church bells, — building fences across the road, hanging cake and beer signs at magistrates and elders doors, — burning in effigy; fights at country weddings and dances, — exploring expeditions in the mountain and caverns, professedly for geological but really for depredating purposes, shooting house dogs — expeditions upon the water, and skating upon the ice, swimming, duelling, fighting, biting, scratching, firing crackers and cannon in college entries, — heavy meat suppers, with oceans of strong waters, then headache, thirst, soda and Congress water in the morning, and perhaps a visit from the doctor or president, — presentments by the grand jury for playing at cards and overturning apple carts, personating ghosts with winding sheets and getting knocked on the head for their pains, — serenading sweethearts, and taking linchpins out of wagons, — making sober people drunk and drunken people sober, — battling with watchmen, constables, and sheriffs — running away from tailors and tavern keepers, — kissing country girls and battling with their beaux, — tricks upon the tutors and shaving the tails of the president's horses, — stealing away the lion or the elephant at an animal show, and pelting strolling players — putting hencoops upon churches, painting out signs, and carrying off platforms, — throwing hot rolls under the table, and biscuit at the steward's head, — playing musical seats at prayers, and saying prayers at rows, — gambling in study hours, and filching at recitation, — having one face for the president and another for the fellows, — and finally being sent home with a letter to your father, informing him that you are corrupting the morals of your teachers in these pranks. These are a few of the classical studies into which the dear little innocents are never initiated, while they form no small part of collegiate education in America.[257]

A long catalogue of educational Americana that should be read by every pious critic of today's collegians! A time-study of the daily experiences of today's collegians would hardly record happenings as flamboyant, picaresque, and hedonistic as those deeds of derring-do enacted by their peers of more than a century ago.

Poe Asks the South to Reform Its Education

Gambling was Edgar Allan Poe's nemesis at the University of Virginia. Expelled for incurring gambling debts, and deliberately forcing his own expulsion from West Point, Poe died without a college degree. His readings and his imaginative mind, however, synthesized in his tales, reveal an intelligence that many an academic mind might envy.

In the short story "William Wilson," Poe follows the educational itinerary of a young American in England. From a grammar school presided over by a paradoxical schoolmaster, Wilson learns early that a man may be a tyrant in the schoolroom and a model of benignity in the pulpit.[258] At Eton the boy is introduced to a dissolute life which he continues at Oxford, the most dissolute university in Europe. Is Poe using Oxford to express his unhappiness at the University of Virginia and at West Point?

Poe did not allow his former association with the South to moderate his censure of Southern education. His criticism in the *Southern Literary Messenger*, December, 1835, appealed to Southerners to equal New England's system of public education:

The most lukewarn friend of the State must perceive — if he perceives anything — that the glory of the ancient Dominion is in a fainting — is in a dying condition. Her once great name is becoming, in the North, a byword for imbecility — all over the South, a type for "the things that have been." And tamely to ponder upon times gone by is not to meet the exigencies of the times present or to come. Memory will not help us. . . . Let us act while we have a resource, let us make it of avail. Memory will not help us. . . . Let us proceed at once to the establishment throughout the country of district schools, upon a plan of organization similar to that of our New England friends.[259]

Lanier on the Emotions and Education

Another poet of the South, the versatile Sidney Lanier, addressed himself to psychological foundations of education. In a letter to his father (December 6, 1860), he asked rhetorically: "What are we going to educate?" Obviously, man. "But what is man? A body, an intellect, an emotional faculty."[260] The whole of man must be educated — his intellect, his emotions, and his body — but amazingly, from the earliest Bible days to the nineteenth century, man educated his intellect only. Since man must feel right before he can think right, he must educate his emotions, and because public opinion depends upon soundness of public emotion, it follows that a meaningful educational system must educate the public to develop sound emotions. Lanier's concern in his youth for the cultivation of public emotions is a challenging concept, but the questions that follow are not easily resolved. Who shall administer a system of public education of the emotions? Are the characteristics of human emotions sufficiently understood by those who would administer this sensitive course of education? And is there an essential difference between reason and educated emotions? Lanier did not pursue this line of inquiry formally. His poetic, musical, and fictional interests consumed his waning energies, and he died before his fortieth birthday, a victim of tuberculosis he had contracted as a Confederate soldier in the Civil War. He is remembered in educational history as one of the fathers of academic adult education in America. Because of his interest in "Schools for Grown People," he succeeded in having President Coit Gilman of Johns Hopkins establish extension courses at the university for adults.[261]

Mark Twain, Huck Finn, and Tom Sawyer

Like Poe, Mark Twain was a Southerner who wrote and published most of his books in the North. Self-educated, self-reliant, and yet markedly self-conscious in the presence of Boston's Brahmins, Twain's popularity never dims. The world of Huck Finn is Twain's universe, and what better place to shed innocence than on an epic voyage down the Mississippi accompanied by an illiterate but sensitive black slave? And what better teacher could an apprentice pilot have than first mate Bixby aboard a palatial river steamer to guide him through the ABC's of navigation and the frightening ordeal of piloting the expensive boat on his own? The river, the boat, the pilot, and his apprentice constitute a unique school. What young Twain learned on the river few students could learn in school.

Twain's amusing autobiography cannot always be taken seriously, but his recollection of his early schooling need not be questioned. At four and a half years he attended Mrs. Horr's small log schoolhouse. A middle-aged New England lady, Mrs. Horr opened each lesson with a prayer and a chapter from the New Testament.[262] Later, he

attended Dawson's school in Hannibal, a typical country school harboring pupils of every age, including a twenty-five-year-old
"regular" student and an eighteen-year-old Latin scholar.[263] When
he was seven, he spent several months on his uncle's farm four miles
from Flouder. From the farm he trekked three miles to the country
school only to be ridiculed because he did not chew tobacco. This
memory occasioned Twain to note: "Children have but little charity
for one another's defects."[264]

Twain knew many unfortunate Huckleberry Finns in his Missouri
days. Orphaned Huck had a low estimate of himself. He attended
school faithfully in autumn and winter, could spell and write a little,
and admitted that though he "could say the multiplication table up
to six times seven is thirty-five . . . I don't reckon I could ever get any
further than that if I was to live forever."

For talking to Huck Finn, the class pariah, Tom Sawyer was given
the ultimate punishment by the schoolmaster — sitting with the
girls. Crafty Tom uses this opportunity to flirt with Becky Thatcher.
But the alert master, chary of encouraging amours in class, yanks
Tom by the ear and draws the hapless lad to his own seat. There "by
love obsessed," he reads poorly, turning lakes into mountains and
mountains into rivers. Soon the class is quiet. An idyllic warmth per-
vades the classroom as the pupils read and write: "The drowsing
murmur of the five and twenty studying scholars, soothed the soul
like the spell that is in the murmur of bees."[265]

Examination day was a highlight of the school year. At 8:00 p.m.,
the townsfolk assembled in the adorned, brilliantly lighted
schoolhouse. The master sat regally on a great chair upon a raised
platform. Tonight he would be compensated for the year's slights,
for his pupil's pranks, for their parents' indifference. To the master's
dismay, Tom forgot the lines of the "Give me Liberty or Death"
speech, but the succeeding declaimers performed well. The proud
parents listened attentively to "Mary Had a Little Lamb," "The Boy
Stood on the Burning Deck," and "The Assyrian Came Down Like
the Wolf on the Fold," and for a time the tormented master forgot
about Tom's mishap.[266]

The festivities continued. Reading exercises and original compositions followed in train. The themes hearkened back generations,
probably to the Crusades, numbering among them such rhetorical
gems as "Friendships," "Memories of Other Days," "Religion in
History," "Advantages of Culture," "Filial Love," and "Heart
Longings." Stylistically, they were "nursed and petted melancholy"

written affectedly in hackneyed diction — a species of insincere sermon. Twain editorializes on these inane compositions: "There is no school in all our land where the young ladies do not feel obliged to close their compositions with a sermon; and you will find that the sermon of the most frivolous and least religious girl in the school is always the longest and the most relentlessly pious." Twain will have his joke at the expense of the village Philistines: "The essay 'A Vision,' read by a dark-complexioned girl, occupied some ten pages of manuscript and wound up with a sermon so destructive of all hope to non-Presbyterians that it took the first prize."[267]

The climax of the examination day was the revenge exacted by the scholars upon their tipsy master, whose hand slipped as he tried to draw a map of the United States on the blackboard. When the tottering don sat down, a cat descended slowly from the rafters above to rest upon his head. As the enthralled congregation watched, "the cat was within six inches of the absorbed teacher's head — down, down, a little lower, and she grabbed his wig with her desperate claws, clung to it, and was snatched up into the garret in an instance with the trophy still in her possession! And how the light did blaze abroad from the master's bald pate for the sign painter's boy had gilded it."[268]

Twain had compassion for slaves and wished to see them free. To have a white southern boy assist a runaway slave to escape was heresy in the South, but Huck's humanity overcame his sectional prejudices when he teamed up with Jim on their river odyssey.

Grayson Compares the Life of the Slave with that of the Worker

Twain's attitude toward the slave was not shared by William J. Grayson, the author of the "Hireling and the Slave," a classical southern apology for slavery. He criticized education in the North, which "seemed to consist in making the most money with the least annoyance to teacher and scholar." Of his own education, he confessed, "I became a bachelor of arts with the usual inaptitude of the tribe for any definite or useful employment."[269] His analysis of the plight of the liberal arts graduates is still applicable: "They become authors or schoolmasters"; but, he adds, "the South fifty years ago, offered no field for authorship."[270] Thus, the candidates for teaching are legion and the market price for their services is generally low.

Grayson's "The Hireling and the Slave" contrasts the allegedly superior life of the slave in America with the miserable life of the European peasant or factory hand. "Under the master's care, the miserable black savage has been fed, clothed, instructed in useful arts, and made an important contributor to the business and enjoyments of the world."[271] The education of the slave is beneficial to him and to his master:

> Instructed thus, and in the only school
> Barbarians ever knew — a master's rule,
> The Negro learns each civilizing art,
> That softens and subdues the savage heart,
> Assumes the tone of those with whom he lives,
> Acquires the habit that refinement gives,
> And slowly learns, but surely, while a slave,
> The lessons that his country never gave.[272]

Europe is no model to follow. The slave is so much happier a paternal ward:

> Still Europe's saints, that mark the motes alone
> In other's eyes yet never see their own,
> Grieve that the slave is never taught to write,
> And reads no better than the hireling white;
> Do their own plowmen no instruction lack,
> Have whiter clowns more knowledge than the black?
> Has the French peasant, or the German boor,
> Of learning's treasure any larger store?
> Have Ireland's millions, flying from the rule
> Of those who censure, ever known a school?
> A thousand years and Europe's wealth impart
> No means to mend the hireling's head or heart;
> They build no schools to teach the pauper while,
> Their toiling millions neither read nor write,
> Whence, then, the idle clamor when they rave
> Of schools and teachers for the distant slave?[273]

Grayson, in effect, is condoning one evil on the grounds that a similar or worse evil exists elsewhere. In praising the alleged paternalism of the white planter he champions agrarian aristocracy as a more humane society than the ugly capitalism of Europe that dehumanizes the worker. Why should the United States become a battleground between conservative and radical factions? Let Europe engage in these fruitless rivalries. To ensure their continued prosperity and power it would be profitable for northern property owners and capitalists to ally themselves with southern aristocracy, accept slavery, and stave off proletarian revolution. Besides, had not pious Puritans enriched themselves in the slave trade? And how sensitive were abolitionists to the cries of the children laboring in northern factories and mines? Lashing out at the hypocrisy of northern foes of slavery, southern theologians quoted Scripture to justify divine sanction of slavery, citing Saint Paul, Saint Peter, and Christ as advocates of slavery.[274]

In the North, abolitionists looked upon paternalistic slavery as a myth. John Brown died for his militancy in opposing slavery, and Wendell Phillips, impervious to the slanders and threats of violence of his enemies, fought for black equality all his life. But the temper even in the North for emancipation was lukewarm. Separate schools, separate churches, and growing sympathies for colonization of blacks and against miscegenation revealed that the South was not alone in the nation's antiblack sentiment. What was apparently lacking among the country's middle and upper classes was a deep-rooted conviction that all forms of social injustice, including forced or wage slavery, were evil and contributory to political and economic upheavals. Eventually, the dispute between Grayson and Phillips would be temporarily resolved on the battlefield. But the successors of these antagonists, unhappy with the consequences of the Civil War, would continue the battle for their respective ideologies.

James Hall Helps Educate the West

The West lured thousands to its boundless prairies. Dreams of land, gold, business adventure, escape, curiosity, and science drew the energetic American to the new states and territories. For example, James Hall, a Philadelphia lawyer who settled in Cincinnati, wrote extensively on Indian and western wildlife, published backwoods novels, and participated fully in the educational development of the West. While residing in Vandalia, Illinois, in 1830, he sponsored a high school for all Christian sects, helped establish Illinois College four years later, and encouraged the opening of lyceums.[275] In Cincinnati he labored to advance education as trustee of Catherine and Harriet Beecher's Western Female Institute, examiner of Woodward High School, and standing committeeman of the Western Literary Institute and College of Professional Teachers. Addressing the Erodolphian Society of Miami (Ohio) University, he entreated the one thousand listeners "to devote your hearts to the great purpose of popular education and national literature," because "in any country where a few are educated, and the great mass of the people ignorant, the uninstructed many will be governed by the enlightened minority."[276]

Hall was dissatisfied with the school readers of his day that stressed writers of eastern America. In his school textbook, *The Western Reader* (1883), he included twenty-three eastern and twenty-six western writers. He was motivated to write an entertaining book because as a boy he had acquired "a deep-seated disgust against schools and schoolmasters." Friendliness should replace whipping and native authors should replace foreign writers, two characteristics of his book that he hoped would enthrall students.[277]

His educational precepts were progressive for his age. He advocated equalization of teachers' salaries with laborers' wages, the establishment of normal schools, the creation of departments of education to train and test teachers, and extension of requirements for licensing of teachers.[278]

Howells Recalls His Early Education

In his autobiographical novel, *A Boy's Town*, William Dean Howells can recall only one kind of teacher, his first schoolmaster in a small town on the Ohio River, who taught classes in the basement of a church. When the teacher left, the young boy lost a friend and a confidant. The academy was disappointing, beginners were assigned to a lower room, punishments were administered in the ill-smelling chemistry room, and older boys were whipped for misbehaving.[279] Rather than suffer humiliation before their peers, older boys who were put back from the Third to the Second Reader left the school. Public whipping was practiced by the teachers, but the students revenged themselves upon the hapless new teachers by whispering and giggling in class, passing notes, and leaving the room without permission. None of the teacher's reasoning prevailed; the class was bent on breaking him. To cap their acts of insolence, students beat the teacher with his own rod, and from time to time barred him from his own classroom — "a cruel band of ingrates," concludes the author.[280]

Schooling in Indiana

Because Edward Eggleston's father disliked schools, the boy had irregular glimpses of schools and teachers. He attended an academy in Virginia, but refused to enroll in the University of Virginia because it supported slavery.[281]

Eggleston's novel *The Hoosier Schoolmaster* offers a classic depiction of elementary education in Indiana. The hero, Ralph Hartsook, applies for a teaching position at Flat Creek. Jack Means, a trustee, informs him that there are no other applicants, that there is no insurance for beatings, and "you'll hev to board roun'."[282] Ralph is not deterred. He will make Flat Creek remember him.

The students test their new master by having one of their toughs place a pup in Ralph's desk. He is equal to the situation: "I am sorry that any scholar in this room could be so mean . . . as to shut up his *brother* in such a place as that!"[283] Laughter! The pupils are his. But the trustees are not fond of the soft technique of the new master:

"Don't believe he'll do," was Mr. Pete Jone's comment to Mr. Means. "Don't thrash enough. Boys won't larn less you thrash 'em, says I. Lay it on good. Don't do no harm. Licken' and larnin' goes together. No lickin' no larnin', says I. Lickin' and larnin', licken and larnin' is the good ole way."[284]

The master is retained, though, and now trustees, masters, parents, and students prepare for the great educational treat of the term — the spelling bee. At this festival of words, Squire Hawkins expounds: "Spelling is the corner-stone, the grand underlying subterfuge of a good education. I put the spellin' book prepared by the great Daniel Webster alongside the Bible. I do, raley."[285] But Ralph, a cultured young man, is smitten by the considerable charms of Hannah Thomson, the exploited maid of the Meanses. Gallantly, he loses his will to win and exults in her victory as the Meanses and the squire look on in consternation.[286]

The Picaresque Professor Stiles

It is a pity that Ross Lockridge died soon after writing his great novel, *Raintree County*. The nation lost a fine historical novelist in Lockridge, for he succeeds in giving the reader a sense of history that historians cannot impart. In *Raintree County* Lockridge brilliantly depicts life in Indiana of the 1850's. Professor Stiles, a picaresque Emersonian, founded Pedee Academy, once "a place of young voices and tattered books." John Shawnessey, a pupil of Stiles, recalls the school's beginnings as advertised in *The Free Enquirer*, September, 1857. Proclaiming that "Republican institutions cannot be maintained without universal enlightenment," Professor Jerusalem Webster Stiles, a student of Harvard, a traveler, and a linguist, opens an institution of higher learning in the former Taylor Boarding House. Students would be taught Latin, English, rhetoric, philosophy, natural history, mathematics, ancient and modern history.[287]

A formidable curriculum, indeed, for one teacher to administer, but Professor Stiles was of heroic stock and announced that progressive methods would be employed, "female as well as male students desiderated," and two-year diplomas would be granted to successful students. Also, a night school would be instituted for illiterate adults.

Stiles taught what he loved. To his immature worshipers he tried to explain the mysteries of transcendentalism, extolling Emerson as the greatest living American. To young John Shawnessey he taught Latin and Greek — "the plastic rhythm of Homer, the togaed majesty of Virgil."[288] He had his students debate the slave question and freely quoted Lincoln and Douglas during the proceedings. John's father is proud when his son graduates:

"Yesiree, John," he said. "I wish I had had just half your advantages when I was your age. I always did want to know a little Latin and Greek. I tell you, with Latin and Greek, and with your natural aptitudes and faculties, John, I take a very hopeful view of your future."[289]

The fetish of Latin and Greek runs through our literary history, and those who could not become devotees of the sacred tongues often felt themselves intellectual amputees. Today, those who cannot read the grammar of science and mathematics feel singularly isolated from the intellectual community. The mark of today's scholar, at least in the popular sense, is his badge of accomplishment in the sciences.

General Lew Wallace on Education

General Lew Wallace, author of the spectacular *Ben-Hur*, recorded pre-Civil War schooling in Indiana in his *Autobiography*. He was not happy in the two-room brick schoolhouse in which an Irish master used the rod too often. When he was dismissed the students rejoiced, but a new problem arose when a female teacher replaced him. Was it manly to submit to a woman? The new teacher gave him Olney's *Geography* to read. The book fascinated the boy, and he remembered this delightful practice of his teacher faithfully: "to catch a boy and hold him fast one has only to set up the delicate machinery of the wonder-box in him at work. The suggestion is respectfully submitted to teachers. Mothers, with better understanding, practice it when lullabies fail."[290]

Wallace opposed flogging a boy of spirit, but considered punishment of a dull boy as less traumatic: "The schoolmaster who cannot discriminate between pupils lacks the first essential to perfection in an honorable calling."[291] He should be fair; for example, a careless teacher of a country school often allowed the older students to monopolize the desirable areas near the fire on cold days. Perhaps it was more fear than carelessness that prompted the teacher to ignore the plight of his younger students.

Young Wallace attended the college at Crawfordsville at nine, but the term "college" was a hyperbole. The school, an Episcopalian seminary, was in effect a prep school, administered by a teacher who loved to feel the crack of his busy ferrule on hapless students' skin and bones. Fortunately his experiences at Centreville Academy were happier. Professor Samuel K. Hoshaur, a disciplinarian who taught well, discovered talent where it had flourished unseen by others. Hoshaur, seeing that Lew was not a mathematical genius, devoted himself to Lew's writing talent and nurtured it until the boy acquired skill and fluency. Hoshaur's dictum was: "In writing everything is to be sacrificed to clearness of expression."[292]

Millard Kennedy Writes about Hoosier Teachers

Millard Fillmore Kennedy writes about Hoosier education in *Schoolmaster of Yesterday,* a biographical history of the Kennedys as pioneer schoolteachers. He describes midwestern teachers as a motley group of unlettered Yankees, Englishmen, Scotchmen, and Irishmen, most of them drifting into teaching since it was "the special province of chaps who were too lazy to work."[293] Among this uninspiring band were one-eyed, one-legged, epileptic, alcoholic, and lecherous pedagogues. These schoolmasters used haphazard texts, failed to discipline classes, neglected to teach arithmetic, which they didn't understand, but they passed licensing examinations because their examiners knew even less than they. The schoolhouses were mostly log cabins, but some classes were held in barns, smokehouses, and smithies. In 1852, the state superintendent of education reported that the school buildings were mostly

. . . dilapidated log buildings situated in some out-of-the-way place in the woods, frequently in the midst of the largest and deepest mudhole of the county, surrounded by stagnant pools and heaps of logs and underbrush, infecting the air with their deadly miasma, a place . . . selected for this purpose because the land can be turned to account in no other way.[294]

Kennedy includes amusing examples of teaching tests given to candidates for positions in the schools of Franklin, Indiana (1856): "When and by whom was America discovered?" "If sugar is six and a quarter cents a pound, how many pounds could be purchased with fifty cents?" "Correct this sentence: 'Me and Mary is playing.' "295 And yet, Indiana has contributed a fair share of writers to America, undoubtedly owing to the scattered presences of serious Professor Hoshaurs and eccentric nonconforming Professor Stileses.

John Muir Dislikes Rural Teachers in Wisconsin

In 1860, John Muir, later to become one of America's great naturalists, dabbled in poetry as an undergraduate at the University of Wisconsin. His poem "The Old Schoolhouse" adds little to the reputation of such schools. The schoolhouse has heard some humorous arithmetic and

> With grammar, too, old schoolhouse, thou hast suffered,
> While Plato, Milton, Shakespeare have been murdered,
> Torn limb from limb in analytic puzzles
> And wondrous parsing, passing comprehension,
> The poetry and meaning blown to atoms
> Sad sacrifices in the glorious cause
> Of higher all-embracing education.296

Muir took a turn at teaching in 1860, but hated whipping the children. He had contempt for rural teachers: "You know it does not require much sapience to be a district school philosopher."297 But in 1862, his criticism of the nation's general intelligence was even more caustic: "The war seems farther from a close than ever. How strange that a country with so many schools and churches should be desolated by so unsightly a monster."298 Muir was young and politically naïve; can schools and churches really act independently of the reigning political regimes that demand their allegiances, overtly or discreetly?

Bret Harte Turns to Writing from Teaching

In the Far West, education developed slowly. There were no public schools in San Francisco before 1851. As late as 1859, Horace Greeley estimated that only six hundred of the estimated two thousand schools needed in California would be erected. The "get rich" mania of Gold Rush days was still in the public's mind. Consequently, children grew up in the streets in "precocious depravity."[299] Bret Harte, who tried teaching at Lagrange in 1854-1855 and found the profession wanting, took up reporting and writing instead.[300] When he was offered a professorship of recent literature by the University of California in 1870, he turned down the offer because teaching would interfere with his writing.[301]

Harte added a new twist to educational fiction in "The New Assistant at Pine Clearing School." In that story, teaching candidate Twing has a strange interview with Mrs. Martin, the principal. She asks, "Have you any teaching experience?" "Not much," he responds. Nevertheless, she hires him, probably because of his bluntness and charm.[302]

Twing's unconventional ways disarm the "toughs" who come late to class bent upon trouble. The fearful Mrs. Martin finds Twing uncannily proficient. He is prepared by heart for all the day's exercises, his students excel in declamation, and he fascinates her with his dialectal vulgarity.[303] Finally Twing's secret is out — he is an actor who enthralls his students with his singing, dancing, dramatics, declamations, and sleight of hand, virtues not usually associated with teachers. Even Mrs. Martin succumbs to Twing's love songs and becomes Mrs. Twing.[304]

The most interesting educational event in "New Assistant at Pine Clearing School" is the declaration of their educational rights by the practical "toughs" who assess their new teacher:

We ain't hankerin much for grammar and dictionary hogwash and we don't want no Boston parts o' speech rung in on us the first thing in the mo'nin! We reckon to do our sums and our figgerin' and our sale and our barter, and our interest tables, and weights and measures when the time comes, and our geography when it's on, and our readin' and writin' and the American Constitution in regular hours, and then we calkillate to git up and git afore the po'try and the Boston airs and graces come round.[305]

Conclusions

American writers were generally very critical of the schooling they received and few of them enjoyed teaching as a profession. Undoubtedly, the artist is temperamentally unsuited for teaching. Emerson refused to remain in a profession that is dominated by conservative trustees and administrators whose perennial shibboleths are large classes and low budgets. He professed to have learned little at academy and college, and his proposals for changing society by education are exciting but vague. Amos Bronson Alcott, who thought peddling was more instructive than degree-questing, promoted educational notions that were too radical for his fellow New Englanders. His child-oriented progressivism and his religious mysticism troubled practical Bostonians, and they resented his admission of a colored child to his school. But his daughter, Louisa, perpetuated his educational thought in two novels, *Little Men* and *Little Women*, that reached millions of Americans.

Orestes Augustus Brownson and Henry David Thoreau saw the scholar's mission as a unending battle with error. The scholar, they said, must be brave, independent, and schooled in experience more than in books. At Brook Farm School George Ripley emphasized learning by doing and by cooperation; here children were loved and taught to love, a way of school life that was alien to Emerson, Thoreau, and Richard Henry Dana in their childhood.

The catalogue of criticisms is long. Lowell, Longfellow, and Henry Adams wrote belittlingly of Harvard — a mere secondary school to them. Lowell repeated the ancient truism that great teachers are rare because the schools will not pay for them. Oliver Wendell Holmes concurred.

Two New Englanders, Whittier and Judge Pierce Thompson, had kinder words about teachers. In "Snowbound," Whittier idealizes the gentle rural schoolmaster, the antithesis of the more common Ichabod Cranes that rule their unhappy classes with rattan, birch rod, and ferrule. Judge Thompson's noble teacher, Locke Amsden, endures the physical and psychological punishment of teaching in a rural school in Vermont, and when he prospers in business and politics, he dedicates himself to bettering public education.

Margaret Fuller forsook teaching for writing, but when she taught she tried to impart many of Amos Bronson Alcott's principles to her pupils. Emily Dickinson found Amherst Academy and Mount Holyoke Seminary to her liking, but her poetic interests occupied her after she left school, leaving her with little time to write on educational themes.

Melville saw early that educational theory and educational practice have little resemblance. He left teaching for the sea and writing, a happy decision that enriched the world with *Moby Dick*, but, says Ishmael, "the transition is a keen one, I assure you, from a schoolmaster to a sailor." Undoubtedly, the transition to writer was just as keen.

Henry James, educated in a variety of lower schools, gave little credit to them for his later fictional flowering, and Harvard, he thought, was an impediment to his development as a writer. Walt Whitman labored in many schools on Long Island, New York, thought little of the teachers with whom he associated, and minimized the importance of formal learning in some of his poems.

In the South, William A. Caruthers satirized collegiate education mercilessly; Sidney Lanier speculated on education and the emotions; and Poe exhorted the South to improve the quality of its public education. William J. Grayson compared the plight of the European peasant with that of the American in his poem "The Hireling and the Slave," and found the slave happier, better cared for, and better educated than the European peasant.

The midwestern writer was unhappy with the education of his region. William Dean Howells, James Hall, Edward Eggleston, Donald G. Mitchell, Lew Wallace, and Millard Fillmore Kennedy agreed that teachers were unkind, incompetent, and apathetic, that trustees were sometimes illiterate, and that support of public education was given grudgingly. In Wisconsin, John Muir wrote that teachers flogged students and lacked the ability to communicate with their indifferent pupils. In California, Bret Harte left teaching for writing. His stories are not complimentary to teaching but in one tale, "The New Assistant at Pine Clearing School," the new teacher excels in class, although he is not academically trained to teach. Finally, Twing, the extraordinary teacher, confesses that he is an actor, an admission that explains his unusual success with a mischievous class.

Although Mark Twain was not a lettered man and never taught school, many of his books include passages that educational psychologists might ponder. Twain's own education as an apprentice pilot on the Mississippi is a remarkable record of Mr. Bixby's pedagogical art. Huck Finn matures on his epic journey with Jim down the Mississippi. The crudities of medieval thinking are lampooned in *A Connecticut Yankee in King Arthur's Court*. Mark Twain is not designedly didactic, but he teaches pleasantly when he informs us that "a cauliflower is a cabbage with a college education."

Emerson, Thoreau, Longfellow, Lowell, Oliver Wendell Holmes, Henry Adams, Margaret Fuller, Louisa May Alcott, Melville, Whitman, John Muir, and Bret Harte all taught at one time in their lives. Holmes alone seemed to enjoy his teaching; Longfellow sorrowed because teaching deprived him of time to write. Today, Longfellow would be awarded a writer-in-residency at a major university, an academic sinecure that allows the writer-teacher to fulfill both his needs comfortably.

The cry of the major writers of this period that teaching is synonymous with poverty is still heard today. Talented intellectuals refuse to work in mediocre settings. Caring for children is nerve-racking, time consuming, and poorly esteemed. The paradox remains. Parents want the best schooling for their children, but they cannot or will not pay for the competent, enthusiastic, and entertaining artists, who are enticed into more lucrative professions.

Notes and References

CHAPTER ONE

1. Merle Curti, *The Social Ideas of American Educators*, (Paterson, N.J.: Pageant Books, 1959), p. 10.
2. Lawrence A. Cremin, *American Education: The Colonial Experience*, p. 397.
3. John C. Miller, *Origins of the American Revolution* (Boston: Little, Brown, 1943), p. 193.
4. Max Savelle, *Is Liberalism Dead?* (Seattle: University of Washington Press, 1967), p. 41.
5. Richard Hofstadter, *The American Political Tradition*, pp. 6 - 7.
6. *Ibid.*, p. 5.
7. Cremin, p. 26.
8. Savelle, p. 41.
9. Moses Coit Tyler, *The Literary History of the American Revolution*, II, p. 15.
10. Thomas J. Wertenbaker, *The Golden Age of Colonial Culture* (Ithaca, N. Y.: Great Seal Books, 1959), p. 13.
11. *Ibid.*
12. Adolphe E. Meyer, *An Educational History of the American People*, p. 56.
13. Charles Francis Adams, ed., *The Works of John Adams*, II, p. 22.
14. Wertenbaker, pp. 47 - 48; Van Wyck Brooks, *The World of Washington Irving* (New York: E. P. Dutton, 1944), p. 28.
15. Meyer, pp. 73 - 74.
16. Bayard Still, *Mirror for Gotham* (New York: New York University Press, 1956), pp. 27 - 28.
17. Tyler, II, p. 209.
18. Henry Bamford Parkes, *The American People*, p. 98.
19. *Ibid.*, pp. 96 - 97.
20. Max Lerner, *America As a Civilization*, p. 21.
21. Hofstadter, p. 11.
22. Meyer, pp. 154 - 155.

23. Charles F. Adams, IV, p. 199.

24. James Madison, *Letters and Other Writings of James Madison*, III, p. 279.

25. David Hosack, *Memoir of De Witt Clinton* (Ann Harbor: University Microfilms, 1967, from the original edition of 1829), p. 162.

26. *Ibid.*, p. 157.

27. Albert J. Beveridge, *The Life of John Marshall* (Boston: Houghton Mifflin, 1919), IV, pp. 471 - 472.

28. Henry Adams, *The Education of Henry Adams* (New York: Modern Library, 1931), p. 302.

29. Meyer, p. 94.

30. *Ibid.*, p. 135.

31. A. O. Hansen, *Liberalism and American Education in the Eighteenth Century*, p. 4.

32. *Ibid.*, p. 23.

33. Elwood P. Cubberley, *Public Education in the United States*, p. 57.

34. Fisher Ames, "American Literature," in *The American Literary Revolution, 1783 - 1837*, ed. Robert Spiller, p. 87.

35. Cubberley, p. 52.

36. Rush Welter, *Popular Education and Democratic Thought in America* (New York: Columbia University Press, 1962), p. 27.

37. Cubberley, p. 77. Revolutionary soldiers were not spelling-bee champions as these examples from their diaries indicate, but they probably read well enough for their limited cultural needs:

whept — whipped	splet — split	sarten — certain
for teague — fatigue	jine — join	ridgment — regiment
arams — arms	lave — leave	wint — went

(From Charles K. Bolton, *The Private Soldier under Washington*, p. 220).

38. Charles and Mary Beard, *The Rise of American Civilization*, I, pp. 183 - 184.

39. Bolton, p. 24.

40. John Spencer Bassett, ed., *Correspondence of Andrew Jackson* (New York: Kraus Reprint Co., 1969), II, p. 141.

41. J. B. Hubbell, *The South in American Literature*, p. 68.

42. Hansen, p. 63.

43. Meyer, p. 71.

44. Charles L. Sanford, ed., *The Quest for America* (New York: New York University Press, 1964), pp. 276 - 278.

45. Curtis Dahl, *Robert Montgomery Bird* (New York: Twayne Publishers, 1963), p. 112.

46. Samuel Miller, "A Brief Retrospect of the Eighteenth Century," in Spiller, *The American Literary Revolution*, pp. 48 - 49.

47. *The Poetical Works of Fitz-Greene Halleck* (New York: Redfield, 1859), V, p. 82.

48. In Fred Lewis Pattee, *The First Century of American Literature*, p. 139.

49. In Barrows Mussey, ed., *Yankee Life by Those Who Lived It*, p. 51.

50. *Ibid.*, pp. 57 - 62.

51. Kenneth and Anna M. Roberts, eds., *Moreau de St. Mery's American Journey, 1793 - 1798* (Garden City, N.Y.: Doubleday, 1947), p. 171.

52. Henry Wansey, *The Journal of an Excursion to the United States of North America in the Summer of 1794* (New York: Johnson Reprint Corp., 1969), p. 206.

53. Henry Onderdonk, *Queens County in Olden Times* (Jamaica, 1865), pp. 79 - 80. A lugubrious notice appears in a Long Island newspaper that doesn't speak well of the tutor as a gentleman: "Charles Gallifor, schoolmaster, going from Hog Island to Oak Neck, being intoxicated with liquor, fell into the bay and was drowned instantly." *Ibid.*, p. 82.

54. Thomas Paine, "The Age of Reason," in *Thomas Paine: Representative Selections*, ed. Harry Hayden Clark (New York: Hill and Wang, 1969), pp. 267 - 270.

55. Edward Tyrell Channing, "On Models in Literature," in Spiller, pp. 160 - 161. Richard Henry Dana supported Channing's criticism of the curriculum, attributing the emphasis upon the classical curriculum to traditionalists in the university who frowned upon change (Spiller, p. 220).

56. Cremin, I, p. 267.

57. Charles Jared Ingersoll, "A Discourse of the Influence of America upon the Mind," in Spiller, pp. 240 - 243.

58. Samuel Miller, in Spiller, pp. 48 - 51.

59. Ingersoll, in Spiller, p. 240.

60. Hubbell, p. 177.

61. Frances Wright, *Views of Society and Manners in America*, p. 215.

62. Curti, p. 35.

63. Paul Goodman, *The Community of Scholars*, p. 38.

64. Frederick Mayer, *American Ideas and Education*, p. 82.

65. Ruth Miller Elson, *Guardians of Tradition* (Lincoln: University of Nebraska Press, 1964), p. 225.

66. Samuel Eliot Morison and Henry Steele Commager, *The Growth of the American Republic*, pp. 148 - 149.

67. Francis Calley Gray, "Phi Beta Kappa Address, September 1816," in Spiller, p. 171.

68. Richard Henry Dana, Sr., in Spiller, p. 216.

69. George Tucker, "On American Literature," in Spiller, p. 92.

70. William Ellery Channing, "Remarks on National Literature," in Spiller, p. 365.

71. Morison and Commager, p. 176.

72. Harold Milton Ellis, *Joseph Dennie and His Circle* (New York: AMS Press, 1971), pp. 34 - 41.

73. Charles R. King, ed., *The Life and Correspondence of Rufus King* (New York: Da Capo, 1971), VI, pp. 345 - 347.

74. Orie Long, *Literary Pioneers*, pp. 74 - 75.

75. Eliphalet Pearson, "A Journal of Disorders" (1778) in *The Harvard Book*, ed. William Bentinck-Smith (Cambridge: Harvard University Press, 1961), pp. 110 - 113.

76. Mussey, pp. 79 - 80.

77. Roberts and Roberts, p. 105.

78. Mussey, p. 92.

79. William K. Bottorf, ed., *The Miscellaneous Works of David Humphreys* (Gainesville, Fla.: Scholar's Facsimiles and Reprints, 1968), p. 112.

80. John Melish, *Travels Through the United States of America in the Years 1806 - 1811* (London, 1818, reprinted by the Johnson Reprint Corp., 1970), p. 111.

81. Francisco de Miranda, *The New Democracy in America* (Norman: University of Oklahoma Press, 1963), p. 70.

82. Beard and Beard, I, p. 537.

83. Cubberley, p. 342.

84. Virgil A. Clift *et al.*, *Negro Education in America*, p. 36.

85. C. G. Woodson, *The Education of the Negro Prior to 1861*, p. 64.

86. Benjamin G. Brawley, *Early Negro American Writers*, pp. 36 - 37.

87. Richard C. Wade, *Slavery in the South, 1820 - 1860* (New York: Oxford University Press, 1964), p. 175.

88. *Ibid.*, p. 176.

89. George W. Williams, *History of the Negro Race in America* (New York: Arno Press, 1968, from the 1883 edition), II, p. 149.

90. Benjamin Brawley, *A Short History of the American Negro*, pp. 35 - 36.

91. Woodson, pp. 79 - 80.

92. Cubberley, p. 86.

93. Woodson, p. 77.

94. Roberts and Roberts, p. 357.

95. Woodson, p. 124.

96. Cubberley, p. 88.

97. Jonathan Messerli, *Horace Mann*, p. 47.

98. Morris Birbeck, *Notes on a Journey in America* (Ann Harbor: University Microfilms, 1966), p. 47.

99. Thomas Woody, *A History of Women's Education in the United States*, I, p. 93.

100. George F. Willison, *Saints and Sinners*, p. 387.

101. Meyer, p. 54.

102. Woody, I, p. 133.

103. Willison, p. 478.

104. Meyer, p. 214.

105. From a letter by President Jared Sparks of Harvard, April 25, 1849, in *The Harvard Book*, ed. Bentinck-Smith.
106. Wright, p. 218.
107. *Ibid.*, p. 222.
108. Messerli, p. 74.
109. Samuel Miller, in Spiller, pp. 39 - 40.
110. Cubberley, p. 115.

CHAPTER TWO

1. Henry T. Tuckerman, "A Sketch of American Literature," in *Outlines of English Literature* by Thomas B. Shaw, pp. 433 - 434.
2. Johann Schoepf, *Travels in the Confederation, 1784 - 1788*, p. 213. The three references are from selections in Robert Spiller, *The American Literary Revolution:* Walter Channing, p. 117; Edward Tyrell Channing, p. 117; Charles Brockden Brown, pp. 36 - 37.
3. John Calley Gray, in Spiller, p. 168.
4. Moses Coit Tyler, *The Literary History of the American Revolution*, I, p. 6.
5. Richard Henry Dana, Sr., in Spiller, p. 217; George Tucker, *ibid.*, p. 90; and Samuel Miller, *ibid.*, p. 53.
6. Fred Pattee, *The First Century of American Literature*, p. 22.
7. Henry Bamford Parkes, *The American People*, p. 46.
8. *Ibid.*, p. 56.
9. For strong criticism of America's commercial tone, see these authors in Spiller: Francis Calley Gray, p. 167; Fisher Ames, p. 68; Henry Wadsworth Longfellow, p. 388; Samuel Miller, p. 56; Richard Henry Dana, Sr., p. 217; George Tucker, p. 98; Walter Channing, p. 129. Interestingly, in his rejoinder to the Report of the Committee on Composition and Rhetoric to the Board of Overseers of Harvard College, 1892 — a report very critical of the compositional skills of Harvard's entering freshmen — B. A. Hinsdale attributes some of the alleged rhetorical deficiences of Harvard's freshmen to the nation's practical tone: "The industrial, commercial, and political tension of American society is the highest known in the world. In this respect we are keyed up to the highest note. But in science, philosophy, and literature — that is, in the intellectual sphere proper — our tension is distinctly lower than that of England, France, or Germany" (B. A. Hinsdale, *Teaching the Language Arts* [New York: D. Appleton, 1897], p. xvi).
10. William Cullen Bryant, in Spiller, p. 198.
11. American critics of American writers were plentiful. See these writers in Spiller: Fisher Ames, p. 25; Washington Irving, p. 404; and Philip Freneau, p. 6.
12. Schoepf, p. 211.
13. *Ibid.*, p. 212.
14. Interestingly, Adam Smith, a contemporary of Trumbull, wrote warmly in defense of the novel: "The poets and romance writers who best

paint the refinements and delicacies of love and friendship, and of all other private and domestic affections, Racine and Voltaire, Richardson, Marivaux, and Ricciboni, are in this case much better instructors than Zeno, Chrysippus, or Epictetus" (quoted by Isaac Disraeli, *Curiosities of Literature* [Boston: William Veazie, 1858], II, p. 129).

15. Pattee, p. 12.

16. Samuel Miller, in Spiller, pp. 56 - 57; also, Dana, *ibid.*, p. 215.

17. Jared Ingersoll, in Spiller, p. 247.

18. *Ibid.*, p. 246.

19. Samuel Miller, in Spiller, p. 42.

20. Charles and Mary Beard, *The Rise of American Civilization*, I, p. 183.

21. Earl L. Bradsher, *Mathew Carey* (New York: AMS Press, 1966), pp. 11 - 12.

22. In *Quest for America*, ed. Charles L. Sanford, pp. 95 - 96.

23. Robert Spiller *et al.*, *Literary History of the United States*, p. 43.

24. William Tudor, in Spiller, *The American Literary Revolution*, p. 133.

25. Henry W. Longfellow, in *ibid.*, p. 390.

26. Charles Brockden Brown, in *ibid.*, p. 25.

27. Richard Henry Dana, Sr., in *ibid.*, p. 226.

28. Spiller *et al.*, *Literary History of the United States*, p. 44.

29. Darrel Abel, *American Literature*, I, p. 142.

30. Beard and Beard, I, p. 188.

31. Adrienne Koch, ed., *The American Enlightenment*, p. 44.

32. James Fenimore Cooper, in Spiller, *The American Literary Revolution*, p. 40.

CHAPTER THREE

1. Quoted by William Linn, *The Life of Thomas Jefferson*, p. 173.

2. John Hardin Best, ed., *Benjamin Franklin on Education*, p. 18.

3. Adrienne Koch and William Peden, eds., *The Selected Writings of John and John Quincy Adams*, p. 134.

4. Patrick Henry refused to serve because he feared ratifying a Constitution that might give the executive dictatorial powers (Malcolm Townsend, *Handbook of United States Political History* [Boston: Lothrop, Lee, & Shepard, 1905], p. 99.). Thomas Jefferson was serving as minister to France and Samuel Adams was not chosen as a delegate. Thomas Paine was abroad, exhibiting an iron bridge he had designed, and continuing his war against European despotism. The Convention was composed primarily of practical men, interested in financial schemes and speculation in public lands (Charles and Mary Beard, *The Rise of American Civilization*, I, p. 311).

5. Bruce Ingham Granger, *Benjamin Franklin, An American Man of Letters* (Ithaca: Cornell University Press, 1964), p. 27.

6. *Ibid.,* p. 33.

7. Carl Van Doren, *Benjamin Franklin,* p. 21.

8. David B. Tyack, ed., *Turning Points in American Educational History,* p. 54.

9. Merle Curti, *The Social Ideas of American Educators* (Paterson: Pageant Books, 1959), p. 36.

10. Adrienne Koch, ed., *The American Enlightenment,* p. 77.

11. Max Savelle, *Is Liberalism Dead?* (Seattle: University of Washington Press, 1967), p. 60.

12. Thomas J. Wertenbaker, *The Golden Age of Colonial Culture* (Ithaca: Great Seal Books, 1959), p. 3.

13. Leonard Labarree *et al.,* eds., *The Autobiography of Benjamin Franklin,* p. 193. But Franklin distributed his pamphlet to leading members of the community and worked diligently to have them approve his academy (Van Doren, p. 192). Interestingly, the twenty-four trustees elected Franklin president. Perhaps his modesty was somewhat affected, for he well knew that his readers would readily identify him as the pamphlet's author.

14. Tyack, p. 30.

15. Carl Holliday, *The Wit and Humor of Colonial Days* (New York: Frederick Ungar, 1960), p. 89.

16. John Hardin Best, ed., *Benjamin Franklin on Education,* p. 161.

17. Samuel G. Goodrich, *The Life of Benjamin Franklin* (Philadelphia: Thomas, Cowperthwait, 1838), p. 161.

18. Van Doren, p. 152.

19. Labarree, pp. 60 - 61, 162.

20. Koch, p. 150.

21. Granger, p. 13.

22. Albert Baugh, *A History of the English Language,* p. 439.

23. *The Life of Benjamin Franklin,* p. 63.

24. Edwin E. Slosson, *The American Spirit in Education,* p. 76.

25. Victor Robinson, M.D., *The Story of Medicine* (New York: Tudor, new printing; 1935), p. 448.

26. *Ibid.,* p. 455.

27. Paul Monroe, *A Text-Book in the History of Education,* p. 456.

28. Dagobert Runes, ed., *The Selected Writings of Benjamin Rush,* p. 116.

29. *Ibid.,* pp. 97 - 98.

30. Richard D. Mosier, *American Temper,* p. 136.

31. Runes, p. 91.

32. Mosier, p. 141.

33. *Ibid.,* p. 136.

34. Runes, p. 88.

35. *Ibid.*, p. 130.

36. L. H. Butterfield, ed., *The Letters of Benjamin Rush*, I, p. 414.

37. Runes, pp. 93 - 94.

38. Butterfield, I, p. 607.

39. Runes, p. 113.

40. *Ibid.*, p. 114.

41. Butterfield, I, pp. 544 - 555. For example, to hire Charles Nesbet to come to Dickinson, Rush wrote to him that in addition to superintending the college he would have to preach a weekly sermon and teach two or three hours daily (Butterfield, I, p. 323).

42. Runes, pp. 109 - 112.

43. Butterfield, I, p. 622.

44. Runes, p. 99.

45. Beard and Beard, I, p. 488.

46. Runes, p. 156.

47. Butterfield, I, p. 491.

48. *Ibid.*, p. 353.

49. *Ibid.*, pp. 364 - 366.

50. C. G. Woodson, *The Education of the Negro Prior to 1861*, p. 67.

51. Runes, p. 93.

52. William V. Wells, *The Life and Public Services of Samuel Adams*, II, p. 328.

53. *Ibid.*, III, p. 328.

54. *Ibid.*, p. 367.

55. Charles Francis Adams, *The Works of John Adams*, VI, pp. 423 - 424.

56. Slosson, p. 91.

57. Richard Hofstadter and Wilson Smith, *American Higher Education*, I, p. 158.

58. Washington Irving, *The Life of George Washington*, V, p. 361.

59. *Ibid.*, V, pp. 360, 362.

60. Norman Cousins, ed., *In God We Trust*, p. 65. This book is an admirable compilation of the religious beliefs of the Founding Fathers, especially useful to students of the history of controversy between the factions for and against state aid to religious schools. Cousins sums up the opposing views neatly: "It is contended on one hand — and Supreme Court decisions have supported this view — that almost any action by the Federal Government in support of religion is a violation of the First Amendment. The opposing contention is that the Constitution speaks for itself, and that if the Founding Fathers, who declared against an established state church, were opposed to any or all Federal concern for religious activities in America, they would have said so" (Cousins, p. 14).

61. Benjamin Brawley, *A Short History of the American Negro*, p. 23.

62. Woodson, pp. 378 - 379.

63. Esther E. Brown, *The French Revolution and the American Man of Letters*, p. 56.
64. Koch and Peden, pp. 18 - 19.
65. *Ibid.*, p. 19.
66. Koch, p. 232.
67. Charles F. Adams, VI, pp. 494 - 496.
68. *Ibid.*, IX, pp. 425 - 426.
69. *Ibid.*, p. 434.
70. Koch, p. 273.
71. Hofstadter and Smith, p. 232.
72. Samuel Eliot Morison and Henry Steele Commager, *The Growth of the American Republic*, p. 260.
73. Koch, p. 166.
74. *Ibid.*, p. 162.
75. Koch and Peden, pp. 184 - 185.
76. James Madison, *Letters and Other Writings of James Madison*, III, p. 278.
77. *Ibid.*, p. 184.
78. Hofstadter and Smith, I, p. 177.
79. Madison, III, p. 232.
80. Edmund Coty Burnett, *The Continental Congress*, p. 124.
81. Cousins, p. 309.
82. *Ibid.*, pp. 310 - 313.
83. Adrienne Koch, *Madison's Advice to My Country* (Princeton: University of Princeton Press, 1961), pp. 35 - 36.
84. *Ibid.*, pp. 46 - 47.
85. Andrew A. Lipscomb, ed., *The Writings of Thomas Jefferson*, II, p. 207.
86. *Ibid.*, pp. 84 - 85.
87. Lester J. Cappon, ed., *The Adams-Jefferson Letters* (Chapel Hill: University of North Carolina Press, 1959), II, p. 484.
88. Saul H. Padover, *A Jefferson Profile*, p. 127.
89. Koch, *The American Enlightenment*, p. 311.
90. Bernard Mayo, ed., *Jefferson Himself* (Boston: Houghton Mifflin, 1942), p. 297.
91. *Ibid.*
92. H. A. Washington, ed., *The Writings of Thomas Jefferson*, VII, p. 94 - 95.
93. Paul Leicester Ford, ed., *The Works of Thomas Jefferson*, IV, p. 61.
94. James B. Conant, *Thomas Jefferson and the Development of American Public Education*, p. 17.
95. *Ibid.*, p. 18.
96. Elwood P. Cubberley, *Public Education in the United States*, p. 335.
97. Linn, pp. 9 - 10.

98. Cubberley, p. 258.
99. Lipscomb, XII, p. 413.
100. *Ibid.*, XV, p. 289.
101. Conant, p. 24.
102. Washington, I, pp. 47 - 48.
103. Lipscomb, II, p. 203.
104. *Ibid.*, p. 71.
105. Richard Beale Davis, *Intellectual Life in Jefferson's Virginia*, p. 66.
106. Roy John Honeywell, *The Educational Work of Thomas Jefferson* (New York: Russell and Russell, 1964), p. 155.
107. Mayo, p. 292.
108. Linn, p. 250.
109. Orie Long, *Literary Pioneers*, pp. 34 - 35.
110. Davis, pp. 64 - 65.
111. Washington, I, p. 467.
112. *Ibid.*, pp. 467 - 468.
113. *Ibid.*, II, p. 176.
114. *Ibid.*, pp. 244 - 245.
115. Lipscomb, VIII, pp. 274 - 275.
116. Conant, p. 25.
117. Edwin M. Betts and James A. Bear, Jr., *The Family Letters of Thomas Jefferson* (Columbia: University of Missouri Press, 1966), p. 436.
118. Paul Goodman, *The Community of Scholars*, p. 57.
119. Washington, VI, p. 565.
120. Lipscomb, II, pp. 205 - 206.
121. *Ibid.*, pp. 256 - 257.
122. Washington, I, p. 399.
123. Padover, p. 304.
124. *Ibid.*, p. 305.
125. Slosson, p. 86.
126. Earl L. Bradsher, *Mathew Carey* (New York: Columbia University Press, 1912, reprinted by AMS Press, 1966), p. 122.
127. Robert M. Healey, *Jefferson on Religion in Public Education* (New Haven: Yale University Press, 1962), p. 249.
128. *Ibid.*, pp. 248 - 249.
129. *Ibid.*, p. 245.
130. Henry S. Randall, *The Life of Thomas Jefferson*, III, pp. 467 - 468.
131. *Ibid.*, pp. 470 - 471.
132. *Ibid.*, p. 465.
133. *Ibid.*, p. 467.
134. Washington, V, p. 543.
135. Goodman, p. 59.
136. Randall, III, p. 517.
137. *Ibid.*, p. 513.
138. *Ibid.*, pp. 518 - 519.

139. John M. Dorsey, *The Jefferson-Dunglison Letters* (Charlottesville: University of Virginia Press, 1960), p. 33.

140. Davis, p. 65.

141. Esther Brown, p. 53.

142. Washington, VI, p. 356.

143. Lipscomb, XV, p. 154.

144. Tyack, p. 103.

145. Beard and Beard, I, p. 652.

146. Padover, pp. 100 - 101.

147. Honeywell, p. 24.

148. Lipscomb, XIX, p. 218.

149. Cubberley, p. 252.

150. Washington, VII, p. 188.

151. Ford, X, p. 317; Koch, *The American Enlightenment*, p. 409.

152. Washington VI, p. 517.

153. Padover, p. 171. In 1818 the State of Virginia granted $45,000 for public education, a sum hardly worthy of Jefferson's carefully planned project for universal elementary education in the state.

154. Merrill D. Peterson, *The Jefferson Image in the American Mind* (New York: Oxford University Press, 1960), p. 244.

155. Albert J. Nock, *Memoirs of a Superfluous Man* (New York: Harper and Brothers, 1943), p. 86.

156. Curti, p. 234.

157. Howard Mumford Jones, *Jeffersonism and the American Novel*, p. 5.

158. Honeywell, p. xv.

159. Adolphe E. Meyer, *An Educational History of the American People*, p. 128.

160. Conant, p. 25.

161. Lipscomb, XV, p. 45.

162. Mayo, p. 298.

163. Washington, IV, p. 317.

164. Lipscomb, XIX, p. 258.

165. Arthur Bestor, "Thomas Jefferson and The Freedom of Books" in *Three Presidents and Their Books*, p. 16.

166. Conant, p. 29.

167. Linn, p. 247.

168. Davis, p. 69.

169. Rupert Hughes, "Washington, Franklin, Adams, Hamilton, Jefferson," in *American Writers on Literature*, ed. John Macy, p. 57.

CHAPTER FOUR

1. Edwin T. Bowden, *The Satiric Poems of John Trumbull*, p. 1.

2. Alexander Cowie, *John Trumbull*, p. 44; Vernon L. Parrington, *Main Currents in American Thought*, I, p. 249.

3. Leon Howard, *The Connecticut Wits*, pp. 45 - 46.
4. Moses Coit Tyler, *The Literary History of the American Revolution*, I, p. 289.
5. Cowie, p. 108.
6. Howard, p. 55.
7. Frank Lewis Pattee, *The First Century of American Literature*, p. 49.
8. John Trumbull, "The Progress of Dulness," ed. Edwin T. Bowden, p. 31.
9. *Ibid.*, p. 32.
10. *Ibid.*, p. 33.
11. *Ibid.*, p. 37.
12. *Ibid.*, p. 38.
13. *Ibid.*, pp. 38 - 39.
14. *Ibid.*, p. 39.
15. *Ibid.*, p. 40.
16. *Ibid.*, p. 41.
17. *Ibid.*
18. *Ibid.*, p. 54.
19. *Ibid.*, p. 56.
20. *Ibid.*, p. 64.
21. *Ibid.*, p. 65.
22. *Ibid.*
23. *Ibid.*, p. 68.
24. *Ibid.*, p. 69. Arthur Hobson Quinn accords Dick Dashaway, a college fop in A. B. Lindley's dramatic satire, "Love and Friendship or Yankee Notions, 1807 - 1808," the dubious distinction of being the first characterization of a college dandy on the American stage (*History of the American Drama from the Beginnings to the Civil War* [New York: Appleton-Century, 1943], p. 160).
25. *Ibid.*, p. 74.
26. *Ibid.*, p. 75.
27. *Ibid.*, p. 78.
28. *Ibid.*, p. 81. Cummin is a low plant of the carrot family cultivated for its aromatic seeds. It is now spelled "cumin."
29. *Ibid.*, p. 94.
30. *Ibid.*, p. 97.
31. In Robert Spiller, ed., *The American Literary Revolution*, p. 199.
32. Parrington, I, p. 249.
33. Carl Holliday, *The Wit and Humor of Colonial Days* (New York: Frederick Ungar, 1960), p. 206.
34. Cowie, p. 101.
35. William Rose Benét, ed., *The Readers' Encyclopedia* (New York: T. Y. Crowell, 1948), II, p. 243.

36. Van Wyck Brooks, *The World of Washington Irving* (New York: E. P. Dutton, 1944), p. 60.

37. James Woodress, *A Yankee's Odyssey*, p. 260.

38. Parrington, I, p. 385.

39. Woodress, p. 39.

40. *Ibid.*, pp. 44 - 45.

41. Charles Burr Todd, *Life and Letters of Joel Barlow* (New York: Da Capo, 1970), p. 254.

42. *Ibid.*, pp. 253 - 254.

43. Vernon L. Parrington, *The Connecticut Wits* (Hamden: Archon Books, 1963), pp. 323 - 324.

44. *Ibid.*, p. 323.

45. Howard, p. 329.

46. Todd, pp. 208 - 209.

47. Howard, p. 327.

48. Woodress, pp. 242 - 243.

49. Russell Nye, *American Literary History*, p. 221.

50. Joseph Gostwick, *Handbook of American Literature* (Port Washington, N. Y.: Kennikat Press, 1971), p. 33. Reprinted from the 1856 edition. Gostwick dismisses Freneau after according him a five-line notice and space for two stanzas of his "Indian Burying Ground."

51. Henry T. Tuckerman, "A Sketch of American Literature," in *Outlines of English Literature* by Thomas B. Shaw, p. 469. In three widely used college anthologies of American literature, thirty of Freneau's poems are included.

52. Claude Milton Newlin, *The Life and Writings of Hugh Henry Brackenridge*, p. 25.

53. Fred Lewis Pattee, ed., *The Poems of Philip Freneau*, I, xxi - xxii.

54. *Ibid.*, I, xxxiii.

55. Philip Freneau, in Spiller, *The American Literary Revolution*, p. 9.

56. Philip Marsh, ed., *The Prose of Philip Freneau*, p. 119.

57. *Ibid.*, pp. 119, 120, 121 - 122.

58. Pattee, *Freneau*, I, p. 182.

59. "The Time-Piece," in Pattee, *The First Century of American Literature*, p. 42.

60. "The Indian Student," in Pattee, *Freneau*, II, pp. 371 - 374.

61. Marsh, p. 55.

62. Pattee, *Freneau*, III, p. 121.

63. Marsh, p. 59.

64. *Ibid.*, p. 38.

65. *Ibid.*, p. 59.

66. Pattee, *Freneau*, III, pp. 33 - 35.

67. Brooks, p. 64.

68. Fred C. Prescott and John Nelson, *The Prose and Poetry of*

the Revolution, p. 169. Dwight had a great admirer in Lyman Beecher, who wrote ecstatically of his teacher: "Oh, how I loved him! I loved him as my own soul, and he loved me as a son! And once at Litchfield I told him all that I owed to him. 'Then', said he, 'I have done a great and satisfying work. I consider myself amply rewarded.' " In Burrows Mussey, ed., *Yankee Life by Those Who Lived It,* p. 94.

69. Parrington, *American Thought,* I, p. 364.
70. Brooks, p. 65.
71. *Ibid.,* pp. 39 - 40.
72. William J. McTaggart and William K. Sottoroff, eds., *The Major Poems of Timothy Dwight,* including "Greenfield Hill," originally published in 1794, p. 414.
73. *Ibid.,* p. 408.
74. *Ibid.*
75. *Ibid.*
76. Washington Irving, "The Legend of Sleepy Hollow," in Walter Blair *et al., The Literature of the United States,* pp. 252 - 264.
77. Daniel Marder, ed., *A Hugh Brackenridge Reader,* p. 7.
78. *Ibid.*
79. *Ibid.,* p. 9.
80. *Ibid.*
81. *Ibid.,* p. 117.
82. Hugh Henry Brackenridge, *Modern Chivalry,* ed. Claude M. Newlin (New York: American Book Co., 1937 from original 1815 edition), p. 108.
83. *Ibid.,* pp. 366 - 369.
84. *Ibid.,* p. 125.
85. *Ibid.,* p. 523.
86. *Ibid.*
87. *Ibid.,* p. 447.
88. Marder, p. 45.
89. William Hill Brown, *The Power of Sympathy,* p. 62.
90. Susanna H. Rowson, "Essay on Female Education," in *Harper's Literary Museum,* ed. Ola E. Winslow, pp. 211 - 215.
91. Charles and Mary Beard, *The Rise of American Civilization,* I, pp. 475 - 476.
92. David Lee Clark, *Charles Brockden Brown,* pp. 19 - 20.
93. *Ibid.,* p. 22.
94. *Ibid.,* p. 119.
95. George S. Hillard, ed., *Life, Letters, and Journals of George Ticknor* I, pp. 7, 25, 72.
96. David B. Tyack, *George Ticknor and the Boston Brahmins* (Cambridge: Harvard University Press, 1967), p. 55.
97. Hillard, I, p. 348.
98. Tyack, *George Ticknor,* p. 103.

99. *Ibid.*, p. 92.
100. *Ibid.*, p. 95.
101. Hillard, I, p. 356.
102. Tyack, *George Ticknor*, pp. 96 - 97.
103. Hillard, I, p. 362.
104. Tyack, *George Ticknor*, p. 91.
105. Hillard, I, p. 363.
106. Tyack, *George Ticknor*, p. 99.
107. Noah Webster, "On the Education of Youth in America," in *Essays on Education in the Early Republic*, ed. Frederick Rudolph, p. 45.
108. *Ibid.*, p. 66.
109. David B. Tyack, ed., *Turning Points in American Educational History*, p. 87.
110. Noah Webster, pp. 17 - 71, *passim.*
111. Adolphe Meyer, *An Educational History of the American People*, p. 140.
112. *Ibid.*, p. 170.
113. Russell B. Nye, *George Bancroft* (New York: Alfred A. Knopf, 1945), pp. 53 - 78, *passim.*
114. Charles Crowe, *George Ripley*, p. 21.
115. Annie Russel Marble, *Heralds of American Literature*, pp. 54 - 55.
116. Royall Tyler, *The Algerian Captive*, pp. 34 - 144, *passim.*
117. James Fenimore Cooper, *Lionel Lincoln* (New York: volume twenty of the Leather-Stocking Edition, n.d.), p. vi.

CHAPTER FIVE

1. Quoted by Richard Hofstadter in *The American Political Tradition*, p. 57, from *The Americans in Their Moral, Social, and Political Relations* by Francis Joseph Grund, an Austrian immigrant who published his book in 1837.
2. Samuel G. Goodrich, *Parley's Common School History*, rev. ed., p. 317.
3. Frederick Jackson Turner, *The United States, 1830 - 1850*, pp. 576, 580.
4. Edwin C. Rozwenc, ed., *Jackson's Farewell Address* (Boston: D. C. Heath, 1963), pp. 3, 10.
5. Turner, pp. 575 - 576, 578.
6. Samuel G. Goodrich, *Peter Parley's Pictorial History of North and South America*, p. 784.
7. Perry Miller, "Emersonian Genius and the American Democracy," in *Emerson*, eds. Milton R. Konvitz and Stephen E. Whicher (Englewood Cliffs, N. J.: Prentice Hall, 1962), p. 73.
8. Harold Rugg, *Culture and Education in America* (New York: Harcourt, Brace, 1931), p. 154.

9. Alfred E. Cave, *Jacksonian Democracy and the Historian* (Gainesville, Fla.: University of Florida Press, 1964), p. 8.

10. Quoted by Edward Emerson in "Emerson and Scholars," *The Harvard Graduate Magazine*, XIV (March, 1906), p. 309.

11. Spencer Bassett, ed., *Correspondence of Andrew Jackson* (New York: Kraus Reprints, 1969), IV, p. 416.

12. John Quincy Adams, *The Diary of John Quincy Adams*, ed. Allen Nevins (New York: Frederick Ungar, 1951), p. 439.

13. Charles Francis Adams, ed., *Memoirs of John Quincy Adams* (Freeport, N.Y.: Books for Libraries, 1969), VIII, p. 547.

14. Carlos Martyn, *Wendell Phillips* (New York: Funk and Wagnalls, 1890), p. 290.

15. Turner, p. 591.

16. *Ibid.*, p. 17.

17. John Stryker, ed., *The American Quarterly Register and Magazine* (Philadelphia: March, 1849), pp. 111 - 112.

18. Horace Mann, "The Indispensable Teacher," in *Horace Mann on the Crisis in Education*, ed. Louis Filler, p. 69.

19. George Ripley and Charles Dana, eds., *The New American Encyclopedia*, IV, p. 552. The charts do not indicate whether they include black children, free or slave.

20. Stryker, p. 64.

21. Ellwood P. Cubberley, *Public Education in the United States*, p. 113.

22. Jay B. Hubbell, *The South in American Literature*, p. 420. Madison and John Adams in later life lost some of their earlier optimism regarding education as a panacea for the world's social ills.

23. Cubberley, pp. 126 - 127.

24. Thomas A. Bailey, ed., *The American Spirit*, p. 323.

25. Cubberley, p. 119.

26. Bailey, p. 323.

27. Irvin G. Wylie, *The Self-Made Man in America* (New York: The Free Press, 1954), p. 95.

28. Turner, pp. 81 - 82.

29. Henry W. Sams, ed., *Autobiography of Brook Farm*, p. 163.

30. Alice Felt Tyler, *Freedom's Ferment*, pp. 189 - 190.

31. Cubberley, p. 112.

32. *Ibid.*

33. Carl Bode, *The American Lyceum*, p. 86.

34. Turner, p. 340.

35. Hubbell, pp. 371 - 372.

36. Turner, pp. 231, 246.

37. Clement Eaton, *The Growth of Southern Civilization*, pp. 114 - 115.

38. Hubbell, p. 346.

39. Turner, p. 83.

40. Harriet Martineau, "Retrospect of Western Travel," in *The Harvard Book*, ed. William Bentinck-Smith (Cambridge: Harvard University Press, 1961), p. 339.

41. Martin Duberman, *James Russell Lowell*, p. 159.

42. Turner, pp. 136 - 137.

43. Maud Howe Elliot, *Uncle Sam Ward and His Circle* (New York: Macmillan, 1938), p. 33.

44. Albert Gallatin, in the *Journal of the Proceedings of a Convention of Literary and Scientific Gentlemen Held in the Common Council of the City of New York, October, 1830* (New York: John Leavitt and G. and C. H. Carvill, 1831), pp. 175, 177.

45. *Ibid.*, pp. 24 - 25.

46. *Ibid.*, p. 243.

47. *Ibid.*, p. 284.

48. Francis Joseph Grund, *The Americans in Their Moral, Social, and Political Relations*, pp. 126 - 127.

49. *Ibid.*, p. 129.

50. *Ibid.*, p. 127.

51. Mann, "The Indispensable Teacher," in Filler, pp. 69 - 71.

52. Adolphe Meyer, *An Educational History of the American People*, p. 378.

53. Horace Mann, "Words, Words, Words," in Filler, p. 140.

54. Stryker, p. 68.

55. Horace Mann, "Remarks at . . . Bridgewater Normal Schoolhouse," in Filler, p. 170.

56. Ripley and Dana, XII, p. 397.

57. Thomas Hamilton, *Men and Manners in America* (Edinburgh: William Blackwood, 1833), I, pp. 93 - 99.

58. Benjamin Quarles, *The Negro in the Making of America*, p. 101.

59. Joseph Sturge, *A Visit to the United States in 1841* (New York: August M. Kelley, 1969, from the 1842 edition), p. 129.

60. C. G. Woodson, *The Education of the Negro Prior to 1861*, p. 96.

61. *Ibid.*, p. 657.

62. Walter M. Merrill, *Against Wind and Tide* (Cambridge: Harvard University Press, 1963), p. 63.

63. Martyn, pp. 201 - 202.

64. Benjamin Brawley, *A Short History of the American Negro*, 4th ed. rev., pp. 108, 131.

65. Meyer, pp. 214 - 216.

66. Stuart H. Holbrook, *Dreamers of the American Dream*, pp. 176 - 177.

67. Meyer, p. 216.

68. Hubbell, p. 293.

69. George Bancroft in *Journal of the Proceedings . . . 1830*, pp. 46 - 47.

70. M. F. Hasler, in *ibid.*, p. 259.

71. Horace Mann, "End Poverty Through Education," in Filler, p. 124.
72. Horace Mann, "Challenges of a New Age," in Filler, p. 88.
73. Alexis de Tocqueville, *Democracy in America*, eds. J. P. Mayer and Max Lerner, trans. George Laurence, p. 279.
74. *Ibid.*, p. 565.
75. Frances M. Trollope, *Domestic Manners of the Americans* (London: George Routledge and Sons, Ltd., 1927, from the 1839 edition), pp. 283 - 284.
76. Hamilton, p. 362.
77. Frederick Von Raumer, *America and the American People* (New York: J. and H. Langley, 1846), p. 275.
78. *Ibid.*, p. 274.
79. Grund, p. 111.
80. Tocqueville, p. 278.
81. *Ibid.*, p. 83.

CHAPTER SIX

1. Quoted in "Education," *The Works of Ralph Waldo Emerson*, ed. James Elliot Cabot (Boston: Houghton Mifflin, 1883), X, p. 133.
2. Cabot, II, p. 59.
3. *Ibid.*, XIII, pp. 72 - 73.
4. Robert L. Gale, *Richard Henry Dana*, p. 22.
5. Cabot, X, p. 55.
6. Stephen E. Wicher *et al.*, eds., *The Early Lectures of Ralph Waldo Emerson*, II, p. 38.
7. Bliss Perry, ed., *The Heart of Emerson's Journals* (Boston: Houghton Mifflin, 1926), p. 41.
8. Cabot, X, p. 136.
9. *Ibid.*, p. 138.
10. *Ibid.*, p. 126.
11. Ralph Waldo Emerson, "Self-Reliance," in *The Romantic Triumph*, ed. Tremaine McDowell (New York: Macmillan, 1940), p. 54.
12. Cabot, VI, p. 135 - 136.
13. *Ibid.*, XI, p. 355.
14. *Ibid.*, X, p. 146.
15. *Ibid.*, p. 142.
16. Ralph Waldo Emerson, "Spiritual Laws," in *The Works of Ralph Waldo Emerson* (New York: Tudor, n.d.), p. 99.
17. Oliver Wendell Holmes, *Ralph Waldo Emerson*, p. 135.
18. Emerson, Tudor edition, p. 219.
19. Cabot, X, p. 152.
20. Emerson, Tudor edition, p. 56.
21. *Ibid.*, pp. 256 - 257.
22. *Ibid.*, p. 405.
23. Holmes, pp. 256 - 257.

24. Cabot, VIII, pp. 125, 137.
25. Emerson, Tudor edition, pp. 92 - 93. Mark Twain and William Faulkner stressed the values of experiential education in *Life on the Mississippi* and "The Bear" respectively. Also, Huckleberry Finn learns more on the river than in school — he comes to wisdom through suffering.
26. Cabot, X, p. 150.
27. *Ibid.*, p. 146.
28. *Ibid.*, p. 147.
29. *Ibid.*, II, p. 127.
30. *Ibid.*, X, p. 148.
31. *Ibid.*, XII, p. 254.
32. *Ibid.*, VI, p. 126.
33. *Ibid.*, III, pp. 244 - 245.
34. Wicher, II, p. 165.
35. *Ibid.*
36. Emerson, "Self-Reliance," in McDowell, p. 191.
37. Vernon L. Parrington, *Main Currents in American Thought*, II, p. 398.
38. Charles and Mary Beard, *The Rise of American Civilization*, I, pp. 781 - 782.
39. Cabot, X, pp. 148 - 149.
40. *Ibid.*, p. 135. Adults who deplore the so-called generation gap that separates them from their children will not find solace in Emerson's indictment of the closed, parental mind, but they will learn that what he brands as a contemporary dichotomy between the mores of the young and old existed also in the "good old days."
41. Holmes, p. 115.
42. Ralph Waldo Emerson, "The American Scholar," in McDowell, p. 158.
43. Frederick Ives Carpenter, *Emerson Handbook*, p. 176.
44. *Ibid.*, pp. 177 - 178.
45. George Ripley and Charles Dana, eds., *The New American Encyclopedia*, I, p. 301.
46. Dorothy McCuskey, *Bronson Alcott, Teacher*, p. 18.
47. *Ibid.*, p. 61.
48. Odell Shepard, *The Journals of Bronson Alcott*, II, p. 444.
49. *Ibid.*
50. McCuskey, p. 23.
51. *Ibid.*, pp. 23 - 24.
52. *Ibid.*, p. 49.
53. Shepard, II, p. 398.
54. McCuskey, p. 143.
55. Richard L. Herrnstadt, ed., *The Letters of Amos Bronson Alcott*, p. 146.
56. *Ibid.*, p. 138.

57. McCuskey, p. 24.
58. *Ibid.*, p. 31.
59. *Ibid.*, pp. 29 - 30.
60. *Ibid.*, p. 33.
61.. *Ibid.*, p. 27.
62. Shepard, I, p. 8.
63. McCuskey, p. 82.
64. *Ibid.*, p. 85.
65. *Ibid.*, pp. 89 - 90.
66. Louise Hall Tharp, *The Peabody Sisters of Salem*, p. 94.
67. McCuskey, p. 99.
68. *Ibid.*, p. 108.
69. Tharp, p. 100.
70. Herrnstadt, p. 48.
71. McCuskey, pp. 147 - 151, *passim.*
72. Shepard, I, p. xxv. See also pp. 6 - 7, 42, and 187.
73. A. Bronson Alcott, *Concord Days* (Philadelphia: Robert Saifer, 1962), p. 53.
74. Shepard, I, p. 195.
75. McCuskey, p. 163.
76. Arthur W. Brown, *William Ellery Channing*, p. 127.
77. Shepard, I, p. 12.
78. McCuskey, p. 22.
79. *Ibid.*, p. 46.
80. A. B. Alcott, p. 155.
81. Ripley and Dana, IV, p. 5.
82. Alvan S. Ryan, ed., *The Brownson Reader*, p. 125.
83. *Ibid.*, p. 107.
84. *Ibid.*, p. 108.
85. *Ibid.*, p. 109.
86. Alice Felt Tyler, *Freedom's Ferment*, p. 181.
87. Ryan, p. 120.
88. *Ibid.*, p. 116.
89. Arthur M. Schlesinger, Jr., *Orestes A. Brownson*, pp. 63 - 64.
90. Orestes A. Brownson, "The Laboring Classes," in *American Philosophical Addresses*, ed. Joseph L. Blau (New York: Columbia University Press, 1947), p. 188.
91. Ryan, pp. 111 - 112.
92. Schlesinger, p. 81.
93. Ryan, p. 129.
94. *Ibid.*, p. 136.
95. *Ibid.*, p. 139.
96. *Ibid.*, pp. 139 - 140.
97. *Ibid.*, p. 144.

98. Henry David Thoreau, *Walden* (New York: New American Library, 1963), p. 11.

99. Walter Harding and Carl Bode, eds., *The Correspondence of Henry Thoreau,* pp. 19 - 20.

100. Walter Harding, *A Thoreau Handbook,* p. 158.

t 101. F. B. Sanborn, *The Life of Henry Thoreau,* pp. 178 - 179.

102. Milton Meltzer and Walter Harding, *A Thoreau Profile,* p. 21.

103. Walter Harding, *The Days of Henry Thoreau* (New York: Alfred A. Knopf, 1965), pp. 32 - 35.

104. *Ibid.,* p. 51.

105. Meltzer and Harding, p. 35.

106. Thoreau, p. 39.

107. *Ibid.,* p. 40.

108. Harding, *Days of Thoreau,* p. 220.

109. Harding, *Thoreau Handbook,* pp. 112 - 113.

110. Harding, *Days of Thoreau,* p. 45.

111. *Ibid.,* pp. 75 - 86.

112. Meltzer and Harding, p. 40.

113. Thoreau, p. 15.

114. Meltzer and Harding, p. 72.

115. *Ibid.,* p. 44.

116. Thoreau, pp. 77 - 78.

117. Meltzer and Harding, p. 45.

118. Annie Russell Marble, *Thoreau: His Home, Friends, and Books* (New York: AMS Press, 1969), p. 69.

119. Harding, *Days of Thoreau,* pp. 267 - 268.

120. Harding, *Thoreau Handbook,* p. 140.

121. *Ibid.,* p. 164.

122. Charles Crowe, *George Ripley,* p. 131.

123. *Ibid.,* pp. 155 - 156.

124. *Ibid.,* p. 130.

125. Gale, p. 28.

126. *Ibid.,* p. 23.

127. *Ibid.,* pp. 25 - 26.

128. Lawrance Thompson, *Young Longfellow,* p. 161.

129. Andrew Hilen, ed., *The Letters of Henry W. Longfellow,* I, pp. 300 - 301.

130. Henry Wadsworth Longfellow, *Hyperion* (New York: AMS Press, 1960), pp. 50 - 51.

131. *Ibid.,* p. 53.

132. Thompson, p. 154.

133. Henry Wadsworth Longfellow, *Kavanagh* (New York: AMS Press, 1960), p. 301.

134. *Ibid.,* p. 304.

135. Edward Wagenknecht, *Henry Wadsworth Longfellow*, p. 100.
136. *Ibid.*, p. 93.
137. *Ibid.*, pp. 98 - 99.
138. Thompson; p. 192.
139. *Ibid.*, p. 173.
140. Hilen, II, p. 175.
141. Wagenknecht, p. 93.
142. William Charvat, *The Profession of Authorship in America, 1800 - 1870*, ed. Matthew Bruccoli (Columbus: Ohio State University Press, 1968), p. 128.
143. Longfellow, *Kavanagh*, p. 416.
144. *Ibid.*
145. *Ibid.*, pp. 291 - 292.
146. Wagenknecht, p. 94.
147. Hilen, I, pp. 328 - 329.
148. *Ibid.*, p. 302.
149. Edward Everett Hale, *James Russell Lowell and His Friends* (New York: AMS Press, 1965), pp. 14, 17.
150. Martin Duberman, *James Russell Lowell*, pp. 14 - 15.
151. Harry Hayden Clark and Norman Foerster, *James Russell Lowell*, p. 436.
152. *Ibid.*, pp. 174 - 175.
153. Duberman, p. 160.
154. Hale, p. 144.
155. Duberman, p. 161.
156. William Smith Clark, ed., *Lowell: Essays, Poems, and Letters*, p. 194.
157. Clark and Foerster, p. 430.
158. *Ibid.*, p. 438.
159. *Ibid.*, p. 439.
160. *Ibid.*, p. 43.
161. *Ibid.*, p. 446.
162. *Ibid.*
163. James Russell Lowell, "Second Biglow Papers," in Jay B. Hubbell, *The South in American Literature*, p. 375.
164. *Ibid.*, p. 340.
165. George E. Woodberry, "James Russell Lowell," in *Authors at Home*, eds. J. L. and J. B. Gilder (New York: Cassell, 1889), p. 232.
166. Robert Spiller *et al.*, *Literary History of the United States*, p. 559.
167. *Ibid.*, p. 600.
168. Oliver Wendell Holmes, *Elsie Venner*, p. ix.
169. *Ibid.*
170. *Ibid.*, p. xi.
171. Clarence P. Oberndorf, M.D., *The Psychiatric Novels of Oliver Wendell Holmes* (New York: Columbia University Press, 1946), pp. 21 - 22.

172. Holmes, *Elsie Venner,* p. 74.
173. *Ibid.,* p. 4.
174. *Ibid.,* p. 6.
175. *Ibid.,* pp. 70 - 71.
176. *Ibid.,* pp. 172 - 173.
177. Henry Adams, *The Education of Henry Adams,* p. 53.
178. *Ibid.,* p. 59.
179. *Ibid.,* p. 67.
180. Worthington Chauncey Ford, ed., *The Letters of Henry Adams* (Boston: Houghton Mifflin, 1931), I, p. 3.
181. Henry Adams, *The Education of Henry Adams,* p. 78.
182. *Ibid.,* p. 79.
183. *Ibid.,* p. 75.
184. *Ibid.,* p. 302.
185. *Ibid.* Every educator learns painfully what Adams and Melville learned in class, namely, that there is a wide gap between the theory and the pràctice of education. In illustration, the National Council of Teachers of English disapproves of school systems that allow freshman composition teachers to carry loads of more than one hundred students. Yet, throughout the nation, English teachers record teaching loads of from 125 to 175 students.
186. John A. Pollard, *John Greenleaf Whittier,* p. 37.
187. *Ibid.,* p. 23.
188. *Ibid.,* pp. 24 - 25.
189. John Greenleaf Whittier, *The Poetical Works of John Greenleaf Whittier,* IV, p. 73. Volume four is dedicated to "my old schoolmaster."
190. *Ibid.,* pp. 149 - 151.
191. Spiller *et al.,* p. 289.
192. Judge D. P. Thompson, "Locke Amsden or the Schoolmaster," in *One Hundred Years Ago Today,* ed. James P. Wood (New York: Funk and Wagnalls, 1947), p. 43.
193. *Ibid.,* p. 344.
194. *Ibid.*
195. *Ibid.,* pp. 366 - 367.
196. *Ibid.,* p. 367.
197. Daniel Roselle, *Samuel Griswold Goodrich,* p. 45.
198. *Ibid.,* p. 43.
199. *Ibid.,* p. 134.
200. Alice Felt Tyler, p. 235.
201. Mason Wade, *Margaret Fuller,* p. 13.
202. Thomas Wentworth Higginson, *Margaret Fuller Ossoli,* p. 75.
203. Wade, p. 35.
204. *Ibid.,* p. 39.
205. Higginson, p. 76.

206. *Ibid.*, p. 77.
207. *Ibid.*, p. 81.
208. *Ibid.*, p. 83.
209. *Ibid.*, p. 91.
210. Stewart H. Holbrook, *Dreamers of the American Dream*, pp. 174 - 175.
211. Jay Leyda, *The Years and Hours of Emily Dickinson*, II, p. 56.
212. Josephine Pollit, *Emily Dickinson*, p. 41.
213. Leyda, I, p. 145.
214. George F. Whicher, *This Was a Poet* (New York: Scribner's, 1938), p. 39.
215. Madeleine B. Stern, *Louisa May Alcott* (Norman: University of Oklahoma Press, 1956), pp. 111 - 112.
216. Louisa May Alcott, *Little Women* (New York: T. Y. Crowell, 1955), pp. 4 - 5.
217. Louisa May Alcott, *Little Women* with a new introduction by Cornelia Meigs (Boston: Little, Brown, 1968), p. ix.
218. L. M. Alcott, Crowell edition, p. 548.
219. Louisa May Alcott, *Little Men* (Boston: Little, Brown, 1899), p. 17.
220. *Ibid.*, p. 28.
221. *Ibid.*, p. 53.
222. William H. Gilman, *Melville's Early Life and Redburn* (New York: New York University Press, 1951), p. 30.
223. *Ibid.*, pp. 70 - 71.
224. Merril R. Davis and William H. Gilman, *The Letters of Herman Melville* (New Haven: Yale University Press, 1960), p. 5.
225. Gilman, p. 85.
226. Jay Leyda, *The Melville Log*, I, p. 72.
227. Herman Melville, *Moby Dick* (New York: Modern Library, 1962), p. 5.
228. *Ibid.*, p. 421.
229. Frederick W. Dupee, ed., *The Autobiography of Henry James* (New York: Criterion Books, 1956), pp. 8, 11, 12.
230. *Ibid.*, pp. 114 - 116.
231. *Ibid.*, p. 120.
232. *Ibid.*
233. Gay Wilson Allen, *The Solitary Singer* (New York: Macmillan, 1955), p. 524.
234. *Ibid.*, pp. 578 - 579,
235. Floyd Stovall, ed., *Prose Works of Walt Whitman*, I, p. 15.
236. Joan Berbrich, *Three Voices from Paumanok*, pp. 132 - 133.
237. Allen, p. 26.
238. Berbrich, pp. 134 - 135.
239. Henry Bryan Binns, *A Life of Walt Whitman*, pp. 29 - 30.
240. Berbrich, p. 135.

241. David B. Tyack, ed., *Turning Points in American Educational History*, p. 329.

242. Berbrich, p. 138.

243. Thomas A. Bailey, ed., *The American Spirit*, p. 330.

244. *The Works of Walt Whitman*, with a prefatory note by Malcolm Cowley (New York: Funk and Wagnalls, 1968), II, pp. 351 - 355.

245. Leadie M. Clark, *Walt Whitman's Concept of the Common Man*, pp. 34 - 35.

246. *Ibid.*, pp. 95 - 97.

247. Berbrich, p. 131.

248. Walter Blair *et al.*, *The Literature of the United States*, p. 692.

249. *Ibid.*, p. 703.

250. Leadie M. Clark, pp. 35 - 36.

251. James E. Miller, Jr., *Complete Poetry and Selective Prose of Walt Whitman*, p. 89.

252. *Ibid.*, pp. 280 - 281.

253. Hubbell, p. 372.

254. James Robert Gilmore, *My Southern Friends*, p. 156.

255. William A. Caruthers, *A Kentuckian in New York*, I, p. 73.

256. Winfield Parks, *Charles Egbert Craddock*, pp. 17 - 18.

257. Caruthers, I, p. 81 - 83.

258. Edgar Allen Poe, "William Wilson," in *The Complete Tales and Poems of Edgar Allen Poe*, pp. 627 - 636.

259. David Kelly Jackson, *Poe and the Southern Literary Messenger*, p. 78.

260. Charles R. Anderson and Aubrey H. Starke, *The Letters of Sidney Lanier, 1878 - 1881*, VIII, pp. 31 - 33.

261. *Ibid.*, III, p. viii.

262. Mark Twain, *The Autobiography of Mark Twain*, ed. Charles Neider, pp. 31 - 32.

263. *Ibid.*, p. 69.

264. *Ibid.*, p. 3.

265. Mark Twain, *The Adventures of Tom Sawyer* in *The Complete Works of Mark Twain*, ed. Charles Neider, I, pp. 426 - 428.

266. *Ibid.*, pp. 492 - 493.

267. *Ibid.*, pp. 493 - 495.

268. *Ibid.*, p. 495.

296. Hubbell, pp. 438 - 439.

270. *Ibid.*

271. William J. Grayson, *The Hireling and the Slave*, p. xi.

272. *Ibid.*, p. 34.

273. *Ibid.*, p. 44.

274. Merle Curti, *The Growth of American Thought* (New York: Harper, 1943), p. 445.

275. James E. Randall, *James Hall: Spokesman for the New West,* pp. 156, 159.

276. *Ibid.,* pp. 205 - 206.

277. *Ibid.,* pp. 207 - 208. Modern educators and publishing houses are now doing for ghetto children what Hall did wisely for western children, namely, providing them with literature that is meaningful to them.

278. *Ibid.,* p. 230.

279. William Dean Howells, *A Boy's Town,* pp. 52 - 53.

280. *Ibid.,* p. 66.

281. Vernon Loggins, in the introduction to Edward Eggleston, *The Hoosier School-Master* (New York: Hill and Wang, 1963), pp. vi - vii.

282. Eggleston, pp. 2 - 3.

283. *Ibid.,* p. 9.

284. *Ibid.,* pp. 10 - 11.

285. *Ibid.,* p. 28.

286. *Ibid.,* p. 34.

287. Ross Lockridge, Jr., *Raintree County,* pp. 143, 145.

288. *Ibid.,* p. 152.

289. *Ibid.,* p. 196.

290. Lew Wallace, *An Autobiography,* I, pp. 13, 25, 26.

291. *Ibid.,* p. 29.

292. *Ibid.,* p. 57.

293. Millard Fillmore Kennedy, *Schoolmaster of Yesterday,* p. 71.

294. *Ibid.,* p. 99.

295. *Ibid.,* p. 121.

296. William F. Badé, *The Life and Letters of John Muir,* I, pp. 66 - 67.

297. *Ibid.,* p. 86.

298. *Ibid.,* p. 93.

299. Henry Child Merwin, *The Life of Bret Harte,* p. 153.

300. George S. Stewart, Jr., *Bret Harte: Argonaut and Exile,* p. 46.

301. *Ibid.,* p. 123.

302. Bret Harte, "The New Assistant at Pine Clearing School," in *Colonel Starbottle's Client* (New York: P. F. Collier, 1892), p. 189.

303. *Ibid.,* p. 205.

304. *Ibid.,* p. 214.

305. Merwin, p. 62.

Selected Bibliography

ABEL, DARREL. *American Literature.* 3 vols. Great Neck, N.Y.: Barron's, 1963.

ADAMS, CHARLES FRANCIS, ed. *The Works of John Adams.* 10 vols. Boston: Little, Brown, 1856.

ADAMS, HENRY. *The Education of Henry Adams.* New York: Modern Library, 1931.

ANDERSON, CHARLES R., and AUBREY H. STARKE. *The Letters of Sidney Lanier, 1878 - 1881.* 10 vols. Baltimore: Johns Hopkins Press, 1963.

BADÉ, WILLIAM F. *The Life and Letters of John Muir.* 2 vols. Boston: Houghton Mifflin, 1924.

BAILEY, THOMAS A. *The American Spirit.* Boston: D .C. Heath, 1968.

BAUGH, ALBERT. *A History of the English Language.* New York: D. Appleton - Century Co., 1935.

BEARD, CHARLES, AND MARY BEARD. *The Rise of American Civilization.* 2 vols. New York: Macmillan, 1928.

BERBRICH, JOAN. *Three Voices from Paumanok.* Port Washington, N.Y.: Ira J. Freedman, 1969.

BEST, JOHN HARDIN, ed. *Benjamin Franklin on Education.* New York: Teachers College Press, 1962.

BESTOR, ARTHUR, DAVID C. MEARNS, and JONATHAN DANIELS. *Three Presidents and Their Books.* Urbana: University of Illinois Press, 1955.

BINNS, HENRY BRYAN. *A Life of Walt Whitman.* New York: E. P. Dutton, 1905.

BLAIR, WALTER, *et al. The Literature of the United States.* Chicago: Scott, Foresman, 1957.

BODE, CARL. *The American Lyceum.* Carbondale, Ill.: Southern Illinois University Press, 1968.

BOLTON, CHARLES R. *The Private Soldier under Washington.* Port Washington N.Y.: Kennikat Press, 1962.

BOWDEN, EDWIN T. *The Satiric Poems of John Trumbull.* Austin: University of Texas Press, 1962.

BRACKENRIDGE, HUGH HENRY. *Modern Chivalry.* Edited by Claude M. Newlin. New York: American Book Co., 1937, from original 1815 edition.

BRAWLEY, BENJAMIN. *Early Negro American Writers.* Freeport, N.Y.: Books for Libraries, 1968.

————. *A Short History of the American Negro*. New York: Macmillan, 1939.

Brown, Arthur W. *William Ellery Channing*. New York: Twayne Publishers, 1961.

Brown, Esther E. *The French Revolution and the American Man of Letters*. Columbia: Curators of the University of Missouri, 1951.

Brown, William Hill. *The Power of Sympathy*. New York: New Frontier Press, 1961, from original 1789 edition.

Burnett, Edmund Coty. *The Continental Congress*. New York: W. W. Norton, 1964.

Butterfield, L. H., ed. *The Letters of Benjamin Rush*. 2 vols. Princeton: Princeton University Press, 1952.

Cabot, James Elliot. *The Works of Ralph Waldo Emerson*. 14 vols. Boston: Houghton Mifflin, 1883.

Carpenter, Frederick Ives. *Emerson Handbook*. New York: Herricks House, 1953.

Caruthers, William A. *A Kentuckian in New York*. 2 vols. Ridgewood: Gregg Press, 1967, from original 1834 edition.

Clark, David Lee. *Charles Brockden Brown*. Durham: Duke University Press, 1952.

Clark, Harry Hayden, and Norman Foerster. *James Russell Lowell*. Boston: Houghton Mifflin, 1947.

Clark, Leadie M. *Walt Whitman's Concept of the Common Man*. New York: Philosophical Library, 1955.

Clark, William Smith, ed. *Lowell: Essays, Poems, and Letters*. New York: Odyssey Press, 1948.

Clift, Virgil A., et al. *Negro Education in America*. New York: Harper and Brothers, 1962.

Conant, James B. *Thomas Jefferson and the Development of American Public Education*. Berkeley: University of California Press, 1962.

Cousins, Norman, ed. *In God We Trust*. New York: Harper and Brothers, 1958.

Cowie, Alexander. *John Trumbull*. Chapel Hill: University of North Carolina Press, 1936.

Cremin, Lawrence A. *American Education: The Colonial Experience*. New York: Harper and Row, 1970.

Crowe, Charles. *George Ripley*. Athens: University of Georgia Press, 1967.

Cubberley, Ellwood P. *Public Education in the United States*. Boston: Houghton Mifflin, 1919.

Davis, Richard Beale. *Intellectual Life in Jefferson's Virginia*. Chapel Hill: University of North Carolina Press, 1964.

Duberman, Martin. *James Russell Lowell*. Boston: Houghton Mifflin, 1966.

Eaton, Clement. *The Growth of Southern Civilization*. New York: Harper and Brothers, 1961.

EGGLESTON, EDWARD. *The Hoosier School-Master.* New York: Hill and Wang, 1963.

EMERSON, RALPH WALDO. *The Works of Ralph Waldo Emerson.* New York: Tudor, n.d.

FILLER, LOUIS, ed. *Horace Mann on the Crisis in Education.* Yellow Springs, Ohio: Antioch Press, 1965.

FORD, PAUL LEICESTER, ed. *The Works of Thomas Jefferson.* 12 vols. New York: G. P. Putnam's Sons, 1964.

GALE, ROBERT L. *Richard Henry Dana.* New York: Twayne Publishers, 1969.

GILMORE, JAMES ROBERT. *My Southern Friends.* Miami: Mnemosyne Publishing Co., 1969.

GOODMAN, PAUL. *The Community of Scholars.* New York: Random House, 1962.

GOODRICH, SAMUEL G. *Parley's Common School History.* Rev. ed. Philadelphia: E. H. Butler, 1857.

———. *Peter Parley's Pictorial History of North and South America.* Hartford: Peter Parley Publishing Co., 1858.

GRAYSON, WILLIAM J. *The Hireling and the Slave.* Charleston: McCarter and Co., 1856.

GRUND, FRANCIS JOSEPH. *The Americans in Their Moral, Social, and Political Relations.* New York: Johnson Reprint Corp., 1968, from original 1837 edition.

HANSEN, A. O. *Liberalism and American Education in the Eighteenth Century.* New York: Octagon Books, 1965.

HARDING, WALTER. *A Thoreau Handbook.* New York: New York University Press, 1959.

HARDING, WALTER, and CARL BODE, eds. *The Correspondence of Henry Thoreau.* New York: New York University Press, 1958.

HERRNSTADT, RICHARD L., ed. *The Letters of Amos Bronson Alcott.* Ames: Iowa State University Press, 1969.

HIGGINSON, THOMAS WENTWORTH. *Margaret Fuller Ossoli.* Boston: Houghton Mifflin, 1884.

HILEN, ANDREW, ed. *The Letters of Henry W. Longfellow.* 2 vols. Cambridge: Harvard University Press, 1966.

HILLARD, GEORGE S., ed. *Life, Letters, and Journals of George Ticknor.* 2 vols. Boston: James Osgood, 1876.

HOFSTADTER, RICHARD. *The American Political Tradition.* New York: Random House, 1955.

HOFSTADTER, RICHARD, and WILSON SMITH. *American Higher Education.* 2 vols. Chicago: University of Chicago Press, 1961.

HOLBROOK, STEWART H. *Dreamers of the American Dream.* Garden City, N.Y.: Doubleday, 1957.

HOLMES, OLIVER WENDELL. *Elsie Venner.* Cambridge: Riverside Press, 1891.

———. *Ralph Waldo Emerson.* Boston: Houghton Mifflin, 1912.

HOWARD, LEON. *The Connecticut Wits*. Chicago: University of Chicago Press, 1943.

HOWELLS, WILLIAM DEAN. *A Boy's Town*. New York: Harper and Brothers, 1890.

HUBBELL, JAY B. *The South in American Literature*. Durham, N.C.: Duke University Press, 1954.

IRVING, WASHINGTON. *The Life of George Washington*. 5 vols. New York: G. P. Putnam's Sons, 1881.

JACKSON, DAVID KELLY. *Poe and the Southern Literary Messenger*. New York: Haskell House, 1970.

JONES, HOWARD MUMFORD. *Jeffersonism and the American Novel*. New York: Teachers College Press, 1966.

KENNEDY, MILLARD FILLMORE. *Schoolmaster of Yesterday*. New York: Whittlesey House, 1940.

KOCH, ADRIENNE, ed. *The American Enlightenment*. New York: George Braziller, 1965.

KOCH, ADRIENNE, and WILLIAM PEDEN. *The Selected Writings of John and John Quincy Adams*. New York: Alfred A. Knopf, 1946.

LABARREE, LEONARD, et. al., eds. *The Autobiography of Benjamin Franklin*. New Haven: Yale University Press, 1964.

LERNER, MAX. *America As a Civilization*. New York: Simon & Schuster, 1957.

LEYDA, JAY. *The Melville Log*. 2 vols. New York: Gordian Press, 1969.

———. *The Years and Hours of Emily Dickinson*. 2 vols. New Haven: Yale University Press, 1960.

LINN, WILLIAM. *The Life of Thomas Jefferson*. Ithaca, N.Y.: Mace, Andrews, and Woodruff, 1839.

LIPSCOMB, ANDREW A., ed. *The Writings of Thomas Jefferson*. 20 vols. Washington: Thomas Jefferson Memorial Association, 1903.

LOCKRIDGE, ROSS, JR. *Raintree County*. Boston: Houghton Mifflin, 1948.

LONG, ORIE. *Literary Pioneers*. New York: Russell and Russell, 1963.

LONGFELLOW, HENRY WADSWORTH. *Kavanagh*. New York: AMS Press, 1960.

McCUSKEY, DOROTHY. *Bronson Alcott, Teacher*. New York: Macmillan, 1940.

McTAGGART, WILLIAM J., and WILLIAM K. SOTTOROFF, eds. *The Major Poems of Timothy Dwight*. Gainesville, Fla.: Scholars' Facsimiles and Reprints, 1969.

MACY, JOHN. *American Writers on Literature*. New York: Horace Liveright, 1931.

MADISON, JAMES. *Letters and Other Writings of James Madison*. 4 vols. Philadelphia: J. B. Lippincott, 1865.

MARBLE, ANNIE RUSSEL. *Heralds of American Literature*. Freeport: Books for Libraries, 1967.

MARDER, DANIEL, ed. *A Hugh Brackenridge Reader*. Pittsburgh: University of Pittsburgh Press, 1970.

MARSH, PHILIP, ed. *The Prose of Philip Freneau*. New Brunswick: Scarecrow Press, 1955.

MAYER, FREDERICK. *American Ideas and Education.* Columbus, Ohio: Charles E. Merrill, 1964.

MELTZER, MILTON, and WALTER HARDING. *A Thoreau Profile.* New York: T. Y. Crowell, 1962.

MERWIN, HENRY CHILD. *The Life of Bret Harte.* Boston: Houghton Mifflin, 1911.

MESSERLI, JONATHAN. *Horace Mann.* New York: Alfred A. Knopf, 1972.

MEYER, ADOLPHE. *An Educational History of the American People.* New York: McGraw-Hill, 1967.

MILLER, JAMES E., JR. *Complete Poetry and Selective Prose of Walt Whitman.* Boston: Houghton Mifflin, 1959.

MONROE, PAUL. *A Text-Book in the History of Education.* New York: Macmillan, 1908.

MORISON, SAMUEL ELIOT, and HENRY STEELE COMMAGER. *The Growth of the American Republic.* New York: Oxford University Press, 1930.

MOSLER, RICHARD D. *American Temper.* Berkeley: University of California Press, 1952.

MUSSEY, BARROWS, ed. *Yankee Life by Those Who Lived It.* New York: Alfred A. Knopf, 1947.

NEWLIN, CLAUDE MILTON. *The Life and Writings of Hugh Henry Brackenridge.* Mamaroneck, N.Y.: Paul Appel, 1971.

NYE, RUSSEL B. *American Literary History, 1607 - 1830.* New York: Alfred A. Knopf, 1907.

PADOVER, SAUL H. *A Jefferson Profile.* New York: John Day, 1956.

PAINE, THOMAS. *Representative Selections.* Edited by Harry Hayden Clark. New York: Hill and Wang, 1969.

PARKES, HENRY BAMFORD. *The American People.* London: Eyre and Spotswood, 1949.

PARKS, WINFIELD. *Charles Egbert Craddock.* Chapel Hill: University of North Carolina Press, 1941.

PARRINGTON, VERNON L. *Main Currents in American Thought: An Interpretation of American Literature from the Beginnings to 1920.* 3 vols, New York: Harcourt, Brace, 1927.

PATTIE, FRED LEWIS. *The First Century of American Literature.* New York: Cooper Square Publishers, 1966.

———. *The Poems of Philip Freneau.* 3 vols. Princeton, N.J.: Princeton University Press, 1902.

POE, EDGAR ALLEN. *The Complete Tales and Poems of Edgar Allen Poe.* New York: Modern Library, 1938.

POLLARD, JOHN A. *John Greenleaf Whittier.* New York: Archon Books, 1960.

POLLIT, JOSEPHINE. *Emily Dickinson.* New York: Harper and Brothers, 1930.

PRESCOTT, FRED C., and JOHN NELSON. *The Prose and Poetry of the Revolution.* New York: T. Y. Crowell Co., 1925.

QUARLES, BENJAMIN. *The Negro in the Making of America.* New York: Collier Books, 1969.

RANDALL, HENRY S. *The Life of Thomas Jefferson.* 3 vols. New York: Derby and Jackson, 1858.

RANDALL, JAMES E. *James Hall: Spokesman for the New West.* Columbus: Ohio State University Press, 1964.

RIPLEY, GEORGE, and CHARLES DANA, eds. *The New American Encyclopedia.* 16 vols. New York: D. Appleton, 1865.

ROSELLE, DANIEL. *Samuel Griswold Goodrich.* Albany: State University of New York Press, 1968.

RUDOLPH, FREDERICK, ed. *Essays on Education in the Early Republic.* Cambridge: Belknap Press of Harvard University, 1965.

RUNES, DAGOBERT, ed. *The Selected Writings of Benjamin Rush.* New York: Philosophical Library, 1947.

RYAN, ALVAN S., ed. *The Brownson Reader.* New York: J. P. Kennedy and Sons, 1955.

SAMS, HENRY W., ed. *Autobiography of Brook Farm.* Englewood Cliffs, N.J.: Prentice-Hall, 1958.

SANBORN, F. B. *The Life of Henry Thoreau.* Detroit: Gale Research Corp., 1968.

SCHLESINGER, ARTHUR M., JR. *Orestes A. Brownson.* New York: Octagon Books, 1963.

SCHOEPF, JOHANN. *Travels in the Confederation, 1784 - 1788.* Philadelphia: William J. Campbell, 1911.

SHAW, THOMAS B. *Outlines of English Literature.* Philadelphia: Blanchard and Lea, 1854.

SHEPARD, ODELL. *The Journals of Bronson Alcott.* 2 vols. Port Washington, N.Y.: Kennikat Press, 1966.

SLOSSON, EDWIN E. *The American Spirit in Education.* New Haven: Yale University Press, 1921.

SPILLER, ROBERT, ed. *The American Literary Revolution, 1783 - 1837.* Garden City, N.Y.: Doubleday, 1967.

SPILLER, ROBERT, et al. *Literary History of the United States.* New York: Macmillan, 1948.

STEWART, GEORGE S., JR. *Bret Harte: Argonaut and Exile.* Port Washington, N.Y.: Kennikat Press, 1964.

STOVALL, FLOYD, ed. *Prose Works of Walt Whitman.* 2 vols. New York: New York University Press, 1963.

THARP, LOUISE HALL. *The Peabody Sisters of Salem.* Boston: Little, Brown, 1950.

THOMPSON, LAWRANCE. *Young Longfellow.* New York: Octagon Books, 1969.

THOREAU, HENRY DAVID. *Walden.* New York: New American Library, 1963.

TOCQUEVILLE, ALEXIS DE. *Democracy in America.* Edited by J. P. Mayer and Max Lerner. Translated by George Laurence. New York: Harper and Row, 1960.

TURNER, FREDERICK JACKSON. *The United States, 1830 - 1850.* Gloucester, Mass.: Peter Smith, 1958.

TWAIN, MARK. *The Autobiography of Mark Twain.* Edited by Charles Neider. New York: Harper and Brothers, 1959.

———. *The Complete Works of Mark Twain.* 2 vols. Edited by Charles Neider. Garden City, N.Y.: Doubleday, 1964.

TYACK, DAVID B., ed. *Turning Points in American Educational History.* Waltham, Mass.: Blaisdell, 1967.

TYLER, ALICE FELT. *Freedom's Ferment.* Freeport, N.Y.: Books for Libraries, 1970.

TYLER, MOSES COIT. *The Literary History of the American Revolution.* 2 vols. New York: Frederick Ungar, 1956.

TYLER, ROYALL. *The Algerian Captive.* Gainesville, Fla.: Scholars' Facsimile and Reprints, 1967.

VAN DOREN, CARL. *Benjamin Franklin.* New York: Viking Press, 1938.

WADE, MASON. *Margaret Fuller.* New York: Viking Press, 1940.

WAGENKNECHT, EDWARD. *Henry Wadsworth Longfellow.* New York: Oxford University Press, 1966.

WALLACE, LEW. *An Autobiography.* 2 vols. New York: Harper and Brothers, 1906.

WASHINGTON, H. A., ed. *The Writings of Thomas Jefferson.* 9 vols. New York: John C. Riker, 1857.

WELLS, WILLIAM V. *The Life and Public Services of Samuel Adams.* 3 vols. Boston: Little, Brown, 1865.

WHITTIER, JOHN GREENLEAF. *The Works of John G. Whittier.* 7 vols. Boston: Houghton Mifflin, 1892.

WICHER, STEPHEN E., et al., eds. *The Early Lectures of Ralph Waldo Emerson.* 3 vols. Cambridge: Belknap Press of Harvard University, 1964.

WILLISON, GEORGE F. *Saints and Sinners.* New York: Reynal and Hitchcock, 1945.

WINSLOW, OLA E., ed. *Harper's Literary Museum.* New York: Harper and Brothers, 1937.

WOODRESS, JAMES. *A Yankee's Odyssey.* Philadelphia: J. B. Lippincott, 1958.

WOODSON, C. G. *The Education of the Negro Prior to 1861*. New York: Arno Press and *The New York Times*, 1968.

WOODY, THOMAS. *A History of Women's Education in the United States*. 2 vols. New York: Octagon Press, 1961.

WRIGHT, FRANCES. *Views of Society and Manners in America*. Cambridge: Belknap Press of Harvard University, 1963.

Index